Wallace Stegner

A Descriptive Bibliography

The Confluence American Authors Series
James R. Hepworth, Series Editor
Lewis-Clark State College

TCAAS 3

photograph of Wallace Stegner by Leo Holub

Wallace Stegner

AMERICAN AUTHORS SERIES
Wallace Stegner

A Descriptive Bibliography

by NANCY COLBERG

Introduction by James R. Hepworth

Confluence Press, Inc.   Lewiston, Idaho

Copyright © 1990 by Nancy Colberg

Printed in the United States of America
First Edition

ISBN 0-917652-80-0
LIBRARY OF CONGRESS CATALOGUE CARD NUMBER 89-82163

Frontispiece photograph of Wallace Stegner courtesy of Leo Holub.
Photographs within the text by Scott Grabinger.

Publication of this book is made possible by generous grants from the Idaho Commission
on the Arts, a state agency, and Lewis-Clark State College
in Lewiston, Idaho.

Typesetting and Design by Judith Heineman Lanphier with
assistance from Tanya Gonzales.

Published by
Confluence Press, Inc.
Lewis-Clark State College
Lewiston, Idaho 83501

for Don

Contents

Preface

This bibliography provides descriptions of all works written by Stegner, covering his more than fifty-year career up to October, 1988. It is a book intended for scholars as well as book collectors and dealers. Since this is a bibliography of an active, prolific writer, it is obviously incomplete.

Section A lists chronologically all books written by Stegner. Additional editions and printings are also arranged by date, with information as verified in publishers' records, agents' correspondence, and the Stegner's own files. Foreign editions of A items are listed separately, in Section F. Lettering on dust jackets, title pages, bindings, and copyright pages has been transcribed in quasi-facsimile, with colors described according to the National Bureau of Standards Centroid Color Chart.

Section B lists all titles edited by or with contributions by Stegner. Contributions include primarily short stories, essays, forewords, and introductions. These are listed chronologically, with cross references to periodicals in Sections C and D. There are also references to other B and to A items where applicable. Not all B items are first appearances in books. Many of his writings appear frequently in collections. Including later appearances gives some indication of the vast territory touched by Stegner's writings. His "Wilderness Letter," for instance, appears in a number of books, newspapers, magazines, posters, and calendars. It has been seen in Africa as well as Nebraska. A number of anthologies are described, but textbooks with reprints and excerpts have been excluded.

In fact, all textbooks have been purposefully excluded from this bibliography. Periodical and first appearances in books are of primary importance in descriptive bibliogoraphy. There are quasi-facsimile transcriptions of all title pages, while copyright information is abbreviated.

Nonfiction periodical articles are included in Section C. Many of these magazines are not indexed and some are virtually inaccessible. In many instances, only Stegner's own records held the clues. For instance, there are a number of small, unsigned articles in Section C which would have been omitted if it hadn't been for his meticulous record-keeping. The author's own records are invaluable to the bibliographer. These articles, with such diversity of topic, demonstrate Stegner's varied talents and interests. History, biography, travel, and conservation are but a few of his nonfiction interests.

Short stories in magazines and newspapers are listed chronologically in Section D. Stegner is known as one of the leading practitioners of the short story. Section B includes O. Henry Award collections with Stegner contributions. Well-known stories such as "The Blue-Winged Teal" and "The Colt" appear in numerous high school and college textbooks. His writing techniques are also presented in such A items as *Teaching the Short Story*.

Section E is a small list of miscellany. Included is the opera of *Angle of Repose*, performed as part of the nation's bicentennial celebration. There are also posters, calendars, pamphlets, and selected sound recordings.

Section F includes translations of novels and stories into foreign languages. These items are arranged alphabetically by language, then chronologically within the language categories.

Section G contains descriptions of collections with substantial Stegner materials. All of these writings are in typescript. Stegner types all drafts and revisions of books, short stories, and periodical articles. Most of his manuscripts, letters, and papers are still in his possession. The University of Iowa, Stanford, and the University of Utah have manuscripts and other materials available to researchers. The University of Nevada, Reno has probably the largest, growing collection of items described in this bibliography.

Appendix 1 is a selective list of the major writings about Wallace Stegner. Included are interviews, dissertations, periodical articles, and a few books. Studies of Stegner have been mainly critical up until this time. Merrill and Lorene Lewis wrote a pamphlet on Stegner as part of the Boise State College "Western Writers Series" (1972), which includes a partial bibliography. It has been invaluable as a source, although limited in scope. The bibliography in Forrest and Margaret Robinson's *Wallace Stegner* (Twayne, 1977) is quite extensive.

Edition. All copies of a book printed from a single setting of type, including reprintings.

Printing. All copies of a book printed at one time (without removing the type or plates from the press).

First English editions are described in full form as are American editions.

Colors for bindings, dust jackets and other important printed matter are based on the *ISCC-NBS Color Names Charts Illustrated with Centroid Colors* (National Bureau of Standards). Centroid numbers have been assigned, even though fading may make exact identification impossible. In most cases, five copies in original bindings were examined and the most exact color determined.

Spines of dust jackets and bindings are printed horizontally unless described otherwise.

Lettering in the descriptions of dust jackets, bindings, and title pages is black, unless noted differently. Type is Roman unless noted.

This bibliography is based upon evidence gathered from personal inspection of multiple copies of Stegner's works.

Symbols used to designate locations are as follows:

LC: Library of Congress
BL: British Library
OX: Bodleian Library, Oxford
FC: Felton Collection (Special Collections, Stanford)
WS: Collection of Wallace Stegner
NC: Collection of Nancy Colberg
SA: Collection of Sylvia Asendorf
JS: Collection of Jean Sickler
JH: Collection of Jim Hepworth

—Nancy Colberg

Acknowledgments

When I first met Wallace Stegner in 1982, I had no idea our meeting would lead to this descriptive bibliography. At that time, like thousands of others, I was simply a Stegner reader. Although generations apart, my own move from the New Almaden area of California to Colorado mirrored the travels of his characters in *Angle of Repose;* that novel, with its skillfully drawn characters and settings, touched me deeply. It struck me then, as it does today, as the work of a true artist, a master.

Collecting works by Stegner, with their numerous printings, is itself an adventure. As my own collection began to grow, I realized that a guide or bibliography was a necessity. My work as a librarian and an amateur book collector naturally led to my interest in descriptive bibliography. Meeting Stephen Tabor, compiler of the Ted Hughes bibliography, proved to be prophetic. Hearing of my friendship with Stegner, Steve Tabor encouraged me to get to work. I thank him for the suggestion and guidance in those early days. To my delight, when I approached Stegner with my plan, he supported my effort wholeheartedly. He gave me a corner desk in his study, granted me open access to his books and papers, and welcomed me with the gracious hospitality both he and his wife, Mary, have extended to so many people across the years.

Having Stegner's support and access to his personal records, book collection, and agent's files made the task possible, yet no less over-whelming. The research involved the products of more than fifty years in Stegner's career as a writer: books, articles, short stories, edited works, and contributions. Perhaps needless to say, I could never have completed the task without the help of others that I am pleased to acknowledge here.

Dr. Robert Harlan of the University of California, Berkley, for example, allowed me to audit his course in descriptive bibliography. I appreciate his encouragement and instruction. Terence Tanner, author of the Frank Waters bibliography, offered numerous suggestions and buoyed my spirits.

Public and private libraries, invaluable to the bibliographer, provided me with hundreds of books and magazine articles acquired through interlibrary loan. My appreciation goes to the late Karen Laurinec, of the Edwin A. Bemis Public Library, Littleton, Colorado; and to Carol Welch, SEMBCS Professional Information Center, Denver, Colorado. Others in Colorado who contributed include the reference librarians at Auraria Library, Denver; Norlin Library, University of Colorado, Boulder; Loretto Heights College Library, Denver; and the Colorado School of Mines Library, Golden.

Special collections librarians gave me access to manuscripts, rare books, and letters. The following librarians were most helpful: Tim Gorelangton, Special Collections, University of Nevada, Reno; Roy Webb, Manuscripts Division, Marriott Library, University of Utah; Walter R. Jones, Special Collections, Marriott Library, University of Utah; Bob McCowan, Special Collections (Iowa Authors Collection), University of Iowa, Iowa City; and the staff, Special Collections (Felton Literature Collection), Stanford University, Stanford, California.

My thanks also extend to librarians and staff members at several national and international libraries, including the British Library, London; the Bodleian Library, Oxford; and the Library of Congress, Washington, D. C. The Copyright Office also deserves credit for guiding me through its files.

Many Stegner collectors in Northern California graciously shared their private libraries with me and came up with original dust jackets and bindings unavailable elsewhere. It appears that most binding variants are in private hands, and, unfortunately, many public holdings have been rebound. My sincere thanks go to Sylvia Asendorf, bookdealer and collector, who encouraged her Stegner fan club to share much with me. Credit also goes to Mr. Maurice Dunbar, who kindly offered me his Stegner checklist.

Publisher's records, of course, are *the* source of publication data. I thank the following publishers who have taken the time to provide me with valuable information: Sally Arteseros, Doubleday; Christine Valentine and Janice Lucas, The Franklin Library; Vicki Austin, Harcourt Brace

Jovanovich; Folcroft; Andrea Colby, G. K. Hall; Karen Mortensen, Houghton Mifflin; McGraw-Hill; Rita Vaughn, Meredith (for Duell, Sloan and Pearce); Stala Georgiades, New American Library; Herman Schein, Parnassus Press; Sam Vaughan and Dante V. Del Col, Random House; Peter Spitzform, Stanford University Press; Willis Regier, University of Nebraska Press; Andre Bernard, Viking Press; Claire Griffin, Viking Penguin; and Kathleen Malley, Warner Books (Popular Library).

A generous share of my gratitude also goes to Scott Grabinger of the University of Colorado at Denver, who skillfully provided all photographs.

Thank you, Jim Hepworth, Stegner scholar and publisher at Confluence Press, for persuading me to publish this bibliography.

Judith Lanphier, your guidance and expertise in book design, have also proven invaluable.

To my husband, Don, who loves books and encouraged me to make this one, I owe my deepest thanks, as well as to my children and friends. They never doubted there would be a Stegner bibliography, and after all these years I am pleased to see their faith in me confirmed. Likewise, the Stegners not only enabled me to gather the information necessary to compile this bibliography—they, too, *believed* in me. I hope this book sustains their faith.

N. C.

Introduction

As Nancy Colberg's volume amply attests, Wallace Stegner has been busier than Aesop's proverbial frog trapped in the milkpond. Indeed, at the age of eighty-one Stegner appears as busy (if not busier) practicing his various trades as he ever was in his youth. Yesterday, for example, he claimed to be at work on his contribution to the next volume in this series, *Wendell Berry*. He is also an advisor for a documentary film on his life and work being produced by Steven Fisher and narrated by Robert Redford. To find more evidence of Stegner's current affairs, I have only to wade through the stacks of books and files in my office: a copy of *Growing Up Western* edited by Clarus Backes (1990), *Collected Stories* (1990), galleys from the University of Utah Press for the second edition of *Conversations with Wallace Stegner on Western History and Literature* (1990), not to mention various audio recordings like *The Sense of Place* (1989) and a recent interview with Kay Bonetti (1987). But why proceed with such a list? Tomorrow, it would be even longer.

"I think you don't choose between the past and the present," Stegner writes in *(TSOMW)*, "you try to find the connections" (200). And those connections, of course, are the sole and exclusive reason for undertaking the publication of Nancy Colberg's bibliography. In its own way, this volume does what Stegner claims nobody had done when he wrote his essay "History, Myth, and the Western Writer": it bridges past and present in the modern American West. According to the Stegner who was writing then, "Nobody has quite made a western Yoknapatawpha County or discovered a historical continuity comparable to that which Faulkner traced from Ikkemotubbe the Chickasaw to Montgomery Ward Snopes. Maybe it isn't possible, but I wish someone would try. I might even try myself" (*TSOMW* 200). When Jackson Benson finishes writing the authorized biography, we will assuredly be able to make many new connections as well as rediscover what we already know about the long life of Wallace Stegner—and much, much more. The roads taken by the sensuous little savage who grew up on the last plains frontier and became the famous virtuoso—novelist, short-story writer, editor, literary critic, historian, biographer, teacher, conservationist—will doubtless surprise and fascinate us with too many twists and turns to imagine now. But that the father of the Stanford Writing Workshop and (in the words of Edward Abbey) "the only living American worthy of the Nobel Prize in literature" is still walking those roads remains for millions of us a source of comfort and immense consolation.

For we live in a time when such solace seems rare, when discontinuity and dislocation, fragmentation and fracture, are the perceived rules of the day. We so commonly see the precious gift of life being squandered by people who know better that a careful examination of a life in which *nothing* seems wasted can astonish us. Yet here it is: the real thing, as Henry James might say, or, at any rate, that part of a life that is the residue and record of a great artist's achievements. "*Je suis une chose qui dure,*" Bruce Mason repeats, echoing Henri Bergson, "I am a thing that lasts. But not," the protagonist of *Recapitulation* adds, "unchanged" (231). And those changes, of course, are an integral part of the record: the failures as well as the victories. But that Stegner's victories and accomplishments so far outweigh their counterparts is more than a matter for celebration. It is genuine cause for hope, especially when we consider the adversity that marks the lives of writers in America. "If you start pretty much at the bottom, at some Neanderthal homestead in Saskatchewan," Stegner told Richard Etulain, "you have to try to come up the whole way in one lifetime, to something like the peak of your civilization, whatever that may be. It's demoralizing" (43). Yet Stegner has done just that. His life itself exemplifies the kind of historical continuity between the American past and the American present that is comparable to a character in a Faulkner novel. And so, to a modest degree, with Stegner's characters. The Metis (mixed-blood Cree) in *Wolf Willow* (1962) share a common fate with Ikkemotubbe the Chickasaw, but anyone who wants to compare Faulkner's Montgomery Ward Snopes with Wallace Stegner's Lyman Ward will realize how quickly such comparisons outlive their usefulness. While Stegner and Faulkner prove comparable in many ways, Nancy Colberg's bibliography underscores their differences with the result that we ought to come away from her reference book with a broader understanding of Stegner's unique place in American letters.

Although not everyone grants Stegner Nobel status in the pantheon, on July 12, 1987, T.H. Watkins, the vice president of the Wilderness Society in Washington, D.C., submitted the name of Wallace Earle Stegner in nomination to the Permanent Secretary of the Swedish Academy, Professor Lars Gyllensten, in Stockholm. Whether the Nobel Prize in literature remains within or beyond the grasp of any American writer before the turn of the century, however, is beside the point here. That time has passed when American critics in particular can refer to Stegner in strictly regional terms and fail to recognize him for what he is—a world class American writer in the tradition of Henry James, Mark Twain, and yes, William Faulkner. Too often, the efforts of critics in the United States have eclipsed our view of Stegner with a narrow lens. In other words, the provinciality of critics on *both* sides of the Mississippi has often distorted rather than enlarged. On the one hand, for example, it took a Pulitzer Prize in fiction and the angry goading of Stegner readers to finally force *The New York Times* into a belated (and snobbish) retrospective review of *Angle of Repose* (1971). Five years later, despite a National Book Award in fiction, *The Times* completely ignored *The Spectator Bird* (1976). No matter. By that date American readers had long since discovered Wallace Stegner for themselves. At the moment the galleys of this volume have appeared before me upon my desk, *The New York Times* ranks *Collected Stories* number fifteen on its Best Sellers list. Other comparable evidence, including Colberg's, points to the fact that Stegner's readership is growing in record numbers.

On the other hand, westerners all too frequently indulge in the kind of defensive chest-beating that has marked American literature for centuries. "We have listened too long to the courtly muses of Europe," Emerson asserted in his American Scholar address in 1837. "It is for the nation's sake, and not for her authors' sake, that I would have America be heedful of the increasing greatness among her writers," Melville wrote in "Hawthorne and His Mosses": "It were the vilest thing you could say of a true American author, that he were an American Tompkins. Call him an American, and have done; for you can not say a nobler thing of him.... Let us away with this leaven of literary flunkyism towards England. If either must play the flunky in this thing, let England do it."

The history of American literature is dominated by provincialism. Indeed, in "The Provincial Consciousness," Stegner claims that American literature in the twentieth century has also been "dominated by a series of sectionalisms either geographical or ethnic: the Midwesterners in the twenties, the Southerners on their heels, the New York school on the heel of the Southerners, the Blacks on the heels of the New Yorkers." He tells us to "Check the writings of the Fugitive group that wrote the script for the South, especially such a book as *I'll Take My Stand*" in order to see "writers making a hate object out of New York, as the early American nationalists made one out of England and Canadians tend to make one out of the United States" (*TSOMW* 93).

"The West is politically reactionary and exploitative," Stegner wrote in "Born a Square": "Admit it, instead of pretending to be the last brave home of American freedom. The West as a whole is guilty of inexpiable crimes against the land: admit that, too. The West is rootless, culturally half-baked. So be it. To deny weaknesses is to be victimized by them and caught in lies forever. But," he reminds us, "while the West is admitting its inadequacy, let it remember its strengths: it is the New World's last chance to be something better, the only American society still malleable enough to be formed" (*TSOMW* 183-4). Unfortunately, too many critics in the West have made their reputations by championing Stegner as a *regional-ist*—as a local boy who somehow happened to make good. Instead of publishing their work in such "national forums for criticism as *American Literature*," Anthony Arthur observes, their articles have appeared "in journals with regional identification such as *Western Humanities Review, South Dakota Review,* and *Western American Literature*" (12). Like the corporate bosses and government slaves who control the timber and mining industries, some of these academics are no strangers to the concepts of strip mining and clear-cutting, the kinds of practices that encourage erosion and threaten to muddy the waters of every major American river.

For years, with few exceptions western critics have mined only the regional veins in Stegner's work for quick personal gains while ignoring the motherlode: Stegner's place in the larger American tradition. Or, to change the metaphor, by treating Stegner's mature growth and development in, say, *Angle of Repose,* as the felling of just another tree in the western forest, they have abused the resource. "He should have deleted more pages," one critic writes of the novel, "This is an age of impatience and novelists must accommodate to that fact, if not acquiesce." What, then, are we to do with all those American anachronisms like *Moby-Dick* and *A Portrait of a Lady?* Or recent novels by John Barth or Larry McMurtry or Joyce Carol Oates? The result of such outlandish statements as the one above has left Stegner criticism in a state of neglect and disrepair, like a ghost town in Idaho or Montana: mostly wind blowing down what was once a main street but is now choked with weeds and crumbling false fronts. While I have no interest in directing readers to critical rantings they can discover for themselves, one of the town characters drunk on strange brew has suggested that Stegner be horsewhipped and hung for a liar and a thief.

Meanwhile, back at the ranch on the hill at the end of South Fork Lane near the "provincial" little town of San Francisco, the old man has quietly been going about his chores. From the 1960's through the 1980's, when other American writers slipped away into metafiction, magical realism, minimalism, fantasy, and historical romance, away from what Thomas Walters calls the "tragically distorted emotional landscape" of contemporary America, Stegner "lowered his lance and charged" (38). Among other things he wrote that powerful series of novels whose complex themes confronted the social problems of the day head on: race and gender, the annihilation of the American family, the realities of marriage and divorce, sexuality and promiscuity, cancer and apocalypse, youth and identity, age and faith, environmental disaster and political chaos. But then, we all know how many times a critic reads a book: less than once. Those who do otherwise will quickly notice that three of the novels—*Angle of Repose, The Spectator Bird,* and *Crossing to Safety*—rely heavily upon transcontinental settings, most notably Mexico, Denmark, and Italy. The other two—*All the Little Live Things* (1967) and *Recapitulation* (1986)—make use of cosmopolitan backdrops—San Francisco and Salt Lake City, two of the most worldly and frankly materialistic cities on the face of the earth. What goes on trial in all five novels, however, has most to do with the profound questions left along the staggering but constantly accelerating path of western civilization: Who is this New Man? And this New Woman? Indeed, who are these Americans? And what, if anything, do they hold sacred?

As Nancy Colberg's work patiently bears witness, Stegner and his books have long been traveling an international circuit. In England, where Stegner has enjoyed a strong following for nearly thirty years and his readers take it for granted that the word *West* can (and perhaps should) be understood metaphorically, C.P. Snow, wrote of Stegner as follows: "You are in the presence of a master. . . one of the deepest, truest, most likeable writers in America" (1961). Elsewhere across the globe, translators have been busy rendering Stegner's books at a steady clip into French, German, Greek, Italian, Polish, Spanish, and Japanese. None of the reviews I have read from abroad ever trouble over Stegner's regional identity. On the contrary, European writers seem to take it as axiomatic that an American writer needs plenty of room in which to tell the truth. These writers freely accept Stegner's settings and his subjects as part of what James called the artist's *donne*. In other words, they are givens. The veritable enemy, as American readers and writers know only too well, is artistic sloth. And Stegner has been anything but slothful.

When we do consider Stegner in regional terms, then, we must exercise extreme caution. As a "regional writer," Wendell Berry notes, Stegner is "exemplary," for he has "worked strenuously to know his region. He has not been just a student of its history, but

one of its historians" (16). Indeed, Stegner may very well qualify
as *the* writer whose voice has literally defined the modern West. But
a close analysis of what some scholars call "Stegner Country"
turns out to include as much of the Midwest—Iowa, Wisconsin, the
Dakotas—and New England—particularly Vermont but also New
York—as it does Utah, Idaho, Colorado, or Montana. Stegner's
so-called "California novels" may be the closest thing he has to
compare with Faulkner's "little postage stamp of soil," the
Yoknapatawpha County seat of the virtually all his great novels. But
"California, it should be said at once," Stegner writes, "is not part
of the West. It is about as much the West as Florida is the South;
it is less a region than an extension of the main line." Toward the
bottom of the same paragraph he adds, "California is a nation of
in-migrants, and its writers are in-migrants too, either writing about
the places they came from or frantically searching around and reading *Sunset* to find specifically Californian patterns to which to
conform. It is the sticks I mean when I speak of the West—the last
of the sticks—the subregions between the ninety-eighth meridian and
the Sierra-Cascades" (*TSOMW* 177).

To think of Stegner as a regional-ist, then, betrays the very brand
of regionalism Faulkner and Stegner exemplify: their universal perspective. Perhaps we ought to remember that it took the help of
the French to legitimize Faulkner not only as an American but as a
citizen of the world. By the time Malcolm Cowley got around to
putting "Count No Count" together again in his *Portable Faulkner*,
many of Faulkner's books were out of print (or OSI, in the par-
lance of contemporary publishers). A number of critics had hooted
rather loudly at some of the most brilliant books of this or any
other century.

No writer, needless to say, can work well in complete isolation,
and while a writer like Stegner may be his own best editor, sometimes an editor like Cowley has made a distinctive difference.
Curiously, for example, it was Cowley to whom Stegner sent the
manuscript of his unclassifiable book, *Wolf Willow* when the
book's scaffolding teetered and threatened to collapse altogether. "It
was an anthology in the first place," Stegner told me in a recent
interview, but until he sent it to Cowley, he "couldn't make it
come together." Stegner reports that Cowley looked and then said,
"'You know, I think if you just move this Dump Ground chapter

from the beginning to the end'—or vice-versa, I've forgotten which—'the book will come together better.' And it did, like a puzzle when you find the key piece" (563).

But in his way, Stegner has exercised his own editorial prowess in his ways that rival Cowley and Perkins and their impact upon the canon of American literature. The list of books, neglected and otherwise, that Stegner's aquisitive nature either helped back into print or got published for the first time is much too long and distinguished to include here. Colberg's superb chronicle, however, provides us with some perspective. I have in mind, for example, two books by John Wesley Powell: his *Report on the Lands of the Arid Region* (1962) and *the Exploration of the Colorado River and Its Canyons* (1875, 1957, 1987). First, by recording, documenting, and *dramatizing* the second opening of the West in *Beyond the Hundredth Meridian* (1954), Stegner did more than insure the nation that Powell's massive importance to American history at last be granted and afterward never again ignored. As DeVoto points out in his introduction to Stegner's book, at the time Stegner published it, "most historians had never even heard of Powell, much less read his work." Afterwards, of course, Powell and his books became a standard requirement for anyone with a serious interest in American studies. To put Stegner's accomplishment in DeVoto's terms, *Beyond the Hundredth Meridian* helped give us "enough basic knowledge . . . to construct a new general synthesis of American history," a history "more realistic and therefore more useful than Turner's"(xxii).

With Stegner's help, Powell's own writing soon became accessible to even the most general reader. When speaking of Stegner's editorial gifts, however, I also have in mind the myriad tasks he set for himself as an editor-at-large for *Saturday Review* and as the editor of *American West*, not to mention the various introductions, prefaces, forewords, and afterwords he provided for the many volumes Colberg lists, as well as those books that bear the distinctive imprint of Stegner's ability to shape material. The case of Stegner's edition of *The Letters of Bernard Devoto* (1975) would serve here, for instance, by way of example, but then, so would others: *This Is Dinosaur* (1954), a book that helped save all that we have left of the Colorado River and its magnificent canyon country. But I also have in mind the sort of editorial assistance only a great and gifted teacher can give a student willing to revise even the most hapless essay into a cogent and powerful work of art, for Stegner has what a recent anthology of fiction and poetry from the Stanford Writing Workshop entitles *The Uncommon Touch* (1989). Like Cowley, he can spot a writer's blind spots at a glance and save him the embarrassment of a lifetime.

We need to remember, for example, what Wayne Ude reminds us in his recent discussion of creative writing programs in America: "In fact, there have been perhaps only three 'generations' of teachers,'" beginning with Paul Engle and Wallace Stegner, who had "more or less to invent the profession" (12). In the foreword to the Stanford Centennial publication dedicated to him—a hefty 512 page tome—Stegner claims that "Of the ninety-eight contributors," he personally knows "only sixty" (xvi). That these sixty writers include the likes of Pulitzer Prize and National Book Award winners in fiction—N. Scott Momaday, Larry McMurtry, Robert Stone—he ignores. Better than 60% of the contributors, nevertheless, passed through the program he founded the year he arrived (1946) and directed until he turned his back on academic life (1971). The other thirty-eight contributors, Stegner insists, are as "remote" from him "as the four-legged Stegners up in Montana who derive from a Red Angus bull that an admirer once named" in his honor. Given this bit of Stegner hyperbole, the bull was aptly named.

In some ways the long and distinguished list of the more than 100 writers who passed through the Stanford Workshops during Stegner's tenure may be less important than the list of those who went on to become professional editors, foreign correspondents, and teachers, for Stegner did much more than teach. To put the matter in Ude's terms, Stegner *invented* a profession. And that took some doing. For one thing, it meant creating a place for the creators of literature within that *sanctum santorum* of the ivory tower from which they had previously been denied access. To this day, the sort of division between critics and creative writers that Ed Loomis alludes to in "Wallace Stegner and Yvor Winters as Teachers" threatens to further alienate writers from readers and readers from writers. Certainly, Stegner and Winters themselves had their differences. But together, they managed to recognize the necessity of the writer's place within American culture and create a literary community that became a model for every other creative writing program in the nation. By securing the endowment that continues to fund fellowships that still bear his name, Stegner gave every fellow who ever passed through Stanford's program the most precious gift any artist requires: *time*. More importantly, by teaching students to view literature from the perspective of its creators, Stegner altered the way students traditionally perceived literature. Consequently, students came away with a new experience and an authentic but very different method of evaluating texts. No student who ever attempted to write a novel or a series of short stories in those workshops could ever view literature again in quite the same way.

It may even be that one of the greatest benefits of the ripple effect generated by the proliferation of creative writing programs in the United States has been to extend the audience for contemporary literature: to insure it a readership. It may also be that the same revolution that created a place for writers within American colleges and universities also dramatically altered the publication of literature in the nation. Certainly, it has helped. We have only to open any one of several directories for writers to find whole constellations of "independent" publishers clustered around intellectual suns. Often, the publication may be only a little magazine with a small circulation like any one of those loosely association with the writers workshops themselves: *The Iowa Review, Columbia, Quarterly West, Triquarterly, Cutbank*. . . . But just as often, the cluster would have to include literary publishing houses whose writers are closely associated with the writing programs, for, as Stegner observes in his Dartmouth interview, American writing itself has moved "into the academy in a big way. As late as the end of the Twenties, the customary way for a writer to get his apprenticeship (both in experience and in actual writing) was to begin as a newspaperman. Many did it. Sinclair Lewis, Dreiser, Hemingway—and before them, Howells and Mark Twain and Richard Harding Davis and Stephen Crane—all wrote their way off newspapers and into books. It is very different now" (50).

Indeed, the same revolution that placed serious writers into colleges and gave them jobs has also produced a "new lecture and reading circuit" in America, one whose cross-currents now run through even the most backwater places on the western map where towns and small cities like Lewiston, Idaho, tend to take much of their character from the academic institutions they nurture. The shock produced from bringing together those who "used to look with some suspicion on writers" as "underbred wild men" (English departments) and those who "used to be somewhat contemptuous of the colleges" (the writers) has generated more suspicion and contempt, but as often as not it has also produced the happy jolt of "warm collaboration." "Whatever the relationship," Stegner says, "colleges are where most of our writers can be found" (51).

For whatever reason, Stegner's views on the art of writing have never been collected into a single comprehensive volume. They remain scattered in dozens of essays, articles, pamphlets, and interviews, including the monograph Dartmouth College published in 1988, the same year Nancy Colberg turned her bibliography over to me. Thanks to her, we can now view the whole of Stegner's own development as a writer through the wide-angle lens of bibliographic scholarship. What such a lens reveals, of course, will depend upon who uses it and how. In the event no editor turns up to collect Stegner's views on the art of writing, now that I have Nancy Colberg's bibliography upon which to rely, I might even try myself. And the same goes for Stegner's conservation career. "Little do you know what a basket of snakes you're getting into," Stegner wrote to me on September 19, 1981, when I volunteered to undertake the bibliography myself. "I've written reams of grocery-buying junk during my lifetime," he said, "and the bibliography shows it."

At that time, of course, the only reliable bibliography of Stegner's work could be found at the end of the Robinsons' *Wallace Stegner* (1977). But the trouble with the "reams of grocery buying junk" theory is something Ann Tyler brings out in her *New York Times* review of Stegner's *Collected Stories*. What she says of the stories tends to hold true for everything Stegner has written: "We can't help but mourn the passing of his short-story days," Tyler writes, "These stories are so large; they're so wholehearted. Plainly, he never set out to write a *mere* short story. It was all or nothing" (2). In other words, risk and literary excellence have been the rule with all that Stegner has written. And that attitude has obvious parallels in his own exemplary life, with the result that Wallace Stegner has also become "one of the central figures of the modern conservation movement" (Watkins 91).

Take the case of the famous "wilderness letter" that Stegner wrote to David E. Pesonen of the Outdoor Recreation Review Commission on December 3, 1960. Although Stegner himself refers to it as "'the labour of an afternoon'" its impact has been profound. According to Watkins, one of the things the infant conservation movement most needed in 1960 was a "manifesto," but long before Stegner could publish "A Coda," former Secretary of the Interior Stewart Udall had made the letter the basis of a keynote speech and *The Washington Post* had picked the letter up "and printed it whole." As Watkins notes (and Colberg confirms), the same letter has also been "found pasted on the wall of an office in a Kenya game park; all or parts of it have appeared on posters in Rhodesia, Canada, and Australia; its last four words, 'the geography of hope,' were used as the title for a book of Eliot Porter photographs; conservation writers. . .have stolen from it shamelessly and quoted it endlessly" (97). Indeed, that little letter may have done as much as anything else to save all that we have left of the remaining wilderness in North America.

Likewise, the sanctity of our National Parks owes a tremendous debt to Wallace Stegner, one of the paper tigers whose early opposition blasted sizeable holes in the formidable fortress erected by the Bureau of Reclamation, the Army Corps of Engineers, Truman's Interior Secretary Chapman, "and after him Eisenhower's man, Douglas McKay, a former automobile salesman from Oregon" (Watkins 96). In 1954, when legislation for the Upper Colorado Project lay pending Congressional approval, Alfred A. Knopf "agreed to publish a book" in order to help block passage of the bill that would have forever destroyed all that remains of the Colorado River and its haunting canyons. As Watkins relays the story, "the Sierra Club's David Brower, who had the face of a child but the heart of a Druid, came down to Stanford and persuaded Stegner to edit the book. The result—a labor of love for all concerned—was *This is Dinosaur: Echo Park and Its Magic Rivers*, with chapters by Stegner, Olaus Murie, and others, including Knopf himself. It was published at breakneck speed in 1955 and sent to every member of Congress" (96). Tragically, the legislation that did pass enabled the government to destroy Glen Canyon, but "it included a stipulation that no national park or monument would be violated by any of its parts; the Echo Park and Split Mountain dams were dead" (96).

Not long after Knopf published *This is Dinosaur,* Stegner accepted an appointment to the publications committee of the Sierra Club, an organization that later made him an honorary life member and for whose board Ansel Adams "talked him into running for election." Watkins notes that Stegner won "and served for two years" (99). But Stegner's service to the cause of conservation extends its roots to grass level with his co-founding of the Committee for Green Foothills (in 1960) and his service to California Tomorrow, Alfred Heller's "muscular little outfit devoted to goading the state's government into producing a land-use plan with teeth" (Watkins 99). On the national level, Stegner has also accepted appointments to the councils of the Trust for Public Land, People for Open Space, and the advisory board for National Parks, Historical Sites, Buildings, and Monuments (1962-1965), chairing the board his last year, before the Reagan Administration dismantled it in one more of its irresponsible attacks on the conservation cause. And in 1961, of course, Stegner served as Special Assistant to former Secretary of the Interior, Stewart Udall, in the Kennedy Administration.

For many Americans, these appointments rival those literary honors Stegner has accumulated over his lifetime, including his memberships in the National Institute and Academy of Arts and Letters, Phi Beta Kappa, and the American Academy of Arts and Sciences. For those of us who need reminding, Stegner is also a three-time recipient of the Guggenheim (1950, 1953, 1960); the recipient of a Rockefeller grant (1950-51); a Wenner-Gren Foundation grant (1954); two Fulbrights (1962, 1968); and a former fellow of the Center for Advanced Study in the Behavioral Sciences (1955). "There are no new ways of being new," Stegner is fond of saying, but given the record of his varied and astonishing achievements Nancy Colberg has recorded here, it may be, as Wendell Berry, T.H. Watkins, and others have been implying for years, that Stegner has become a new *kind* of American writer, one "who does his best to protect" his country, "by writing and in other ways, from its would-be exploiters and destroyers"(Berry 16). "There is an instructive humility in his studentship as a historian of the West," Berry writes, "It is hard to imagine Hemingway researching and writing a history of Michigan or Africa; to him, as to many writers now, history was immediate experience. To Mr. Stegner, it is also memory. He has the care and the scrupulousness of one who understands historical insight and honesty as duties" (16). If, indeed, there is another living American writer, man or woman, any more deserving of the Nobel Prize than Wallace Stegner, then I would like to know where to begin reading.

Even as I make it, I know that statement may cost me a nervous turn in a friendship I value and prize as highly as any other, for generally speaking, Wallace Stegner "has not been a taker of credit" (Berry 14). When Sharon Butala, Mary Scriver, and others associated with the Eastend Arts Council in Saskatchewan wrote to tell me of their project to restore "the Stegner house" and I questioned Stegner about their progress, he only expressed bafflement and muttered embarrassments over what he perceived to be a curious affair. Happily, by January 12, 1989, the group could boast that "The Wallace Stegner House, Eastend, Saskatchewan, is now officially Municipal Heritage Property and belongs to the Eastend Arts Council," complete with new cedar shingles for the roof and plans to "carry on with the restoration." (Unhappily, the shingles had only been "partly paid for." So with the shingles on this house.)

But as Martin Lasden observes in a recent article, the days when Stegner could be easily "typecast as one of those great American novelists doomed to be admired far more than he is read" must now compete fiercely with Stegner's current popularity, for once again another major American writer has proven that literary worth and popularity *can* be compatible. What too many reviewers and critics once smugly viewed as Stegner's "general lack of hipness, his disdain for literary fashion, and his indifference to contemporary taste" (Lasden 23), we must now reconsider in earnest. To do so, we have Nancy Colberg's generous and supportive foundation upon which to continue to build.

"Everything potent," Stegner says in "This I Believe," "from human love to atomic energy, is dangerous: it produces ill about as readily as good"; and "it becomes good only through the control, the discipline, the wisdom with which we use it." On this, the birth date of a man who continues to produce about as much good as any mortal may be capable of, I'm willing to let that statement stand as a testament to the power of Nancy Colberg's volume.

—James R. Hepworth
February 18, 1990

WORKS CITED

Berry, Wendell. "Wallace Stegner and the Great Community." *South Dakota Review* 23.4 (1985): 10-18.

Critical Essays on Wallace Stegner. Ed. Anthony Arthur. Boston: G. K. Hall, 1982.

DeVoto, Bernard. "Introduction." *Beyond the Hundredth Meridian: John Wesley Powell and the Second Opening of the West.* By Wallace Stegner. Boston: Houghton Mifflin, 1954.

Emerson, Ralph Waldo. "The American Scholar." *Essays.* 1841.

Hepworth, James R. "Wallace Stegner's *Angle of Repose:* One Reader's Response." Diss. University of Arizona, 1989.

Lasden, Martin. "On His Own Terms." Stanford (Spring 1989): 23-31.

Loomis, Edward. "Wallace Stegner and Yvor Winters as Teachers." *South Dakota Review* 23.4 (1985): 19-24.

Melville, Herman (Timothy Dwight). "Hawthorne and His Mosses." Travels in New-England and New York. 1821, 1822.

Stegner, Wallace. *Collected Stories of Wallace Stegner.* New York: Knopf, 1990.

Wallace Stegner and Richard W. Etulain. *Conversations with Wallace Stegner on Western History and Literature.* 2nd ed. Salt Lake: University of Utah Press, 1990.

———. "Finding the Place." *Growing Up Western: Reflections by Dee Brown, A.B. Guthrie Jr., David Lavender, Wright Morris, Clyde Rice, Wallace Stegner, Frank Waters.* Ed. Clarus Backes. New York: Knopf, 1990.

———. "Foreword." *The Uncommon Touch: Fiction and Poetry from the Stanford Writing Workshop.* Ed. John L'Heureux. Stanford, Ca.: Stanford Alumni Association, 1989.

Wallace Stegner and Kay Bonetti. An Interview with Wallace Stegner. Audiotape. American Audio Prose Library, 1987.

———. *On the Teaching of Creative Writing: Responses to a Series of Questions.* Ed. Edward Connery Lathem. Hanover, New Hampshire: University Press of New England and Dartmouth College.

———. "The Provincial Consciousness." *One Way to Spell Man: Essays with a Western Bias.* New York: Doubleday, 1982.

———. *Recapitulation.* New York: Doubleday, 1979.

———. *The Sense of Place.* Audiotape. Read by Wallace Stegner. The Audio Press Inc., 1989.

———. *The Sound of Mountain Water.* New York: E.P. Dutton, 1980.

———. "This I Believe." *One Way to Spell Man: Essays with a Western Bias.* New York: Doubleday, 1982.

Tyler, Ann. "The Outsider May Be You." Rev. of *Collected Stories of Wallace Stegner. The New York Times Book Review* 18 March (1990) 2.

Ude, Wayne. "Notes from a Community: Creative Writing Programs in Animation." *AWP Chronicle* 22.5 (1990): 12-15.

Walters, Thomas. "The Spectator Bird." *Magill's Literary Annual 1977.* Ed. Frank N. Magill. Englewood Cliffs, N.J.: Salem Press, 1977. Reprinted in *Critical Essays on Wallace Stegner.* Ed. Anthony Arthur. Boston: G.K. Hall, 1982.

Watkins, T.H. "Typewritten on Both Sides: The Conservation Career of Wallace Stegner." *Audubon* 89 (September 1987): 89-103.

Chronology

1909   Born February 18, 1909, at Lake Mills, Iowa, son of
            George H. and Hilda (Paulson) Stegner.

1910-14   Family moved frequently—in Iowa, North Dakota, and
            Washington State.

1914-20   Lived in East End, Saskatchewan, a tiny village on
            remote plains. Attended grammar school.

1920-21   Fifteen months in Great Falls, Montana.

1921   Moved to Salt Lake City, Utah, where the family lived
            in a dozen houses over the next ten years. Attended
            junior high and high school.

1927   Graduated from high school and entered the University
            of Utah at age sixteen. Was encouraged to write by his
            freshman English teacher, the novelist Vardis Fisher.

1930   Received a B. A. from the University of Utah and began graduate work in English literature at the University of Iowa.

1932 Completed his master's thesis, which consisted of several short stories, and received an M. A. from the University of Iowa. As a graduate student he began teaching courses.

1932-33 Began doctoral work at the University of California at Berkeley.

1933 Left Berkeley because of his mother's illness. After her death that year he returned in February 1934 to Iowa to work on his doctorate at the University of Iowa.

1934 Married a fellow graduate student, Mary Stuart Page, September 1, 1934, and accepted a teaching position at the University of Utah (1934-37). Received his first full-time teaching position at Augustana College in Rock Island, Illinois (a one semester stint).

1935 Completed requirements for the Ph.D. in English with a dissertation on the Utah naturalist Clarence Dutton (later published as *Clarence Dutton: An Appraisal*).

1937 He and his wife became the parents of a son, Stuart Page, their only child. Achieved national success as a writer when *Remembering Laughter* was published after winning the $2500 Little, Brown novelette prize. Began teaching at the University of Wisconsin (1937-39).

1938 *The Potter's House*

1938 Joined the staff of the Bread Loaf Writers' Conference, where he formed friendships with Robert Frost and Bernard DeVoto. Began teaching in the writing program at Harvard (1939-45).

1940 *On a Darkling Plain*

1941   *Fire and Ice*

1942   *Mormon Country*

1943   *The Big Rock Candy Mountain*

1945   Shared the Anisfield-Wolfe Award and received the
        Houghton Mifflin Life-In-America Award for *One
        Nation.* Appointed as Professor of English, Stanford
        University. Directed the eminently successful writing
        program at Stanford University (1945-71).

1947   *Second Growth*

1950   First Prize O. Henry Memorial Short Story Award for
        "The Blue-Winged Teal." (Also received O. Henry
        Awards in 1942 and 1954). Published *The Preacher and
        the Slave* and *The Women on the Wall.*

1950-51 Rockefeller fellowship to conduct seminars with writers
        throughout the Far East.

1951   *The Writer in America*

1954   *Beyond the Hundredth Meridian*

1955   *This is Dinosaur* (ed)

1956   *The City of the Living*

1960   Wrote the famous "Wilderness Letter."

1961   Assistant to the Secretary of the Interior. Published *A
        Shooting Star.*

1962   *Wolf Willow* published.

1962-66 Served as a member of the National Parks Advisory
        Board.

Section

a

A   Items

A1 *Clarence Edward Dutton*

Only printing (1935)

Title page: 'Clarence Edward Dutton / *An Appraisal* / BY / WALLACE E. STEGNER / University of Utah / [typographical orn.] / Published by / UNIVERSITY OF UTAH / Salt Lake City'

Copyright: 'THE UNIVERSITY PRESS / UNIVERSITY OF UTAH / SALT LAKE CITY'

[1]¹²

pp. (1-3) 4-23 (24)

9 7/8″ × 6 13/16″

Contents: p. 1: title; p. 2: copyright; pp. 3-19: text; p. 20: blank; pp. 21-23: bibliography; p. 24: blank.

Paper: Cream wove. No endpapers.

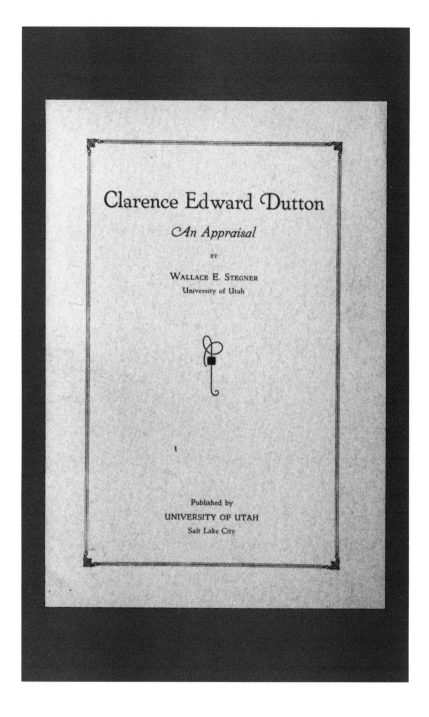

Clarence Edward Dutton

An Appraisal

BY

WALLACE E. STEGNER
University of Utah

Published by
UNIVERSITY OF UTAH
Salt Lake City

Cover for A1

Binding: Light gray paper (c.264) with fiber fleck. Front: '[within decorative double-ruled frame] Clarence Edward Dutton / *An Appraisal* / BY / WALLACE E. STEGNER / University of Utah / [typographical orn.] / Published by / UNIVERSITY OF UTAH / Salt Lake City'. Stapled twice at centerfold.

Dust jacket: None.

Publication: No date on title page or copyright. No record of number of copies. Copyright Office dates it August, 1935.

Location: WS (1), LC (1)

Note: A condensation of Stegner's thesis, *Clarence Edward Dutton, Geologist and Man of Letters*, State University of Iowa, 1935.

A2 *Remembering Laughter*

A2.1

First edition, first printing (1937)

Title page: '[all within a single rule] / [title and author within border of leaves] Remembering / Laughter / WALLACE STEGNER / [publisher's device] / *1937* / LITTLE, BROWN AND / COMPANY [dot] BOSTON'

Copyright page: 'COPYRIGHT 1937, BY WALLACE STEGNER / ALL RIGHTS RESERVED, INCLUDING THE RIGHT / TO REPRODUCE THIS BOOK OR PORTIONS / THEREOF IN ANY FORM / FIRST EDITION / *Published September 1937* / PRINTED IN THE UNITED STATES OF AMERICA'

$(1\text{-}10)^8$

pp. (i-vi) (1-3) 4-154

7 1/2″ × 4 15/16″

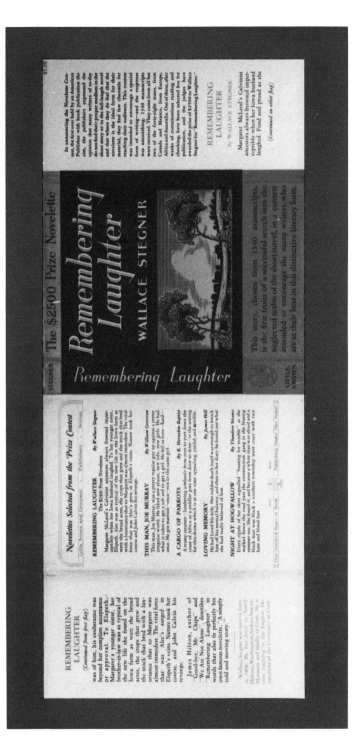

Dust jacket for A2.1

Contents: p.i: half title; p.ii: blank; p.iii: title; p.iv: copyright; p.v: 'TO / MARY STUART PAGE'; p.vi: blank; p. 1: half title; p. 2: 'All characters and all incidents in this novelette are purely fictitious'; pp. 3-8: PROLOGUE; pp. 9-154: text, headed "1".

Paper: Cream wove stock. Edges trimmed. Endpapers of heavier cream stock.

Binding: Medium greenish blue (c.173) V cloth (smooth). Edges trimmed. Front gilt-stamped: '[within gilt-stamped border of leaves] *Remembering* / *Laughter* / WALLACE STEGNER / [publisher's device]'. Spine: '[horizontal gilt-stamped] [gilt rule of leaves] / *Remembering* / *Laughter* / + / STEGNER / [gilt rule of leaves] / LITTLE, / BROWN / AND / COMPANY'.

Dust jacket: Front and spine lettered on panels of black and gold background. Front: '[black on gold panel] The $2500 Prize Novelette / [light greenish blue (c.172) outlined in white on black] *Remembering* / *Laughter* / [black drawing of farmland signed C.G.R. on light greenish blue background] [black on gold panel] This story, chosen from 1340 manuscripts, / is the first fruits of a successful search into the / neglected realm of the short novel, in a contest / intended to encourage the many writers who / are at their best in this distinctive literary form'. Spine: '[black on gold horizontal] STEGNER / [white on black top to bottom] *Remembering Laughter* / [horizontal publisher's device] / LITTLE, / BROWN'. Back: 'Novelettes Selected from the Prize Contest [5 titles]'. Front flap describes the contest. Price in light greenish blue at upper right corner: '$1.25'. Also blurb on RL. Back flap continues front and gives biographical information on Wallace Stegner.

Publication: September 27, 1937. Price: $1.25. First appeared in *Redbook* September, 1937 as a "novelette complete in one issue." A small number of presentation copies were distributed, with an extra page tipped in (pp. vii-viii). This page reads: 'REDBOOK / MAGA-ZINE / *is proud to present you with* / *this complimentary copy of* / "REMEMBERING / LAUGHTER" / [within frame] A FIRST-EDITION COPY OF / THIS PRIZE NOVELETTE / WHICH FIRST APPEARED / IN THE PAGES OF REDBOOK'.

Two LC copies are dated December 13, 1937 and November 18, 1937.

Locations: WS (3), NC (3), LC (2)

A2.2

First English edition, first printing (1937)

Title page: 'REMEMBERING / LAUGHTER / BY / WALLACE STEGNER / [publisher's device] / [rule] / WILLIAM HEINEMANN LTD / LONDON [four dots forming a square] / TORONTO'

Copyright: 'FIRST PUBLISHED 1937 / PRINTED IN GREAT BRITAIN AT THE WINDMILL PRESS / KINGSWOOD, SURREY'

$(A-I)^8 (K)^4$

pp. (i-iv) 1-148

7 7/16″ × 5 1/16″

Contents: p.i: half title; p.ii: blank; p.iii: title; p.iv: copyright; pp. 1-6: 'PROLOGUE'; pp. 7-148: text.

Paper: Cream wove stock. Edges trimmed. Endpapers of heavier stock.

Binding: Gray reddish orange cloth (c.39). Spine stamped in gold: 'WALLACE / STEGNER / [vertical] Remembering Laughter / [horizontal] HEINEMANN'.

Dust jacket: Beige with rust and green. Front: '[rust] REMEMBER-ING / LAUGHTER / [illus. of couple embracing beneath a tree] / WALLACE STEGNER'. Spine: '[rust with black and beige letter-ing] WALLACE / STEGNER / [yellow flower with green stem] / [vertical] [beige] REMEMBERING LAUGHTER [yellow flower] /

[horizontal] HEINEMANN'. Back: ad for John Steinbeck's *Of Mice and Men*. Front flap: blurb for RL. Back flap: 'New Novels from / Heinemann'.

Publication: "6 s. net" Received by BL 13 September 1937.

Locations: WS (1), BL (1), OX (1)

A2.3

Third edition: Dell ($.10), 200,000 copies. December, 1950. Dell Book 17 (pb).

A2.4

Fourth edition: Toronto: Harlequin ($.25), 1952.

Notes: According to Stegner correspondence, the Little, Brown edition has been out of print since 1944. The plates were melted in 1942. Reprinted in *The American Reader* by Simpson & Nevins, Summer, 1941 ($2.50). See B3.

A3   *The*
Potter's House

First edition, first (and only) printing (1938)

Title page: '[within red double-ruled note tacked upon "door"] The / Potter's / House / [blue star] / BY WALLACE / STEGNER / 1938 / *The Prairie Press: Muscatine, Iowa*'

Copyright: '*Copyright, 1938, by Wallace Stegner / Printed in the United States of America / First Edition*'

(1-5)⁸

pp. (1-10) 11-75 (76-80)

9 3/4″ × 6 3/8″

Contents: pp. 1-4: blank; p. 5: half title; p. 6: blank; p. 7: title; p. 8: copyright; p. 9: dedication, '*To Philip and Margaret Gray*'; p. 10: blank; pp. 11-75: text; p. 76: colophon; pp. 77-80: blank.

Typography and paper: Running heads at sides of pages, red page

The Potter's House

*

BY WALLACE
STEGNER

1 9 3 8
The Prairie Press : Muscatine, Iowa

Detail of title page for A3

numbers. 'Colophon / This book has been designed and printed by / Carroll D. Coleman at The Prairie Press. / The type faces are Kennerley and Goudy / Text, both original type designs by / Frederic / W. Goudy. This edition is limited to / four hundred and ninety copies'. Cream laid stock, watermarked 'Strathmore Wayside Text U.S.A.' Edges uncut. Endpapers of heavier cream stock.

Binding: Medium gray cloth (c.265) V cloth (smooth). Front and back covers blank. Spine gilt-stamped: '[leaf designs and short double rules] THE POTTER'S HOUSE [star] STEGNER [reverse of design at top]'.

Dust jacket: Glassine wrapper.

Publication: December 1, 1938 (LC). 490 copies only printed. $2.50.

Locations: WS (2), NC (1), LC (2), FC (1)

Note: See D10. First published in *American Prefaces*, 3 (Summer 1938), 147-151, 165-176. Reviewer raved about format; called it "a desirable gift volume".

A4 *On a Darkling Plain*

A4.1.a

First edition, first printing (1940)

Title page: 'WALLACE STEGNER On a / Darkling Plain / *Men are brothers by life lived, and are hurt for it.* / ARCHIBALD MACLEISH / HARCOURT, BRACE AND COMPANY, NEW YORK'

Copyright page: 'COPYRIGHT, 1939, 1940, BY / WALLACE E. STEGNER / *All rights reserved, including / the right to reproduce this book / or portions thereof in any form.* / *first edition* / *Designed by Robert Josephy* / PRINTED IN THE UNITED STATES OF AMERICA / BY QUINN & BODEN COMPANY, INC., RAHWAY, N.J.'

$(1-15)^8$

pp. (i-vi) (1-2) 3-230 (231-234)

7 15/16″ × 5 5/16″

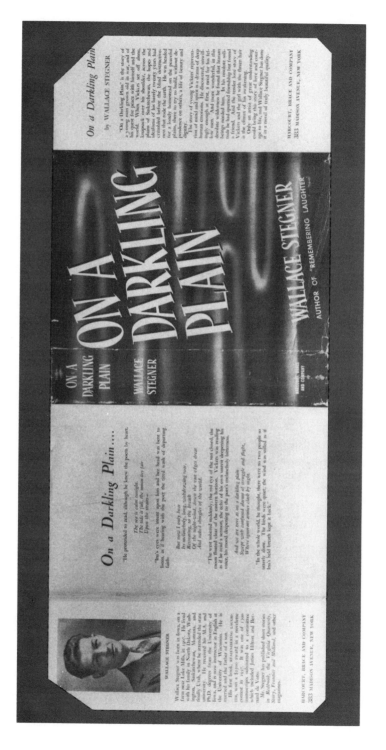

Dust jacket for A4.1.a

Contents: p.i: half title; p.ii: blank; p.iii: title; p.iv: copyright; p.v: dedication, 'TO MARY'; p.vi: blank; p. 1: second half title; p. 2: blank; pp. 3-231: text; pp. 232-234: blank.

Paper: Cream wove stock. Edges trimmed. Endpapers of heavier cream stock.

Binding: Dark greenish blue (c.174) V cloth (smooth) with silver stamped lettering. Front and back covers blank. Spine: 'ON A / DARKLING / PLAIN / WALLACE / STEGNER / HARCOURT, BRACE / AND COMPANY'.

Dust jacket: White with light bluish green (c.163) and medium gray (c.265). Lettering in white. Front: '[lettering slanted to left] ON A / DARKLING / PLAIN / WALLACE STEGNER / AUTHOR OF "REMEMBERING LAUGHTER"'. Spine: 'ON A / DARKLING / PLAIN / WALLACE / STEGNER / HARCOURT, BRACE / AND COMPANY'. Back has blurb on the book. Front flap: blurb. Back flap: photograph of Wallace Stegner and biographical sketch.

Publication: According to *Publisher's Weekly*, date of publication was February 8, 1940. Information received from Harcourt corroborates that date. It went out of print July 1, 1941. The publisher records only one printing, but there was a second printing (see A4.1.b). $2.00.

Locations: WS (1), NC (1), SA (1), LC (2)

Note: First appeared in *Redbook*, November, 1939, under the title, "Clash by Night," as a serial. See D13.

A4.1.b

First edition, second printing (1940)

Title, collation, contents, paper, binding as in A4.1.a.

On copyright page: 'COPYRIGHT, 1939, 1940, BY / WALLACE E. STEGNER / ALL RIGHTS RESERVED, INCLUDING /

THE RIGHT TO REPRODUCE THIS BOOK / OR PORTIONS
THEREOF IN ANY FORM / SECOND PRINTING, January
1940'.

Locations: JS (1)

A5   *Fire and Ice*

First edition, only printing (1941)

Title page: 'FIRE / AND / ICE / WALLACE STEGNER /
DUELL, SLOAN AND PEARCE / NEW YORK'

Copyright: 'COPYRIGHT, 1941, BY / WALLACE STEGNER /
*All rights reserved, including / the right to reproduce this book / or
portions thereof in any form. / first edition /* PRINTED IN THE
UNITED STATES OF AMERICA / BY QUINN & BODEN
COMPANY, INC., RAHWAY, N.J.'

(1-14)⁸

pp. (i-vi) (1-2) 3-214 (215-218)

7 15/16″ × 5 5/16″

Contents: p.i: half title; p.ii: 'Books by Wallace Stegner /
REMEMBERING LAUGHTER / ON A DARKLING PLAIN /
FIRE AND ICE'; p.iii: title; p.iv: copyright; p.v: dedication, 'TO /
M.P.S.'; p.vi: blank; p. 1: second half title; p. 2: blank; pp. 3-214:
text; pp. 215-218: blank.

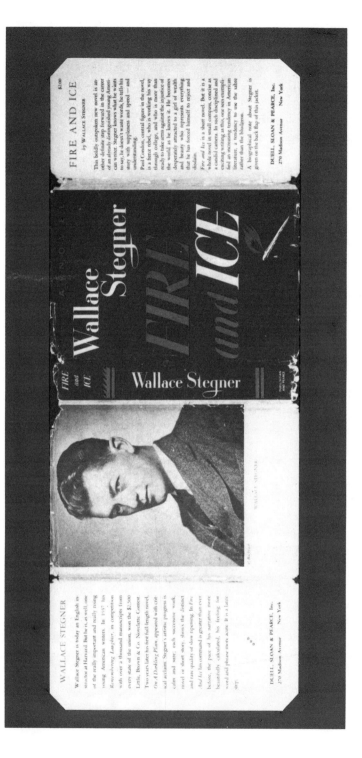

Dust jacket for A5

Paper: Heavy cream wove. Edges trimmed. Endpapers of heavier cream wove stock.

Binding: Grayish purplish blue (c.204) V cloth (smooth). Front and back covers blank. Spine: '[white] *FIRE / and / ICE* [wave rule] / [wide rule] / Wallace / Stegner / DUELL, SLOAN / AND PEARCE'.

Dust jacket: Dark purplish blue (c.201). Front: '[red] A NOVEL / [white] Wallace / Stegner / [red] *FIRE / and* [white] *ICE* / [beneath is a flaming icicle torch]'. Spine: '[white] *FIRE / and / ICE* [red] [thick wave rule] / [rule] / [horizontal] [white] Wallace Stegner / [vertical] [double red rule] / [white] DUELL, SLOAN / AND PEARCE'. Back: photo of Wallace Stegner by Bachrach. Front flap: '$2.00 / [red] FIRE AND ICE / [black] *by* WALLACE STEGNER'. Back flap: biographical note.

Publication: Duell, Sloan & Pearce, has no record of the number of copies printed or date of publication. According to *PW*, it was published May 17, 1941. The two copies housed at the Library of Congress were received March 24, 1941, with a publication date cited as April 24. At most there were 2500 printed and less than 2000 sold. $2.00.

Locations: WS (1 without dj), NC (1), SA (1), JS (1), LC (2 without dj)

Note: Wallace Stegner estimates a 2500-copy printing and sale of approximately 1900. This is, perhaps, the rarest of Stegner books to locate, particularly with dust jacket intact. In a letter from his agents, Brandt and Brandt, dated April 15, 1948, Stegner was informed that the text plates, jacket plates, and dies for *Fire and Ice* and *The Big Rock Candy Mountain* were forwarded to the Riverside Press. His agents wrote on April 14, 1948 that "Wally Stegner says, with regret, that he cannot find any immediate use for 515 sets of sheets for *Fire and Ice*. I am afraid, therefore, that you will have to have them pulped."

A6 *Mormon Country*

A6.1.a

First edition, first printing (1942)

Title page: '[within a dark greenish blue (c.174) American Folkways shield device] AMERICAN / FOLKWAYS / [within dark greenish blue panel] [white] EDITED BY ERSKINE CALDWELL / [black] MORMON / COUNTRY / by / WALLACE STEGNER / [white] DUELL, SLOAN & PEARCE [dot] NEW YORK'

Copyright: 'COPYRIGHT, 1942, BY / WALLACE STEGNER / *All rights reserved, including / the right to reproduce this book / or portions thereof in any form. / first printing* / PRINTED IN THE UNITED STATES OF AMERICA'

$(1-31)^6$

pp. (i-viii) ix-x (1-2) 3-349 (350) 351-362

8 7/16″ × 5 5/8″

Dust jacket for A6.1.a

Contents: p.i: half title; p.ii: other books in the American Folkways series; p.iii: title; p.iv: copyright; p.v: dedication, '*For Mary, as all of them are.*'; p.vi: blank; p.vii: '*Acknowledgments*'; p.viii: blank; p.ix-x: '*Contents*'; p. 1: Part I title; p. 2: blank; pp. 3-349: text; p. 350: blank; pp. 351-362: '*Index*'.

Paper: Cream wove. Edges trimmed. Smooth white endpapers with United States map in blue ("Mormon Country" highlighted in white).

Binding: Rough cloth in very deep purplish red (c.257) and black. Front: American Folkways shield device stamped in black in lower right corner. Back cover blank. Spine: '[wide rule] / [4 narrow rules] / [black panel with gold lettering] MORMON / COUNTRY / [dot] WALLACE / STEGNER / [black] [4 narrow rules] / [wide rule] / [4 narrow rules] / [lower edge] [4 narrow rules] / [small black panel with gold lettering] DUELL, SLOAN / AND PEARCE'. / [4 narrow rules] / [wide rule]'.

Dust jacket: Beige with medium greenish blue (c.173) and medium reddish brown (c.43). Top and bottom edge trimmed in brown. Front: '[map of Western United States in background] [letters slanted to left] [beige edged in brown] MORMON / COUNTRY / [brown] WALLACE STEGNER'. Spine: '[brown] [4 narrow rules] / [on blue panel] [brown] MORMON / COUNTRY / [beige] [dot] / WALLACE / STEGNER / [brown and beige] [American Folkways series shield device superimposed on narrow and wide rules] / [blue-green trees] / [brown] [4 narrow rules] [narrow panel with beige lettering] DUELL, SLOAN / AND PEARCE / [brown] [4 narrow rules]'. Back: blurb on American Folkways series. Front flap: blurb on MC. Back flap: blurbs on other American Folkways titles.

Publication: *Publisher's Weekly* gives September 24, 1942 as the date of publication. "Duell, Sloan & Pearce 3.00 372p. Map, O (8 vo: 25 cm). An anecdotal, descriptive account of the Mormons, their way of life, customs and leaders, and of the country where they settled." LC cites same pub date. No Duell, Sloan & Pearce records available. Stegner correspondence mentions 4,000 to 5,000 sold by 1951.

Locations: WS (1), NC (2), LC (2)

A6.1.b

Second printing (1942)

On copyright page: 'COPYRIGHT, 1942, BY / WALLACE STEGNER / *All rights reserved, including / the right to reproduce this book / or portions thereof in any form.* / Second printing / PRINTED IN THE UNITED STATES OF AMERICA'.

Binding: Light blue (c.181) cloth, rather than the red used in the first printing.

Dust jacket: Same, with some changes in the American Folkways advertisement on the back. Instead of a paragraph by Erskine Caldwell, there are portions of reviews by Harold Rugg and Lewis Gannett. On the front flap is "Second Large Printing".

A6.1.c

Third printing (1942)

Note: Not seen. Assumed third printing since there is a fourth printing (Location: Hepworth).

A6.1.d

Fourth printing (1942)

Light blue (c.181).

A6.1.e

Fifth printing: New York: Bonanza (MCMXLII).

Hardcover reprint by Bonanza, a division of Crown publishers, by arrangement with Meredith Press (who bought out Duell, Sloan, & Pearce).

A6.1.f

Sixth printing: New York: Hawthorn, (1975).

"Reprint of the edition published by Duell, Sloan & Pearce, New York. In series American Folkways." $3.95 paperback.

A6.1.g

Seventh printing: Lincoln: University of Nebraska, (1981).

Bison book. BB778. Dec., 1981 - 3,510 - $6.95 pap.
                    Nov., 1984 - 2,532 - $8.50 pap.
                    May 1988 - 2,164 - $8.50 pap.

Cloth edition published March, 1982 - 264 copies - $21.50. Plain library binding. No dust jacket.

A7 *The Big Rock Candy Mountain*

A7.1.a

First edition, first printing (1943)

Title page: 'THE / BIG ROCK CANDY / MOUNTAIN / WALLACE STEGNER / DUELL, SLOAN AND PEARCE / NEW YORK'

Copyright: 'COPYRIGHT, 1938, 1940, 1942, 1943, BY / WALLACE STEGNER / *All rights reserved, including / the right to reproduce this book / or portions thereof in any form.* / *first edition* / PRODUCING BOOKS IN WARTIME / This book has been produced in conformity / with war-time economy standards. The pub-/lishers will do their utmost in meeting the / objectives of the War Production Board to-/ wards the successful prosecution of the war. / PRINTED IN THE UNITED STATES OF AMERICA / BY AMERICAN BOOK-STRATFORD PRESS, INC., NEW YORK'

$(1-11)^{16} (12-17)^{14}$

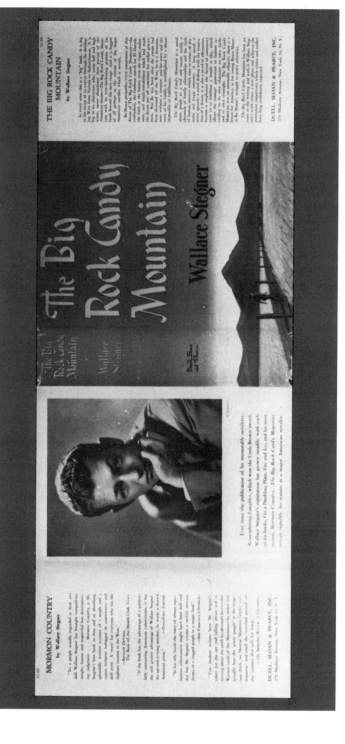

Dust jacket for A7.1.a

pp. (i-iv) (1-2) 3-515 (516)

8 1/4″ × 5 1/2″

Contents: p.i: half title; p.ii: '*Books by Wallace Stegner*'; p.iii: title; p.iv: copyright; p. 1: second half title; p. 2: blank; pp. 3-515: text; p. 516: blank.

Paper: Cream wove. Edges trimmed. Endpapers of heavier cream wove stock.

Binding: Very deep red (c.14) cloth. Also seen in dark purplish red, rust color, and green. Front and back covers blank. Spine gilt-stamped: 'The Big / Rock Candy / Mountain / Wallace / Stegner / DUELL, SLOAN / AND PEARCE'. All edges trimmed.

Dust jacket: Beige with medium greenish blue (c.173) and light yellow (c.86). Front: '[illus. of man walking down a road through fields of wheat towards the mountains] [yellow lettering on blue sky background] The Big / Rock Candy / Mountain / [black] Wallace Stegner'. Spine: '[yellow on blue] The Big / Rock Candy / Mountain / Wallace / Stegner / [black] Duell, Sloan / and Pearce'. Back: photo of Wallace Stegner by Bachrach and paragraph on him. Front flap: blurb on BRCM. Back flap: portions of reviews of *Mormon Country*.

Publication: From *Publisher's Weekly*: "September 25, 1943. *The Big Rock Candy Mountain*. 515p. O (8 vo: 25 cm). (c. '38-'43). New York: Duell, Sloan & Pearce. $3.00). The developing West, from Minnesota to Saskatchewan, is the setting of the story of dynamic Bo Mason, a pioneer born too late, and of his wife who wanted security." LC dates it September 24, 1943. Advance sales numbered 12,000. First printing was at least 15,000 copies. Agent (Brandt and Brandt) correspondence of December 2, 1943 stated that sales were over 26,000 copies. Stegner's own estimate is "somewhere between 25,000 and 28,000."

Locations: WS (2), NC (3), SA (1 red, 1 green), LC (1)

Note: This is Wallace Stegner's big book. Unfortunately, it was written during the War years, when production was difficult. Many copies were sold and this massive work has been reprinted numerous times. It was featured on the front cover of *PW* August 23, 1943. This book was the first to make an impact on the foreign market and was published in French, German, and Rumanian (not seen in Rumanian edition).

An edition, in wrappers, came out simultaneously. Both hardcover and paper-bound copies are designated as "first edition" on the copyright page. Only one paper copy has been seen (WS). The cover is identical to the dust jacket of the first edition. These paper-back copies are not uncorrected proofs. A small number of paper-back copies were used by Duell, Sloan, and Pearce to fill orders as late as November 21, 1947.

A7.1.b

Second printing (1943)

Title, collation, contents, paper, binding as in A7.1.a.

Printing size unknown. Binding in both red and green. The second printing has a "2" on the copyright page.

A7.1.c

Third printing: Cleveland: World Publishing Co., 1945.

In 1945 2,800 sets of sheets of the first printing were given to World "on completion of the Cheap Edition deal." 'FORUM BOOKS EDITION / First Printing February 1945'. There was another printing in December, 1945.

A7.2

Second edition: New York: Editions for the Armed Services, (1944?) N-32. 4 1/2″ × 6 1/2″

Abridged by Louis Untermeyer for "wartime reading." Date on the copyright page is 1943, but correspondence shows that the cut version was scheduled for October, 1944.

A 7.3

First English edition, first printing (1950)

Title page: 'WALLACE STEGNER / The Big / Rock Candy / Mountain / LONDON / HAMMOND, HAMMOND & CO. LTD / 87 GOWER STREET W.C.I'

Copyright: *'Copyright by Wallace Stegner / First published 1950 / Printed in Great Britain by / Richard Clay and Company, Ltd., Bungay, Suffolk / 5.50'*

(1-20)^{16}

pp. (1-4) 5-631 (632-640)

7 3/4″ × 5 13/16″

Contents: p. 1: half title; p. 2: *'Other Books by Wallace Stegner*; p. 3: title; p. 4: copyright; pp. 5-631: text; p. 632: blank; pp. 633-639: publisher's advertisement, including Stegner's *Second Growth*; p. 640: blank.

Paper: Cream wove. Edges trimmed. Endpapers of heavier cream stock.

Binding: Medium reddish brown (c.43) rough cloth. Front and back covers blank. Spine: '[gilt-stamped] THE / BIG ROCK / CANDY / MOUNTAIN / [star] / Wallace / Stegner / [publisher's device] / HAMMOND / HAMMOND'.

Dust jacket: Beige with medium purplish blue (c.200) and shades of brown. Front: '[white letters on blue sky background] The BIG ROCK CANDY / MOUNTAIN / [drawing of a mother and two children travelling West in a covered wagon] / [blue] Wallace /

Dust jacket for A7.3

Stegner'. Spine: '[within a square white panel] The / BIG ROCK / CANDY / MOUNTAIN / [illus. of a man leaning against a car] / [white panel] WALLACE / STEGNER / [sketch of wheat] / [within small white panel] [publisher's device] / HAMMOND / HAMMOND'. Back: '[within orange triple-ruled rectangle] photograph of WS and quotations from English journals re: *Second Growth*'. Front flap: blurb on BRCM. Back flap: 'RECENT FICTION TITLES'.

Publication: Published in Great Britain in June, 1950. Price: 15s. Reprinted in September and October, 1950. "Daily Mail Choice" for June. By June 30, Hammond and Hammond sold 2,460 copies. Received by the British Library 5 June 1950.

Locations: BL (1), OX (1) Later printings: WS (1), NC (2)

A7.4.a

Fourth edition, first printing: New York: Sagamore Press, 1957.

According to *PW*: 563p. size D (12 mo: 20 cm). (American Century Series, S-19) 57-12439. '57, c'38-'43. pap., 1.95. A new text setting with excised matter in the opening section.

A7.4.b

Second printing: New York: Hill and Wang (1962?)

Reprint of 1,000 in white wrapper for University of Wisconsin bookstore. Not priced.

Sagamore was taken over by Hill and Wang and acquired BRCM when they bought the rights from Sagamore.

A7.4.c

Third printing: Lincoln: University of Nebraska, (1983) Bison book. BB855. July, 1983 - 5,088 copies - $9.95 pap. Reprint of Sagamore edition.

A7.4.d

Fourth printing: Lincoln: University of Nebraska, (1983).

Bison book. BB855. November 6, 1987 - 2,576 copies - $9.95.

A7.5

Fifth edition: New York: Doubleday, 1973. $8.95.

Publication date of 5,000 copies was February 9, 1973.

A7.6

Sixth edition: New York: Pocket Books, 1977.

On copyright page: 'THE BIG ROCK CANDY MOUNTAIN / Doubleday edition published 1973 / POCKET BOOK edition published March, 1977'. Paperback $2.50. On the back is written "Over 1,000,000 copies sold!"

A7.7

Seventh edition: Franklin Center, Pennsylvania: Franklin Library, 1978.

"Signed Limited Edition" from The Franklin Library. Binding is rust leather. 55-pound high opaque book paper specially milled for the volume. Signed by WS on the limitation page. The illustrations are from paintings by Charles Reid. Printing of 12,500 copies. March, 1978.

Note: Portions of *The Big Rock Candy Mountain* appear in many periodicals, anthologies, and textbooks. Permissions were numerous, particularly for "The Colt," which was published as a separate short story. See D24.

The manuscript was sent to the Iowa Author collection in June, 1957.

A8 *One Nation*

A8.1.a

First edition, first printing (1945)

Title page: '[extending over pp.ii-iii] [black and white crowd photo] / One Nation / [p.ii] *BOOKS BY WALLACE STEGNER:* / *Remembering Laughter* / *Potter's House* / *On a Darkling Plain* / *Fire and Ice* / *Mormon Country* / *Big Rock Candy Mountain* / *One Nation* / [p.iii] BY WALLACE STEGNER / AND THE EDITORS OF LOOK / *A Life-in-America Prize Book* / 1945 / HOUGHTON MIFFLIN COMPANY [dot] BOSTON / [publisher's device] / [Gothic] The Riverside Press'

Copyright: 'COPYRIGHT 1945, BY COWLES MAGAZINES, INC. / PRINTED IN THE UNITED STATES OF AMERICA / BY THE INTAGLIO GRAVURE PROCESS AT / THE ULLMAN COMPANY, INC., BROOKLYN, N.Y.'

$(1-11)^{16}$

pp. (i-iv) v (vi) vii (viii-x) (1) 2-15 (16-18) 19-43 (44) 45-67 (68)
69-91 (92-94) 95-115 (116) 117-137 (138-140) 141-167 (168)
169-193 (194-196) 197-221 (222) 223-236 (237) 238-249 (250)
251-269 (270-272) 273-299 (300) 301-327 (328) 329-340 (341-342)

9 9/16" × 6 9/16"

Illustrations: 324 black and white photographs.

Contents: p.i: half title; pp.ii-iii: title; p.iv: copyright; p.v: Foreword
signed: 'Harlan Logan / Editor of LOOK'; p.vi: blank; p.vii:
'Contents'; p.viii: blank; p.ix: second half title; p.x: photo; pp.
1-336: text; p. 337: 'Acknowledgments subscribed 'Wallace
Stegner'; pp. 338-340: 'Pictures Credits'; pp. 341-342: blank.

Paper: Cream wove. Edges trimmed. Endpapers of heavier cream
stock.

Binding: Yellow gray (c.93) cloth. Front: '[within a square
medium reddish orange (c.37) panel within three narrow rules]
[black] One / Nation'. Back cover blank. Spine: '[three narrow
medium reddish orange rules] / [within medium reddish orange
panel] [black] One / Nation / WALLACE / STEGNER / AND
THE / EDITORS / OF LOOK / [three narrow medium reddish
orange rules] / [publisher's device] / HOUGHTON / MIFFLIN /
COMPANY'.

Dust jacket: Beige with red, white, and blue. Front: '[red] one /
nation / [along left side twisted rope in red, yellow, blue, and
green] / [lower half of front in deep gray purple (c.229) with map
of the U.S. in red, white, and blue] / [beige] WALLACE
STEGNER / and the EDITORS of "LOOK" / [white] A
text-and-picture study of eight of the most / colorful of our
minorities which together make the / majority of our people.'
Spine: '[vertical] [yellow orange c.66)] one nation [beige]
WALLACE STEGNER / and the EDITORS of "LOOK" /
[horizontal] [white] H.M.CO.' Back: photograph and biographical
sketch of WS. Front flap: blurb on ONE NATION. / Price at upper right, '$3.75'; below: *Jacket by George Kelley*. / ad for war

bonds and stamps. Back flap: blurb on *When Johnny Comes Marching Home* by Dixon Wecter.

Publication: *Publisher's Weekly* (September 25, 1945): "*One Nation.* 347p. O (8 vo: 25 cm) (Life-in-America prize book) c. Boston, Houghton 3.75. A picture-and-text presentation of the problem of status of minorities—Negroes, Filipinos, Jews, Catholics, Mexicans, Japanese—in the United States; the injustice and violence these minorities now suffer, the hope for future." LC has copies dated September 10 and September 25. According to Houghton Mifflin, first printing was 10,000.

Locations: WS (2), NC (2), LC (2)

A8.1.b

Second printing: 9/5/45 - 5,000 copies.

A8.1.c

Third printing: 10/17/45 - 5,000 copies.

A8.1.d

Fourth printing: 9/16/46 - 3,500 copies.

Note: This book was made up of articles which were intended for serial publication in "LOOK" first. The series of articles was instead "boiled down into one quite long, but thoroughly innocuous—and I would think, ineffective—article." (Stegner in *Conversations*, p. 66). Houghton Mifflin published the book, which won the Life-in-America award. *One Nation* shared the *Saturday Review* Anisfield-Wolf Award for the year's best book on race relations.

A9 *Second Growth*

A9.1.a

First edition, first printing (1947)

Title page: '[within yellow panel] WALLACE STEGNER / Second / Growth / [publisher's device] / HOUGHTON MIFFLIN COMPANY / Boston [dot] 1947 [gothic] The Riverside Press Cambridge'

Copyright: 'Copyright, 1947, by Wallace Stegner / All rights reserved including the right to reproduce / this book or parts thereof in any form / A Note on Fictional Character / The making of fiction entails the creation of places and persons / with all the seeming of reality, and these places and persons, no / matter how a writer tries to invent them, must be made up piece-/meal from sublimations of his own experience. There is no other material out of which fiction can / be made. / In that sense, and in that sense only, the people and the village / of this story are taken from life. The village I have tried to make / one that would exist anywhere

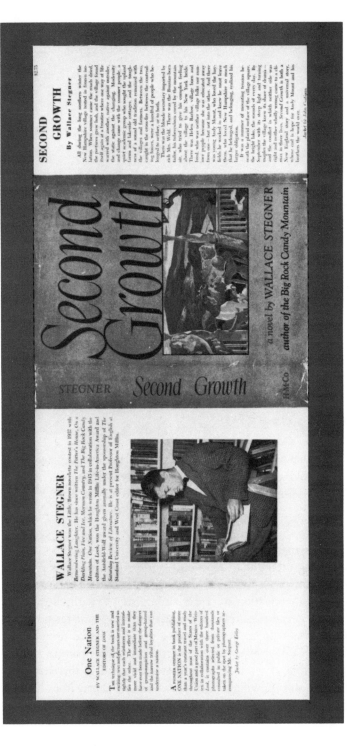

Dust jacket for A9.1.a

in rural New England; though it is / placed in northern New
Hampshire, I hope it would have been just / as much at home in
Vermont or Maine, or even in western Massa- /chusetts. The
people are such people as this village seems to me / likely to
contain, and the cultural dynamism, the conflict on the / frontier
between two ways of life, which is its central situation, is / one
that has been reproduced in an endlessly changing pattern all / over
the United States. It should be, if I have been successful, as /
visible in Carmel-by-the-Sea or Taos or Charlevoix as on the
ficti-/tious Ammosaukee River. These people and their village took
form / in my mind not as portraits but as symbols. There are no
portraits, / personal or geographical, in the novel. / [Gothic] The
Riverside Press / [Roman] Cambridge [dot] Massachusetts / Printed
in the U.S.A.'

$(1)^{10} (2\text{-}16)^8$

pp. (i-xvi) 1-240 (241-244)

8 1/4″ × 5 1/4″

Contents: pp.i-iii: blank; pp.iv-v: double-paged map of the 'Town of
Westwick'; p.vi: blank; p.vii: half title; p.viii: 'BOOKS BY
WALLACE STEGNER'; p.ix: title; p.x:: copyright; p.xi: dedication,
'For Mary'; p.xii: blank; p.xiii: 'Contents'; p.xiv: blank; p.xv:
second half title; p.xvi: blank; pp. 1-240: text; pp. 241-244: blank.

Paper: Cream wove. Edges trimmed. Endpapers of heavier cream
stock.

Binding: Light green (c.144) V cloth (smooth). Dark blue (c.183)
panels on front and spine. Front: '[light green on a dark blue square
panel] SECOND / GROWTH / [below panel] [dark blue]
STEGNER'. Back cover blank. Spine: '[light green within dark blue
horizontal panel] SECOND / GROWTH / [below panel] [dark
blue] STEGNER / HOUGHTON / MIFFLIN CO.'

Dust jacket: Beige with light gray olive (c.109) front and spine.

Lettering in medium brown (c.58) and olive black (c.114). Front: '[olive black] Second / Growth / [illus. of people gathered, overlooking the hills] [framed in olive black rule] / [brown] a novel by [olive black] WALLACE STEGNER / author of the Big Rock Candy Mountain'. Spine: [vertical] [brown] STEGNER [olive black] Second Growth / [horizontal] [brown] H.M.Co.' Back: biographical sketch and photograph of Wallace Stegner. Front flap: blurb on SECOND GROWTH. *'Jacket by John Costigan'*. Back flap: blurb on *One Nation*.

Publication: WS estimates the printing size as 6,000-8,000 copies. *Publisher's Weekly* information: "August 23, 1947. *Second Growth*. 240p. (map) O (8 vo: 25 cm) c. Boston, Houghton 2.75. A story of summer in a northern New Hampshire village, a summer of emotional crisis for individuals among the villagers and summer people." LC copies dated July 15 and August 30. Houghton Mifflin records show one printing of 10,000 copies.

Locations: WS (2), NC (2), LC (2)

Note: Two sets of bound galleys exist with the first title; *The Walls of Westwick*. These are owned by Wallace Stegner. Other titles originally considered were *Country Dance* and *Landscape with Figures*.

A9.1.b

Second printing: Lincoln: University of Nebraska, 1985.

Bison book. BB940. Sept., 1985 - 3,072 copies - $6.95 pap.

Cloth edition published October, 1985 - 218 copies - $18.95. Plain library binding. No dust jacket.

A9.2

Second edition: New York: Popular Library, 1947.

"FIRST TIME IN PAPERBACK". .75 #75-1291. Reprinted 1969.

Dust jacket for A9.3

A9.3

First English edition, first printing (1948)

Title page: 'WALLACE STEGNER / [star] / SECOND GROWTH / [star] / LONDON / HAMMOND, HAMMOND & CO. LTD. / 87 GOWER STREET, W.C.I'

Copyright: '*Copyright, 1948, by Wallace Stegner / Printed in Great Britain / by Latimer Trend & Co. Ltd., Plymouth / 6.48*'.

(1-14)^8

pp. (1-6) 7-221 (222-224)

7 7/8" × 5 1/8"

Contents: p. 1: half title; p. 2: '*Also by Wallace Stegner*'; p. 3: title; p. 4: copyright; p. 5: 'Contents'; p. 6: dedication, 'FOR / MARY'; pp. 7-221: text; p. 222: blank; p. 223: 'TO THE READER' (reviews of other books published by Hammond and Hammond); p. 224: '*This book is produced in complete / conformity with the authorized / economy standards*'.

Paper: Cream wove. Edges trimmed. Endpapers of heavier cream stock.

Binding: Gray olive green (c.127) cloth, rough. Stamped in gilt. Front: 'SECOND GROWTH / WALLACE STEGNER'. Back cover blank. Spine: '[star] / SECOND / GROWTH / [star] / Wallace / Stegner / [publisher's castle device] / HAMMOND / HAMMOND'.

Dust jacket: Light gray olive (c.109) with dark brown (c.59) and white print. Front: '[illus. of a rooming house and tailor shop with figures] [white] Second / Growth / [brown] Wallace Stegner / STEIN [dust jacket artist]'. Spine: '[brown] Second / Growth / WALLACE / STEGNER / [white] [publisher's castle device] /

[red] HAMMOND / HAMMOND'. Back: 'NEW FICTION
TITLES'. Front flap: blurb on SECOND GROWTH. Back flap:
blurb on book by another author.

Publication: '9s.6d.NET' Received at BL 11 June 1948.

Locations: WS (4), NC (1), BL (1), OX (1)

A10 *The*
Women on the Wall

A10.1.a

First edition, first printing (1950)

Title page: '[typographical orn.] / The Women / on the Wall / [rule] / by Wallace Stegner / HOUGHTON MIFFLIN COMPANY [dot] BOSTON'

Copyright: 'Copyright, 1940, 1941, 1942, 1943, 1944, 1945, 1946, / 1947, 1948, by Wallace Stegner / ALL RIGHTS RESERVED INCLUDING THE RIGHT TO REPRODUCE / THIS BOOK OR PARTS THEREOF IN ANY FORM / [Gothic] The Riverside Press / CAMBRIDGE [dot] MASSACHUSETTS / [Roman] Printed in the U. S. A.' Verso of half title: '1950 / [rule] / [Gothic] The Riverside Press Cambridge'.

$(1-18)^8$

pp. (i-v) vi (vii-x) 1-227 (278)

8 1/8″ × 5 1/2″

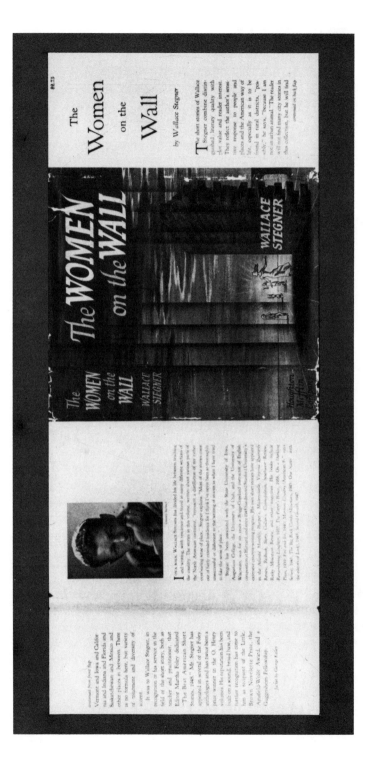

Dust jacket for A10.1.a

Contents: p.i: half title; p.ii: 'BOOKS BY WALLACE STEGNER';
p.iii: title; p.iv: copyright; pp.v-vi: 'Acknowledgments'; p.vii:
'Contents'; p.viii: blank; p.ix: second half title; p.x: blank; pp.
1-277: text; p. 278: blank.

Text Contents: "Beyond the Glass Mountain," "The Berry Patch,"
"The Women on the Wall," "Bugle Song," "Balance His, Swing
Yours," "Saw Gang," "Goin' to Town," "The View From the
Balcony," "The Volcano," "Two Rivers," "Hostage," "In the
Twilight," "Butcher Bird," "The Double Corner," "The Colt,"
"The Chink," "Chip Off the Old Block," "The Sweetness of the
Twisted Apples." All short stories have appeared previously, in
either periodicals or incorporated into the novel *The Big Rock
Candy Mountain*.

Paper: Cream wove. Edges trimmed. Endpapers of heavier wove
stock.

Binding: Light bluish green (c.163) cloth. Front stamped with
typographical ornament in red. Back covers blank. Spine stamped in
dark green with small red ornament: '[orn.] / The / [orn.] Women
/ [orn.] / on the / [orn.] / Wall / [orn.] / [orn.] / STEGNER /
[orn.] / HOUGHTON / MIFFLIN CO.'

Dust jacket: Cream with yellow gray (c.93), gray yellow (c.90),
dark blue (c.183), and red. Front: '[yellow] The [gray] WOMEN /
[yellow] on the [gray] WALL / [yellow] WALLACE / STEGNER'.
Spine lettered in yellow gray, light gray yellowish brown (c.79), and
dark gray olive green (c.128): '[yellow] The / [light gray yellowish
brown] WOMEN / [yellow] on the / [light gray yellowish brown]
WALL / [yellow] WALLACE / STEGNER / [dark gray olive
green] Houghton / Mifflin / Company'. Back: photo of author
'Courtesy Bachrach' and biographical sketch. Front flap: blurb for
The Women on the Wall. Back flap: 'continued from front flap /
Jacket by George Kelley'.

Publication: According to *Publisher's Weekly*: "January 3, 1950.
Women on the Wall. 283p. O (8 vo: 25 cm) (c. '40-'48) Boston,
Houghton 2.75. Short stories of people and ways of rural

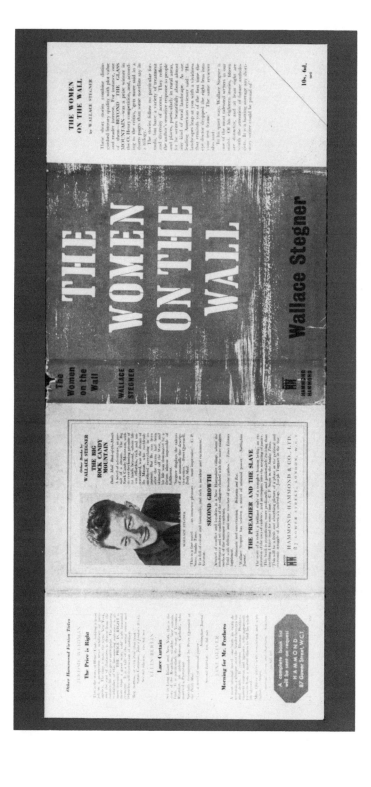

Dust jacket for A10.2

America." Houghton Mifflin records show 4,500 copies published 1/3/50.

Locations: WS (4), NC (1), LC (2)

A10.1.b

Second printing: Lincoln: University of Nebraska, (1981)

Bison book. BB710. Dec., 1980 - 3,036 copies - $5.50 pap.

Cloth copy published January, 1981 - 211 copies - $16.50. Issued in plain library binding, without dust jacket.

A10.1.c

Third printing: Lincoln: University of Nebraska, (1981)

Bison book. BB710. March 1987 - 1,068 copies - $8.95.

A10.2

First English edition, first printing (1952)

Title page: 'THE / WOMEN ON THE / WALL / by / WALLACE STEGNER / LONDON / HAMMOND, HAMMOND & COMPANY'

Copyright: 'COPYRIGHT BY WALLACE STEGNER / *First published in Great Britain 1952 / Printed in Great Britain by / Richard Clay and Company Ltd., Bungay, Suffolk / for Hammond, Hammond & Co., Ltd., / 87 Gower Street, / W.C. I / 3.52'*

$(1-16)^8$

pp. (1-8) 9-255 (256)

7 7/8" × 5 1/8"

Contents: p. 1: half title; p. 2: '*Other Books by Wallace Stegner*'; p. 3: title; p. 4: copyright; p. 5: 'ACKNOWLEDGMENTS'; p. 6: blank; p. 7: 'CONTENTS'; p. 8: blank; pp. 9-255: text; p. 256: portions of reviews of other Stegner books.

Paper: Cream wove. Edges trimmed. Endpapers of heavier cream stock.

Binding: Very red (c.11) pebbled paper-covered boards. Front and back covers blank. Spine: '[gilt-stamped] The / Women / on the / Wall / [dot] / WALLACE / STEGNER / [publisher's castle device] / HAMMOND / HAMMOND'.

Dust jacket: White (c.263) with pale blue (c.185) and light yellowish brown (c.76). Front: '[white lettering on pale blue] THE / WOMEN / ON THE / WALL / [black lettering on light yellowish brown] Wallace Stegner' / Spine: 'The / Women / on the / Wall / WALLACE / STEGNER / [publisher's device] / HAMMOND / HAMMOND'. Back: photo and reviews of other books by Wallace Stegner. Front flap: blurb on *The Women on the Wall*. Back flap: '*Other Hammond Fiction Titles*'.

Publication: Published March 1952. 10s.6d. Received by Bodleian Library (OX) 2 April 1952. Received by British Library 26 March 1952.

Locations: WS (1), NC (1), BL (1), OX (1)

A10.3

Third edition: New York: Viking, (1962)

Compass books, C105. Published January 5, 1962.

A11 *The Preacher and the Slave*

A11.1.a

First edition, first printing (1950)

Title page: '[double title page] / [both] [beige rules spaced at 1″ intervals] / [left] [beige] [publisher's device] / [black] BOOKS BY WALLACE STEGNER / Remembering Laughter / The Potter's House / On a Darkling Plain / Fire and Ice / Mormon Country / The Big Rock Candy Mountain / One Nation (in collaboration with the editors of *Look* Magazine) / Second Growth / The Women on the Wall / The Preacher and the Slave / [right] THE / PREACHER / AND THE / SLAVE / BY WALLACE / STEGNER / HOUGHTON MIFFLIN COMPANY / BOSTON [dot] The Riverside Press Cambridge / 1950'

Copyright: 'Copyright, 1950 by Wallace Stegner / All rights reserved including the right to reproduce / this book or parts thereof in any form / [Gothic] The Riverside Press / [Roman] CAMBRIDGE [dot] MASSACHUSETTS / Printed in the U.S.A.'

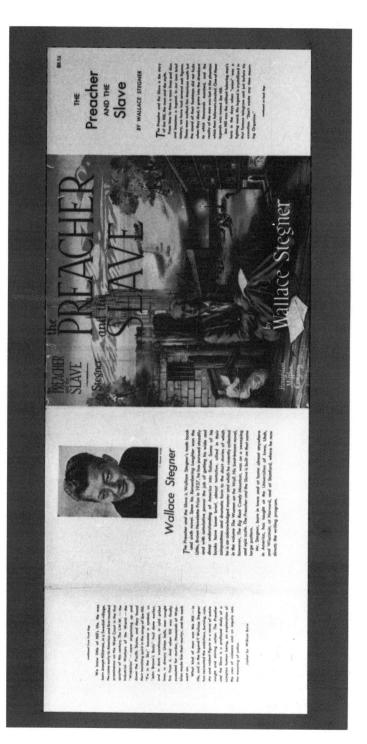

Dust jacket for A11.1.a

$(1-13)^{16}$

pp. (i-iv) vii-x (xi-xii) 1-403 (404)

8 5/16″ × 5 9/16″

Contents: p.i: half title; pp.ii-iii: title; p.iv: copyright; p.v: dedication, 'To My Wife and Son'; p.vi: 'CONTENTS'; pp.vii-x: 'FOREWORD'; p.xi: half title; p.xii: blank; pp. 1-403: text; p. 404: blank.

Paper: Cream wove stock. Edges trimmed. Top edged stained brown. Endpapers of heavier cream stock.

Binding: Medium reddish orange (c.37) cloth with thin horizontal black rules spaced one inch apart on front and spine. Back cover blank. Spine stamped in blue: 'THE / PREACHER / AND THE / SLAVE / STEGNER / H.M.Co.'

Dust jacket: Beige with illus. of Joe Hill writing songs in a shipyard with other scenes depicted: mountains, picking apples, and playing the piano. Front: 'the / PREACHER / and the / SLAVE / [white] by / Wallace Stegner'. Spine: '[continuation of picture from the front] the / PREACHER / and the / SLAVE / [short broken rule] / Stegner / [white] Houghton / Mifflin / Company'. Back: photo of Wallace Stegner by Roland Wolfe and biographical sketch. Front flap: blurb on *The Preacher and the Slave*. Back flap: 'continued from front flap / Jacket by William Barss'.

Publication: September 5, 1950 (*Publisher's Weekly*). "Weekly Record" reads: "*The Preacher and the Slave*". 413. O (8 vo: 25 cm) 50-8708 c. Boston, Houghton $3.75. Joe Hill, the militant labor leader of the "Wobblies" (IWW) who became an American legend, is the central figure in this historical novel. Stegner attempts through fiction to recreate the character of the man who has been called both martyr and murderer." LC copies are dated July 12 and August 17, 1950. Houghton Mifflin records indicate a first printing of 6,000 on 9/5/50. Second printing of 2,500 copies also dated 9/5/50.

Locations: WS (1), NC (2), LC (2)

Note: Review copies were sent to Sinclair Lewis and John Dos Passos, among other eminent literary figures. The printer's setting copy typescript is part of the State Library of Iowa's "Iowa Author manuscript collection".

A11.1.b

Second printing: 2,500 copies (9/5/50).

A11.2

First English edition (1951)

Title page: 'WALLACE STEGNER / The Preacher / and the / Slave / LONDON / HAMMOND, HAMMOND & CO. LTD / 87 GOWER STREET W.C. I'

Copyright: '*Copyright by Wallace Stegner / First published in Great Britain 1951 / Printed in Great Britain by / Richard Clay and Company, Ltd., Bungay, Suffolk / 3.51*'

$(1\text{-}14)^{16}$

pp. (1-9) 10-445 (446-448)

7 3/4″ × 5 3/16″

Contents: p. 1: half title; p. 2: '*Other Books by Wallace Stegner*'; p. 3: title; p. 4: copyright; p. 5: dedication, 'TO / MY WIFE AND SON'; p. 6: blank; p. 7: 'CONTENTS'; p. 8: blank; pp. 9-12: 'FOREWORD'; pp. 13-445: text, headed 'MAY DAY, 1916'; pp. 446-448: reviews of *The Big Rock Candy Mountain* and *Second Growth*.

Paper: Cream wove. Edges trimmed. Heavier stock endpapers.

Binding: Dark red (c.16) rough cloth. Front and back covers blank. Spine gilt-stamped: 'THE / PREACHER / AND THE / SLAVE / [star] / Wallace / Stegner / [publisher's device] / HAMMOND / HAMMOND'.

Dust jacket for A11.2

Dust jacket: Illustrated with IWW's—the "Preacher" and "the Slave." Lettering in deep reddish orange (c.36) and deep yellowish green (c.132). Front: '[red] THE PREACHER AND THE SLAVE / [green] WALLACE STEGNER'. Spine lettered in red, green, and black: '[red] THE / PREACHER / AND THE / SLAVE / [green] WALLACE / STEGNER / [black] [publisher's device] / HAMMOND / HAMMOND'. Back: Reviews of *The Big Rock Candy Mountain* and *Second Growth*. Front flap has blurb for *The Preacher and the Slave*. Back flap: 'RECENT FICTION TITLES' published by Hammond.

Publication: March, 1951. 12s.6d. Received by Bodleian Library (OX) 25 May 1951. Received by British Library 16 May 1951.

Locations: WS (2), NC (1), BL (1), OX (1)

A11.3.a

Third edition, first printing (1969)

Title page: 'Wallace Stegner / JOE HILL / A Biographical Novel / [short narrow rule] / First published as / *The Preacher and the Slave* / 1969 / [short narrow rule] / Doubleday & Company, Inc., Garden City, New York'

Copyright: 'Library of Congress Catalog Card Number 69-15576 / Copyright 1950 by Wallace Stegner / All Rights Reserved / Printed in the United States of America'

$(1-16)^{12}$

pp. (1-11) 12-381 (382-384)

8 3/16″ × 5 7/16″

Contents: p. 1: blank; p. 2: '*By Wallace Stegner*'; p. 3: half title; p. 4: blank; p. 5: title; p. 6: copyright; p. 7: dedication, 'To My Wife and Son'; p. 8: blank; p. 9: 'Contents'; p. 10: blank; p. 11: 'Foreword'; pp. 12-381: text; pp. 382-384: blank.

Paper: Cream wove. Edges trimmed. Endpapers medium brown (c.58) heavier stock.

Dust jacket for A11.3.a

Binding: Very deep red (c.14) rough cloth with medium reddish brown (c.43) spine. Front: '[gilt-stamped] W / S [within narrow ruled vertical panel]'. Back cover blank. Spine: '[gilt-stamped] [narrow double rule] / WALLACE / STEGNER / [narrow rule] / Joe Hill / A / Biographical / Novel / [double narrow rule] / Doubleday'.

Dust jacket: Deep reddish orange (c.36) with black and white lettering. Front: '[white] by / *Wallace* / *Stegner* / [black] *Joe* / *Hill* / *A BIOGRAPHICAL NOVEL BY THE AUTHOR OF* / *"THE SOUND OF MOUNTAIN WATER"*'. Spine: '*Joe* / *Hill* / [white] *by Wallace* / *Stegner* / [black] Doubleday'. Back: quotation from the Foreword to *Joe Hill*. Front flap: blurb on *Joe Hill*. Price in upper right: $6.95. Back flap: photograph and biographical data on Wallace Stegner. / 'JACKET BY PATRICIA SAVILLE VOEHL / *Printed in the U.S.A.*'

Publication: *The Preacher and the Slave* was republished by Doubleday as *Joe Hill* in 1969. Only the title was changed. One printing of 4,000 copies. Price: $6.95.

Note: *Joe Hill* won the Irving and Jean Stone Award for best biographical novel of 1969.

A11.3.b

Third edition, second printing (Joe Hill):   Lincoln: University of Nebraska, (1980)

Bison book.   BB728   Oct., 1980 - 3,480 copies - $5.95 pap.
                          April, 1985 - 1,521 copies - $8.50 pap.

Cloth edition published October, 1980 - 212 copies - $25.95. Plain library binding without dust jacket.

A11.4

Fourth edition (Joe Hill):   New York: Ballantine, (1972)

"A Comstock Edition." First printing: February, 1972.

A12   *The Writer in America*

A12.1.a

First edition, first printing (1952)

Title page: 'THE / WRITER IN AMERICA / By / WALLACE
STEGNER / *with Notes by* / M. HIRAMATSU / THE
HOKUSEIDO PRESS'

Copyright: Copyright information supplied in Japanese on a stamp
on the inside of the back flyleaf.

(1)⁴ (2-9)⁸ (10)⁸ (a leaf is missing from gathering 10)

pp. (4 pp.) i-ii (iii-iv) 1-102 (103) 104-133 (134)

8 1/4″ × 5 7/8″

Contents: p. (1): half title; p. (2): blank; p. (3): title; p. (4): blank;
pp. i-ii: 'FOREWORD'; p.iii: 'CONTENTS'; p.iv: blank; pp. 1-102:
text; pp. (103)-133: 'NOTES'; p. 134: blank.

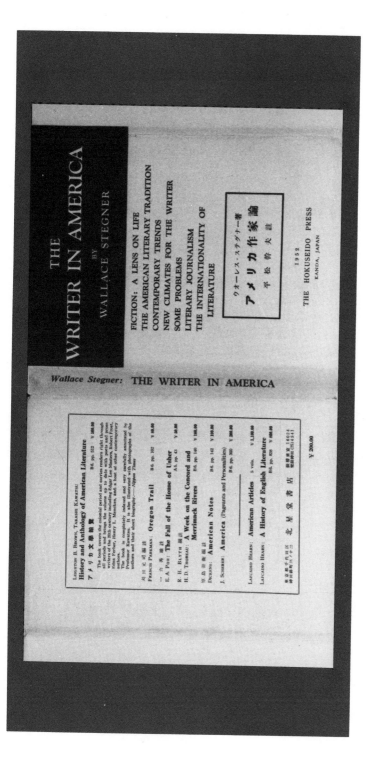

Dust jacket for A12.1.a

Text Contents: Seven lectures: "Fiction: A Lens on Life," "The American Literary Tradition," "Contemporary Trends," "New Climates for the Writer," "Some Problems," "Literary Journalism," "The Internationality of Literature."

Paper: Light-weight cream wove. Edges trimmed. Endpapers pale yellow (c.89) smooth stock.

Binding: Dark reddish brown cloth (c.44). Front and back covers blank. Spine: '[gilt-stamped] THE / WRITER / IN / AMERICA / WALLACE / STEGNER / HOKUSEIDO'.

Dust jacket: Pale yellow (c.89) with gray brown (c.61). Front: '[upper one-half pale yellow lettering on gray brown] THE / WRITER IN AMERICA / BY / WALLACE STEGNER / [lower two-thirds brown print on beige] FICTION: A LENS ON LIFE / THE AMERICAN LITERARY TRADITION / CONTEM-PORARY TRENDS / NEW CLIMATES FOR THE WRITER / SOME PROBLEMS / LITERARY JOURNALISM / THE INTERNATIONALITY OF / LITERATURE / [within narrow-ruled rectangle] [in Japanese].../ 1952 / THE HOKUSEIDO PRESS / KANDA, JAPAN'. Spine: '[vertical] [brown] *Wallace Stegner*: THE WRITER IN AMERICA'. Back: ads for other books published by Hokuseido Press. Flaps: narrow and blank.

Publication: First edition only published in Japan. There is no copy at LC nor any copyright information. Not in *PW*. Price: Y200.00.

Locations: WS (3)

Note: '...six lectures, slightly reworked for print...delivered at Keio University in Tokyo between January 24 and February 4, 1951...'

A12.1.b

Second printing: Folcroft, Pa.: Folcroft Press, (1969)

A12.1.c

Third printing: Folcroft, Pa.: Folcroft Press, (1976)

Reprint of the 1952 edition. One printing of 200 copies.

A12.1.d

Fourth printing: Brooklyn, N.Y.: Haskell House, (1977)

A12.1.e

Fifth printing: Norwood Editions, (1979)

A13 *Beyond the Hundredth Meridian*

A13.1.a

First edition, first printing (1954)

Title page: 'Beyond the / Hundredth Meridian / JOHN WESLEY POWELL / AND THE SECOND OPENING OF THE WEST / *by Wallace Stegner* / WITH AN INTRODUCTION BY / BERNARD DEVOTO / [publisher's device] / *illustrated* / HOUGHTON MIFFLIN COMPANY BOSTON / [Gothic] The Riverside Press Cambridge / 1954'

Copyright: '*Copyright, 1953, 1954, by Wallace E. Stegner* / *All rights reserved including the right to reproduce* / *this book or parts thereof in any form* / *Library of Congress* / *catalogue card number: 53-9245* / [Gothic] The Riverside Press / [Roman] CAMBRIDGE [dot] MASSACHUSETTS / *Printed in the U.S.A.*'

(1-29)⁸

pp. (i-ii) (iii-vi) vii-x (xi-xiii) xiv-xxiii (xxiv-xxvi) (1) 2-115 (116)

117-201 (202) 203-242 (243)) 244-293 (294) 295-350 (351)
352-367 (368-369) 370-419 (420) 421-438

8 3/16″ × 5 7/16″

Illustration: Fold-out panorama of the Grand Canyon between pp.
ii and iii. Map, blank between 38 and 39, 56 and 57, 72 and 73,
90 and 91. Twelve plates between 92 and 93. Map, blank between
118 and 119. Double page map between 217 and 218. Four plates
between 238 and 239.

Contents: p.i: half title; p.ii: 'BY WALLACE STEGNER'; p.iii:
title; p.iv: copyright; p.v: dedication, *'For Bernard DeVoto'*; p.vi:
blank; pp.vii-x: 'AUTHOR'S NOTE'; p.xi: 'CONTENTS'; p.xii:
blank; p.xiii-xiv: 'ILLUSTRATIONS'; pp. xv-xxiii:
'INTRODUCTION'; p.xxiv: blank; p.xxv: half title; p.xxvi: blank;
pp. (1)-38: text; pp. 39-56: text; pp. 57-72: text; ; pp. 73-90: text;
(map, blank); pp. 91-92: text; ['THE CANYON COUNTRY /
[rule] / *The Artists' View*']; (blank); (12 plates); pp. 93-118: text;
(map, blank); pp. 199-217: text; (double page map); pp. 218-238:
text; ['THE CANYON COUNTRY / [rule] / *The Camera's View* /
Portraits']; (blank); (4 plates); pp. 239-367: text; p. 368: blank; pp.
369-419: 'NOTES'; pp. 420-438: 'INDEX'.

Paper: Cream wove. Edges trimmed. Front endpapers: map of the
U.S. 'Beyond the Hundredth Meridian / and the Plateau Province'.
Back endpapers heavier cream stock.

Binding: Light brown (c.27) cloth. Front stamped in gilt: '[short
rule] Beyond the / Hundredth Meridian / [short rule]'. Back cover
blank. Spine stamped in gilt: 'Stegner / [rule] / Beyond / the /
Hundredth / Meridian / [rule] / H.M.Co.'

Dust jacket: Dark gray brown (c.62) with pale orange yellow (c.73)
and light gray yellowish brown (c.79) lettering. Panorama of the
Grand Canyon across the top of entire jacket. Front: '[c.79]
WALLACE STEGNER / [portion of Grand Canyon panorama] /
[c.73] BEYOND the Hundredth / MERIDIAN / [c.79] John
Wesley Powell and the Second Opening / of the West'. Spine:

'[c.79] STEGNER / [portion of panorama] / BEYOND / the / Hundredth / MERIDIAN / HOUGHTON / MIFFLIN / COMPANY'. Back: [panorama] / blurb on *Beyond the Hundredth Meridian*. Front flap: quotations by Edward Weeks and Wallace Stegner. Back flap: quotation by Bernard DeVoto on John Wesley Powell.

Publication: *Publisher's Weekly* gives a September 9, 1954 publication date. "Beyond the Hundredth Meridian. 461p. (51p. bibl. notes) il (pt. col.) maps. O (8 vo: 25 cm) 53-9245 '54 c.'53,'54 Boston, Houghton 6.00. A biography of John Wesley Powell, 19th century scientific pioneer, an explorer, surveyor, geologist, and ethnologist, the father of the United States Geological Survey, the founder of the Bureau of American Ethnology, and the leader of the first expedition to descend the Green and the Colorado Rivers through all their canyons in 1869." LC copies dated August 30, 1954; copyright #A150799. Publisher's records indicate a first printing of 6,000 copies on 9/9/54. Voted out of print 5/10/72.

Locations: WS (2), NC (1), LC (2)

Notes: Received the "Geographic Society of Chicago Publication Award," a citation given to "the individual whose book, monograph, or article of a popular nature, does most to encourage a broader public interest in the field of geography."

A13.1.b

Second printing: 5/27/54 - 3,000 copies

A13.1.c

Third printing: 5/20/62 - 500 copies

A13.1.d

Fourth printing: Boston: Houghton Mifflin, (1962)

Sentry edition no. 20. "Bibl. pap. 2.45. June 30, 1962" (*PW*)

5/29/62 - 7,500 copies

A13.1.e

Fifth printing: Sentry edition. 7/31/62 - 5,000 copies

A13.1.f

Sixth printing: Sentry edition. 4/11/68 - 5,000 copies

A13.1.g

Seventh printing: Sentry edition. 3/04/74 - 2,500 copies

A13.1.h

Eighth printing: Sentry edition. 12/30/76 - 2,500 copies

Voted out of print 2/8/80.

A13.1.i

Ninth printing: Lincoln: University of Nebraska, (1982)

Reprint of original HM edition, with new Preface only. This edition limited to 250 copies. $50.00. October, 1982 - 269 copies (according to UNP)

A13.1.j

Tenth printing: Lincoln: University of Nebraska, (1982)

Bison book. BB798. Aug., 1982 - 4,102 copies - $12.50 pap.

A13.1.k

Eleventh printing: Bison. June, 1985 - 2,612 copies - $12.50 pap.

A14   *The City of the Living*

A14.1.a

First edition, first printing (1956)

Title page: 'the city / of / the living / AND OTHER STORIES /
by wallace stegner / HOUGHTON MIFFLIN COMPANY
BOSTON / [Gothic] The Riverside Press Cambridge / 1956'

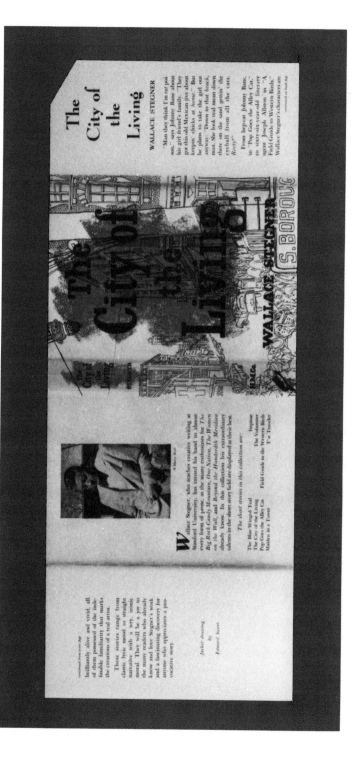

Dust jacket for A14.1.a

/ [Gothic] The Riverside Press / [Roman] CAMBRIDGE [dot] MASSACHUSETTS / PRINTED IN THE U.S.A.'

Perfect bound.

pp.(i-viii) (1)-22 (23) 24-40 (41) 42-66 (67) 68-83 (84) 85-102 (103) 104-125 (126) 127-194 (195) 196-206 (207-208)

7 15/16″ × 5 7/16″

Contents: p.i: half title; p.ii: 'BOOKS BY / WALLACE STEGNER'; p.iii: title; p.iv: copyright; p.v: 'contents'; p.vi: blank; p.vii: second half title; p.viii: blank; pp. (1)-106: text; pp. 207-208: blank.

Includes "The City of the Living" and 7 other stories: "The Blue-Winged Teal," "The City of the Living," "Pop Goes the Alley Cat," "Maiden in a Tower," "Impasse," "The Volunteer," "Field Guide to the Western Birds," and "The Traveler."

Paper: Cream wove. Top and bottom edges trimmed; fore edge uncut. Cream wove endpapers of text paper.

Binding: Green gray (c.255) paper-covered boards. Front and back covers blank. Spine stamped in brilliant greenish yellow (c.98): 'the / city / of / the / living / stegner / h m co.' Perfect bound, glued at the backstrip.

Dust jacket: Black pen and ink drawing of a city street with a splash of red highlighting title in black. Front: 'The / City of / the / Living / WALLACE STEGNER'. Spine: 'The / City of / the / Living / STEGNER / H.M.Co.' Back: photograph of Wallace Stegner by Harry Redl with blurb on his career and publications. Front flap: blurb on *The City of the Living*. Back flap: continuation of front flap, beneath, 'Jacket drawing / by / Edward Sweet'.

Publication: According to *PW*, publication date was October 23, 1956. "City of the Living, and Other Stories. 206p. O (8 vo: 25 cm) 56-12088 ('56, c. '50-'56) Boston, Houghton bds, 3.00. Short stories set in varied sections of the United States, France, and Egypt." LC copies received October 25, 1956. Printing size approximately 4,000 copies, published 10/23/56. Voted OP 4/29/65.

Locations: WS (1), NC (2), LC (2)

A14.1.b

Second printing: Freeport, N.Y.: Books for Libraries Press, (1969).

Short Stories Index reprint series. Received by LC May, 1969. Reprinted approximately 500-1,000 copies.

A14.1.c

Third printing: Freeport, N.Y.: Books for Libraries Press, (1971).

Lifetime Library edition.

A14.1.d

Fourth printing: Freeport, N.Y.: Books for Libraries Press, (1976).

Another reprinting of the Books for Libraries hardcover edition.

A14.2.a

First English edition, first printing (1957)

Title page: 'THE CITY / OF THE LIVING / and other stories / by / WALLACE STEGNER / LONDON / HAMMOND, HAMMOND & COMPANY'

Copyright: 'COPYRIGHT BY WALLACE STEGNER / *First published in Great Britain 1957* / *The following stories appeared originally in Harper's Magazine*: 'The Blue-Winged Teal,' 'The Traveller,' / 'Pop Goes the Alley Cat,' and 'Maiden in a Tower'; / 'Field Guide to the Western Birds' first appeared in *New / Short*

Novels, 2, published by Ballantine Books, Inc.; 'The City of the Living' and 'The Volunteer' are re-/printed by permission of *Mademoiselle*; 'Impasse' is / reprinted by permission of *Woman's Day*, the A & P / Magazine. / Printed in Great Britain by / Ebenezer Baylis & Son, Ltd., The Trinity Press, Worcester, and London / for Hammond, Hammond, & Co. Ltd., / 87 Gower Street, W.C. I / 657'.

$(1-12)^8$

pp. (1-6) 7-189 (190-192)

Contents: p. 1: half title; p. 2: '*Also by Wallace Stegner*'; p. 3: title; p. 4: copyright; p. 5: 'CONTENTS'; p. 6: blank; pp. 7-189: text; pp. 190-192: 'Other books by: WALLACE STEGNER' (and others).

Includes "The City of the Living" and 7 other stories: "The Blue-Winged Teal," "The City of the Living," "Pop Goes the Alley Cat," "Maiden in a Tower," "Impasse," "The Volunteer," "Field Guide to the Western Birds," and "The Traveller."

Paper: Cream wove stock. Edges trimmed. Cream wove endpapers.

Binding: Red (c.12) thin paper-covered boards. Front and back covers blank. Spine stamped in black: 'The City / of the / Living / WALLACE / STEGNER / [publisher's device] / HAMMOND / HAMMOND'. Also bound in gray yellow (c.90) cloth with maroon print.

Dust jacket: Gray and black with red and white lettering. Front: '[white] The / [red and white] CITY / [white] of the / [red and white] LIVING / [white] Wallace Stegner'. Spine: '[white] The / CITY / of the / LIVING / Wallace / Stegner / [publisher's device] / HAMMOND / HAMMOND'. Back: photography of Wallace Stegner and blurbs on four of his books. Front flap has blurb on *The City of the Living*. Back flap: Hammond, Hammond advertisement and price: 12s. 6d.

Publication: Published June, 1957.   12s.6d.   Received by Bodleian Library (OX) 18 April 1958. Received by British Library 24 July 1957.

Locations: WS (1), NC (1 red), LC (2), BL (2), OX (1)

A15 *A Shooting Star*

A15.1.a

First edition, first printing (1961)

Title page: '[upper right corner] Wallace Stegner / [decorative double rule] / [three star rule] / A / SHOOTING / STAR / [publisher's device] / NEW YORK [star] The Viking Press 1961'

Copyright: 'COPYRIGHT © 1961 BY WALLACE STEGNER / ALL RIGHTS RESERVED / FIRST PUBLISHED IN 1961 BY THE VIKING PRESS, INC. / 625 MADISON AVENUE, NEW YORK 22, N.Y. / PUBLISHED SIMULTANEOUSLY IN CANADA BY / THE MACMILLAN COMPANY OF CANADA LIMITED / LIBRARY OF CONGRESS CATALOG NUMBER: 61-7037 / PRINTED IN THE U.S.A. BY VAIL-BALLOU PRESS, INC.'

(1-14)^{16}

pp. (i-x) (1-2) 3-433 (434-438)

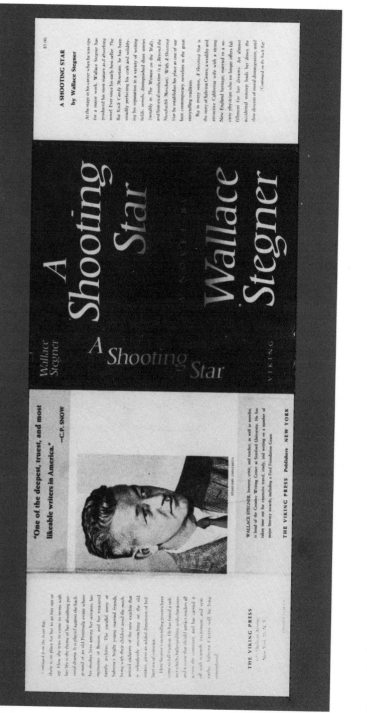

Dust jacket for A15.1.a

8 5/16″ × 5 11/16″

Contents: pp.i-iii: blank; p.iv: '*Other Books by Wallace Stegner*'; p.v: half title; p.vi: blank; p.vii: title; p.viii: copyright; p.ix: dedication, 'For Mary'; p.x: blank; p. 1: half title; p. 2: blank; pp. 3-433: text; pp. 434-438: blank.

Paper: Cream wove stock. Edges trimmed; top edge stained blue. Cream endpapers of heavier stock.

Binding: Blue (c.179) marbled paper-covered boards with black cloth spine. Front cover: 'W' overstamped with larger 'S.' Back cover blank. Spine stamped in gilt: 'WALLACE / STEGNER / [double rule] / [two stars] / A / Shooting / Star / [double rule] / [two stars] / [double rule] / [single rule] / [double rule] / [three stars] / [double rule] / [single rule] / [double rule] / The / Viking / Press'.

Dust jacket: Black with brilliant yellow (c.83) lettering, with blue and green shading. Front: '[yellow] A / Shooting / [green and yellow] Star / [blue] A / NOVEL / BY / [green and yellow] Wallace / [yellow] Stegner'. Spine: '[yellow] Wallace / Stegner / [vertical, uneven lines] / A / [green and yellow] Shooting / Star / [horizontal] [yellow] VIKING'. Back: photograph and biographical information on Stegner. Front flap: blurb on *A Shooting Star*. Back flap: continuation of blurb.

Publication: Official publication date June 30, 1961, but probably came off the press May 15th. Estimated first printing of 20,000 copies. $5.00. OP as of February 13, 1978.

Location: WS (5), NC (3), LC (1), FC (1)

Note: Originally titled *Sabrina*, this was Viking's lead book for Spring. An unknown quantity of advance bound uncorrected page proofs were ordered for distribution to critics. An advance edition was printed and sent out to the trade (printed for "friends of the author and publisher"). The binding is deep red (c.13) marbled paper-covered boards. The front is gilt-stamped at lower right:

'ADVANCE EDITION'. The variant dust jacket is blue, yellow, and red with white lettering. Flaps are blank, book cover text differs. The title page is also variant, page i is a colophon, and pagination differs. This specially-bound edition was a give-away by Viking at the ABA in June. It was a Literary Guild Selection. *Contact* used Chapter 13 prior to publication by Viking. See D53.

A15.1.b

Second printing: (before publication) (1961)

On copyright page: 'SECOND PRINTING BEFORE PUBLI-CATION'

A15.2.a

First English edition, first printing (1961)

Title page: 'Wallace Stegner / [rule] / A / SHOOTING / STAR / [rule] / [publisher's device] / HEINEMANN / LONDON MEL-BOURNE TORONTO'

Copyright: 'William Heinemann Ltd / LONDON MELBOURNE TORONTO / CAPE TOWN AUCKLAND / THE HAGUE / First published in Great Britain 1961 / Copyright ©1961 by Wallace Stegner / *All rights reserved* / Printed in Great Britain / by The Windmill Press Ltd / Kingswood, Surrey'

$(1-14)^{16}$ $(15)^8$

pp. (1-4) 5-464

7 11/16″ × 5 1/16″

Contents: p. 1: description of the story; p. 2: 'BOOKS BY WALLACE STEGNER'; p. 3: title; p. 4: copyright; pp. 5-464: text.

Paper: Cream wove. Edges trimmed. Endpapers heavier cream wove stock.

Binding:　Black cloth (rough). Front and back covers blank. Spine gilt-stamped: 'A Shooting / Star / [rule] / WALLACE / STEGNER / HEINEMANN'.

Dust jacket:　Black with photo of a heavily made-up woman holding a rose next to her cheek. Front: '[white] A SHOOTING STAR / Wallace / Stegner'. Spine: '[vertical] [medium purplish red (c.258)] A SHOOTING STAR / [horizontal] [white] Wallace / Stegner / [medium purplish red] HEINEMANN'. Back: quotation by C.P. Snow on Wallace Stegner as a writer. Front flap: blurb on *A Shooting Star*. Back flap: blank except for names of wrapper designers.

Publication:　Published by Heinemann on 23 May 1961. Received by the Bodleian Library (OX) 6 June 1961. Received by the British Library 17 April 1961. First printing 15,000 copies. 18s.

Location:　WS (3), NC (2), BL (1), OX (1)

A15.3

Third edition:　New York: Dell, (1962).

"First Dell printing - June 1962". Illustrated paper wrappers. $.60.

A15.4

Fourth edition:　London: Transworld, (1962).

Corgi book FN1242. 5/-.

A16 *Wolf Willow*

A16.1.a

First edition, first printing (1962)

Title page: '[double title page] WALLACE STEGNER / Wolf
Willow / A History, a Story, and a Memory of the Last Plains
Frontier / THE VIKING PRESS / New York / [illus. of horses
running across the plains]'

Copyright: 'Copyright © 1955, 1957, 1958, 1959, 1962 by
Wallace Stegner / All rights reserved / Published in 1962 by The
Viking Press, Inc. / 625 Madison Avenue, New York 22, N.Y. /
Published simultaneously in Canada by / The Macmillan Company
of Canada Ltd. / Library of Congress catalog card number:
62-17939 / Printed in the U.S.A. by H. Wolff Book Mfg. Company / "Quiet Earth, Big Sky" and "History Comes to the Great
Plains," / which appear here in somewhat altered form as "The
Question / Mark in the Circle" and "The Medicine Line," first
appeared in / *American Heritage*. "History is a Pontoon Bridge"
first appeared / in *Horizon*. "The Mounties at Fort Walsh,"

Dust jacket for A16.1.a

which makes up part / of the chapter entitled "Capital of an Unremembered Past," and / "The Town Dump" first appeared in *Contact*. "Carrion Spring" first appeared in / *Esquire*. "The Making of Paths," here expanded into the chapter / of the same name, first appeared in *The New Yorker*.'

(1-10)[16]

pp. (i-xii) (1-2) 3-36 (37) 38-123 (124-126) 127-238 (239-240) 241-283 (284-286) 287-306 (307-308)

8 3/8″ × 5 5/8″

Contents: p.i: half title; p.ii: blank; p.iii: '*Other Books by Wallace Stegner*'; p.iv-v: double title page; p.vi: copyright; p.vii: dedication, '*This is in memory of my mother*'; p.viii: blank; pp.ix-x: '*Contents*'; p.xi: half title; p.xii: blank; p. 1: Part I title; p. 2: blank; pp. 3-36: text; pp. 37-38: Part II title; pp. 39-123: text; p. 124: blank; p. 125: Part III title; p. 126: blank; pp. 127-238: text; p. 239: Part IV title; p. 240: blank; pp. 241-283: text; p. 284: blank; p. 285: 'EPILOGUE'; p. 286: blank; pp. 287-306: epilogue; p. 307: '*Acknowledgments*'; p. 308: blank.

Text contents: This "history and story" includes the following periodical articles and short stories:
  "Quiet Earth, Big Sky" - C89.
  "History Comes to the Great Plains" - C98.
  "Child of the Far Frontier" - C119.
  "The Mounties at Fort Walsh" - C102.
  "The Town Dump" - C109.
  "Genesis" - D49.
  "Carrion Spring" - D54.
  "The Making of Paths" - C104.

Paper: Cream wove stock. Top and bottom edges trimmed. Fore edge rough-cut. Top edge stained bluish green. Map endpapers.

Binding: Orange brown cloth (c.54). Front: imprint of an 'S' superimposed over a 'W.' Back cover blank. Spine: '[within brown short panel framed by narrow gilt rule] [gilt-stamped] Wolf / Willow / Stegner / [below panel] Viking'.

Dust jacket: Light bluish green (c.163) with brown, white, and black. Front: 'Wolf / Willow / A HISTORY, A STORY, AND A MEMORY / OF THE LAST PLAINS FRONTIER / WALLACE STEGNER / [illus. of horses running across the plains]'. Spine: 'STEGNER / '[vertical] Wolf Willow / [horizontal] VIKING'. Back: quotations from reviews of *Wolf Willow*, photograph of Wallace Stegner by James Hall, and brief biographical sketch. Front flap: blurb on *Wolf Willow*, 'Jacket design by John Pimlott'. Back flap: continuation of front flap and '*Comments on earlier works / by Wallace Stegner*'.

Publication: Published October 15, 1962. $5.95. OP as of June 29, 1977. Viking estimates printing at 10,000 copies.

Locations: WS (5), NC (4), LC (2)

Notes: Received the Black Hawk Award, given annually by the Midland Booksellers Association to the best book by an Iowa-born writer. Many chapters first appeared in periodicals prior to *Wolf Willow*. See note at end of description.

A16.1.b

Second printing (First English edition) (1963)

Title page: same as A16.1.a, with imprint, 'HEINEMANN / London [dot)] Melbourne [dot] Toronto'

Copyright: '*William Heinemann Ltd* / LONDON MELBOURNE TORONTO / CAPE TOWN AUCKLAND / THE HAGUE / Published in 1963 / Copyright © 1955, 1957, 1958, 1959, 1962 by Wallace Stegner / All rights reserved / PRINTED IN THE U.S.A.'

(1-10)^{16}

pp. (i-xii) (1-2) 3-36 (37) 38-123 (124-126) 127-238 (239-240)
241-283 (284-286) 287-306 (307-308)

8 1/4″ × 5 3/6″

Contents: p.i: half title; p.ii: blank; p.iii: *'Other Books by Wallace
Stegner'*; p.iv-v: double title page: p.vi: copyright; p.vii: dedication,
'This is in memory of my mother'; p.viii: blank; p.ix-x:'Contents';
p.xi: half title; p.xii: blank; p. 1: Part I title; p. 2: blank; pp. 3-36:
text; pp. 37-38: Part II title; pp. 39-123: text; p. 124: blank; p.
125: Part III title; p. 126: blank; pp. 127-238: text; p. 239: Part IV
title p. 240: blank; pp. 241-283: text; p. 284: blank; p. 285:
'EPILOGUE'; p. 286: blank; pp. 287-306: epilogue; p. 307:
'Acknowledgments'; p. 308: blank.

Text contents:
  "Quiet Earth, Big Sky" - C89.
  "History Comes to the Great Plains" - C98.
  "Child of the Far Frontier" - C119.
  "The Mounties at Fort Walsh" - C102.
  "The Town Dump" - C109.
  "Genesis" - D49.
  "Carrion Spring" - D54.
  "The Making of Paths" - C104.

Paper: Cream wove. Edges trimmed. Light gray endpapers of a
heavier stock.

Binding: Dark gray blue paper-covered boards (c.187). Front cover
blank. Back cover with embossed publisher's device in lower right
corner. Spine gilt-stamped: '[three short rules] / Wolf / Willow /
[short rule] / WALLACE / STEGNER / [three short rules] /
HEINEMANN'.

Dust jacket: Yellow gray (c.93) with fiber fleck. Lettering in
medium blue (c.182) and black. Front: '[medium blue] WALLACE
/ STEGNER / [black] Wolf Willow / *A History, a Story, and a
Memory of the Last Plains Frontier'*. Spine: 'WALLACE /
STEGNER / Wolf / Willow / HEINEMANN'. Back: 'RECENT

HEINEMANN / NON-FICTION'. Front flap: blurb on Wallace Stegner and WOLF WILLOW. *'Wrapper design by Brian Russell'*. Back flap: C.P. Snow quotation on Wallace Stegner.

Publication: Heinemann bought and bound sets of sheets from the U.S. The English printing was published April, 1963 (between 1,500 and 2,000 copies). This printing is actually made from first edition, first printing sheets and precedes the American second printing. Bodleian Library copy is dated 7 May 1963. British Library copy was received 16 April 1963. Price: 35s.

Locations: WS, NC (2), BL (1), OX (1)

A16.1.c

Third printing: June, 1963. This is actually the second American printing. Identical to A16.1.a, except the front endpaper map is corrected. The map in the first printing had Saskatchewan too far east.

A16.1.d

Fourth printing: New York: Viking, (1966).

Compass Books. Published in softcover August 24, 1966.

A16.1.e

Fifth printing: Toronto: Macmillan of Canada, (1977).

"First Laurentian Library Edition"

A16.1.f

Sixth printing: Lincoln: University of Nebraska, (1980).

Jan., 1980 - 388 copies - $18.50 cl.

A16.1.g

Seventh printing: Lincoln: University of Nebraska, (1980).

Bison book. BB708. March, 1980 - 3,991 copies - $6.95 pap.

A16.1.h

Eighth printing: Lincoln: University of Nebraska, (1980)

Bison book. BB708. Feb., 1984 - 2,578 copies - $7.95 pap.

A16.1.i

Ninth printing: Lincoln: University of Nebraska, (1980).

Bison book. BB708. New (brown) cover this printing. March 14, 1988 - 1,862 copies - $7.95.

A16.2

Second edition: London: Corgi Books, (1964).

"A Corgi Western" 5/- Later printing: Corgi Modern Reading edition, 1966. 6s.

A16.3

Third edition: Ballantine, (1973).

Printed May, 1973. "A Comstock Edition"

"Genesis" was later incorporated into the film script called "Carrion Spring" for the Canadian National Film Board.

A17 *The Gathering of Zion*

A17.1.a

First edition, first printing (1964)

Title page: '[within double-ruled, framed drawing of trees] THE /
GATHERING / OF ZION / [beneath frame] / *The Story of the
Mormon Trail* / by WALLACE STEGNER / McGRAW-HILL
BOOK COMPANY / NEW YORK TORONTO LONDON /
[framed drawing of Salt Lake City]'

Illustrations: This book has 8 numbered (implied, see contents page)
pages representing illustrated endpapers, frontispiece map, list of
books in Trail Series, and illustrated title page. These and the
8-page gathering of plates (not numbered in pagination) are on
different paper from the text.

Copyright: 'THE GATHERING OF ZION / *The Story of the
Mormon Trail* / *Copyright* © *1964 by Wallace Stegner. All Rights
Reserved. / Printed in the United States of America. This book, or parts
thereof,* / *may not be reproduced in any form without permission of the*

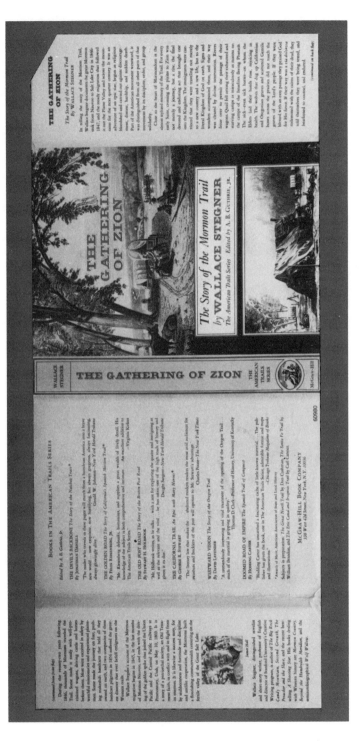

Dust jacket for A17.1.a

publishers. / *Library of Congress Catalog Card Number*: 00-00000 *First Edition* / 64-19216 / 60980'.

(1)^4 (2-6)^{16} (7)^4 (8-11)^{16} (12)^{12} (13)^{16}

pp. (i-xx) 1-148 (1-8) 149-331 (332)

8 15/16″ × 5 15/16″

Contents: p.i: pastedown endpaper recto (blank); p.ii: left half of the endpaper pastedown illus.; p.iii: right half of free endpaper illus.; pp.iv-v: map of Mormon Trail; p.v: 'BOOKS IN THE AMERI-CAN TRAIL SERIES'; p.vii: title; p.viii: copyright; p.ix: '*Contents*'; p.x: '*Acknowledgments*'; pp.xi-xvii: 'CHECKPOINTS ON THE ROAD / TO NEW JERUSALEM'; p.xviii: blank; p.xix: half title; p.xx: blank; pp. 1-13: '*Introduction*'; p. 14: blank; p. 15: chapter title; p. 16: blank; pp. 17-148: text; 8 pp. photographs; pp. 149-312: text; pp. 313-319: 'A Word on Bibliography'; p. 320: blank; pp. 321-331: '*Index*'; p. 332: 'ABOUT THE AUTHOR'.

Paper: Cream wove stock. Edges trimmed. Front endpapers pictorial (see illus. note). Terminal endpapers rougher cream wove. Preliminary pages i-viii and the plates are on different paper from the text (rough stock as in terminal endpapers).

Binding: Medium purple cloth (c.223). Front: at lower right three stamped ovals in gold, silver, and purple gilt; each depicting man, woman, and child moving West. Back cover blank. Spine: '[silver stamped] The / Gather-/ing / of Zion / [silver oval design] / WALLACE / STEGNER / McGraw- / Hill'.

Dust jacket: Cream with gray and medium purplish blue (c.200). Front: [gray] [drawing of covered wagons by a river] [c.200] THE / GATHERING / OF ZION / [within a blue and black ruled rectangle] [black] *The Story of the Mormon Trail* / [c.200] *by* WALLACE STEGNER / [black] *The American Trails Series* Edited by A.B. GUTHRIE, JR. / [illus. of a pioneer campsite within a blue and black ruled rectangle]. Spine: [outlined with double rule of blue and black] WALLACE / STEGNER / [narrow rule] [vertical] [c.200] THE GATHERING OF ZION / [horizontal] [black] THE / AMERICAN / TRAILS / SERIES / [oval design] / McGraw-Hill'. Back: 'BOOKS IN THE AMERICAN TRAILS SERIES'. Front flap: blurb on *The Gathering of Zion*. Price on upper right corner: $6.95. Back flap: blurb continued, photograph of Wallace Stegner by James Hall, and biographical sketch.

Publication: *Publisher's Weekly* announced publication for October, 1964. Copies at the Library of Congress are dated September 14, 1964. $6.95. The cloth edition is out-of-print. Publisher's records are no longer available.

Locations: WS, NC (3), FC (2), LC (2)

A17.1.b

Second printing (First English edition) (1966)

Title page: Same as A17.1.a, except with imprint 'EYRE & SPOTTISWOODE (*Publishers*) LTD. / FRONTIER LIBRARY' beneath author line.

Illustrations: Same as in A17.1.a.

Copyright: 'THE GATHERING OF ZION / *The Story of the Mormon Trail* / *First published in Great Britain 1966* / *Copyright* © *1964 by Wallace Stegner* / *Printed in the United States of America*'

$(1)^4 (2-6)^{16} (7)^4 (8-11)^{16} (12)^{12} (13)^{16}$

pp. (i-xx) 1-148 (1-8) 149-331 (332)

8 15/16″ × 5 15/16″

Contents: p.i: pastedown endpaper recto (blank); p.ii: left half of the endpaper pastedown illus.; p.iii: right half of free endpaper illus.; pp.iv.-v: map of the Mormon Trail; p.vi: 'BOOKS IN / EYRE &

SPOTTISWOODE'S FRONTIER LIBRARY'; p.vii: title; p.viii: copyright; p.ix: 'Contents'; p.x: 'Acknowledgments'; pp.xi-xvii: 'CHECKPOINTS ON THE ROAD / TO THE NEW JERUSALEM'; p.xviii: blank; p.xix: half title; p.xx: blank; pp. 1-13: 'Introduction'; p. 14: blank; p. 15: chapter title; p. 16: blank; pp. 17-148: text; 8 pp. photographs; pp. 149-312: text; pp. 313-319: 'A Word on Bibliography'; p. 320: blank; pp. 321-331: 'Index'; p. 332: 'ABOUT THE AUTHOR'.

Paper: Cream wove stock. Edges trimmed. Front endpapers pictorial. Terminal endpapers rougher stock cream. Preliminary pages i-viii and the plates are on different paper from the text (rough stock as in terminal endpapers).

Binding: Gray reddish brown cloth (c.46). Front and back covers blank. Spine stamped in gilt and red: '[gilt] The / Gathering / of Zion / [red] [double rule] / [gilt] Wallace / Stegner / [red] [publisher's device] / [gilt] E&S'.

Dust jacket: Gold with black and white print. Drawing of covered wagons and river-crossing in black. Front: '[black on gold] WALLACE STEGNER / [super-imposed on picture] [white double letters] THE / GATHERING / OF ZION / [single letters] The Story of the Mormon Trail / [on lower, gold section] FRONTIER LIBRARY'. Spine: '[on gold area near top edge] Wallace / Stegner /[vertical] [white] THE / GATHERING / OF ZION / [horizontal] [on lower, gold area] [publisher's device] / E&S'. Back: [gold and black lettering] blurbs on two other books on the Mormons published in Eyre & Spottiswoode's Frontier Library. Front flap: blurb on *The Gathering of Zion*. Back flap: biographical sketch of Wallace Stegner. Advertisement for two other Frontier Library titles.

Publication: 'PRICE IN U.K. / 42S net'. British Library copy received 24 November 1965. American sheets, therefore, not a true second printing (same sheets as bound in A17.1.a).

Locations: WS (1), NC (2), FC (1), BL (1), OX (1)

A17.1.c

Third printing: New York: McGraw-Hill, (1971)

Paperback. $4.50. According to McGraw-Hill, the paperback edition has sold 8,978 copies since 1971.

A17.1.d

Fourth printing: Salt Lake City: Westwater, (1981)

This is designated as the fourth printing rather than a new edition because only illustrations and dust jacket blurbs have changed. The text remains the same.

The 8 pages of engravings (14 illus.), between pages 148 and 149 in previous editions, have been replaced in the 1981 Westwater printing. A 16-page "Portfolio of Mormon Trail Engravings by Frederick Hawkins Piercy and Thomas Moran" has replaced the original plates and appears between pages 142 and 143. This printing includes the engravings found in the first edition and adds 10 more. Captions have been altered and Moran's and Piercy's names have been added to their works. Jacket blurbs have been rewritten. New illustrations (from Piercy's Route From Liverpool to Great Salt Lake Valley) have been added to the cover (dust jacket in cloth copy) and title page. Also added is a fold-out map at the front of the book.

This printing was issued simultaneously in cloth and paper. $15.95/$7.95.

A18
Teaching the Short Story

A18.1.a

First edition, first printing (1966)

Title page: 'DAVIS PUBLICATIONS IN ENGLISH / *Number Two* / Teaching the Short Story / *by* / WALLACE STEGNER / [tree] / Department of English / University of California / Davis, California 95616 / *Fall, 1965*'

Copyright: The Davis Publications in English was initiated in 1965 by the / Department of English, University of California at Davis, as part of its / continuing program in the training of students and teachers of English. / In the first number of the series, Grammar Instruction Today, / Professor Wayne Harsh of the Davis English faculty summarizes the / approaches to language study offered by descriptive linguistics, tradi-/tional grammar, and generative grammar. In this issue, Wallace Stegner, / Professor of English and Director of the Creative Writing Program at / Stanford University, discusses the style and structure of the short story. / *Copyright* 1966 by Wallace Stegner / Price: $.50'

(1)⁸

pp. (i-ii) (1) 2-13 (14)

8 5/16″ × 5 1/2″

Paper: Cream wove.

Contents: p.i: title; p.ii: copyright; pp. 1-12: text; pp. 12-13: 'BIBLIOGRAPHY'; p. 14: blank.

Binding: Marbled heavy paper wrap. Stapled at centerfold. White with deep red (c.16) print. Front: [deep red] 'DAVIS PUBLICA-TIONS IN ENGLISH / *Number Two* / [thick rule] / Teaching / the / Short Story / *by* / Wallace Stegner / UNIVERSITY OF CALIFORNIA, DAVIS / *Fall, 1965* / [along left side: deep red tree on white and three white trees on deep red area]'. Back: [wide deep red frame with white within. Deep red tree on white near bottom].

Dust jacket: None.

Publication: $.50. Library of Congress copy dated 19 January 1966. Published November 29, 1965 by the Repro-Graphics Department. By 1969 there were four printings of 1,000 each. By 1975 the number of copies totalled 8,105. There were no changes in the text.

Notes: 'Professor Stegner first presented the paper as one of a series of lectures in the / course "The Teaching of English Grades K-12," offered in 1965 through the / University of California Extension, Davis.'

A19
All the Little Live Things

A19.1.a

First edition, first printing (1967)

Title page: 'Wallace Stegner / All the Little / Live Things / *The Viking Press* [diagonal] [slash] NEW YORK'

Copyright: '*Copyright* © *1967 by Wallace Stegner / All rights reserved / First published in 1967 by The Viking Press, Inc. / 625 Madison Avenue, New York, N.Y. 10022 / Published simultaneously in Canada by / The Macmillan Company of Canada Limited / Library of Congress catalog card number: 67-13499 / Printed in U.S.A. /* Grateful acknowledgment is made to Holt, Rinehart and / Winston, Inc. for permission to quote, on page 209, from / "To Earthward" from *Complete Poems of Robert Frost.* / Copyright 1923 by Holt, Rinehart and Winston, Inc. Copy-/right 1951 by Robert Frost.'

(1-11)[16]

pp. (i-vi) (1-2) 3-345 (346)

8 3/8″ × 5 1/4″

Contents: p.i: half title; p.ii: '*Other books by Wallace Stegner*'; p.iii: title; p.iv: copyright; p.v: dedication, '*For Trudy, Franny, Judy, Peg*'; p.vi: William Wordsworth quotation; p. 1: half title; p. 2: blank; pp. 3-345: text; p. 346: blank.

Paper: Cream wove stock. Top edge trimmed and stained yellow. Bottom edge trimmed. Fore edge uncut. Endpapers light gray heavier stock.

Binding: Medium blue (c.182) paper-covered boards with cream cloth spine. Front stamped in dark blue (c.183): 'WS' at upper right with decorative short rule above and below. Back cover blank. Spine stamped in dark blue: '[decorative rule] / *Wallace* / *Stegner* / All the / Little / Live / Things / [decorative rule] / VIKING'.

Dust jacket: Brilliant yellow (c.182) with greenish blue (c.169) borders. Front: 'All the / Little / Live / Things / [deep yellow green (c.118)] A novel by / [black] Wallace / Stegner'. Spine: '[vertical] All the Little Live Things / [horizontal] [green] Viking / [vertical] [black] Wallace Stegner'. Back: Wallace Stegner on *All the Little Live Things*. Front flap: blurb on book and '[greenish blue] JACKET DESIGN BY MEL WILLIAMSON' Price in upper right corner: $5.75. Back flap: biographical sketch.

Publication: Published August 7, 1967. $5.75. Literary Guild alternate for August, 1967. Library of Congress copy (A942121) dated August 7, 1967. Now OP. Viking estimates printing size of 10,000 copies.

Locations: WS (2), NC (5), LC (2)

Notes: First appearance of "All the Little Live Things" was in *Mademoiselle*, 49 (May, 1959). D50.

A19.1.b

Second printing: Lincoln: University of Nebraska, (1979).

Dust jacket for A19.2

Bison book. BB709. Aug., 1979 - 4,103 copies - $4.95 pap.

A19.1.c

Third printing: Lincoln: University of Nebraska, (1979).

October, 1979 - 392 copies - $14.95 cloth (without dj)

A19.1.d

Fourth printing: Lincoln: University of Nebraska, (1979).

Bison book. BB709. Jan., 1982 - 2,979 copies - $6.50 pap.

A19.1.e

Fifth printing: Lincoln: University of Nebraska, (1979).

Bison book. BB709. Jan., 1986 - 2,606 copies - $6.50 pap.

A19.2

Second edition (First English edition) (1968)

Title page: '[double title page] All the Little Live Things / *Wallace Stegner* / Other books by Wallace Stegner / Remembering Laughter / Second Growth / Women on the Wall / Big Rock Candy Mountain / The Preacher and the Slave / The City of the Living / A Shooting Star / Wolf Willow / The Gathering of Zion / [publisher's device] HEINEMANN : LONDON'

Copyright: 'William Heinemann Ltd / LONDON MELBOURNE TORONTO / CAPE TOWN AUCKLAND / The lines on p. 209 are from "To Earthward", reprinted / by permission from *The Complete Poems of Robert Frost,* / published by Jonathan Cape. / First published in Great Britain 1968 / Copyright ©1967 by Wallace Stegner 434 73702 × / Printed and Bound in Great Britain by / Bookprint Limited, Crawley, Sussex'

$(1-11)^{16}$

pp. (i-iv) (1-2) 3-348

7 11/16″ × 5 1/8″

Contents: p.i: half title; p.ii-iii: double title page; p.iv: copyright; p. 1: dedication, '*For Trudy, Franny, Judy, Peg*'; p. 2: quotation; pp. 3-345: text; pp. 346-348: 'A brief glossary. compiled by the author'.

Paper: White wove stock. Edges trimmed. Endpapers heavier white stock.

Binding: Black paper. Front and back covers blank. Spine: '[gilt-stamped] All / the / Little / Live / Things / Wallace / Stegner / Heinemann'.

Dust jacket: Cream with light gray (c.264) and medium greenish blue print (c.173). Illus. in blues and greens. Front: '[gray] WALLACE STEGNER / [black] [narrow rule] / [greenish blue] All the Little Live Things / [illus. of four characters against a background of green hills]'. Spine: '[vertical] [gray] WALLACE STEGNER / [greenish blue] All the Little Live Things / [horizontal] [black] HEINEMANN'. Back: continuation of illus. Front flap: blurb on book. Back flap: photograph of Wallace Stegner by C.P. Noyes and biographical sketch. / '*jacket design: Bruce Macdonald*'.

Publication: Publication date for Heinemann edition July 8, 1968. *1.50 (30s). Remaindered March, 1969. Bodleian Library (OX) copy dated 25 July 1968. British Library copy dated 28 June 1968.

Locations: WS (2), NC (3), BL (1), OX (1)

A19.3.a

Third edition, first printing: New York: New American Library, (1968).

Signet Q3572. $.95. 'FIRST PRINTING, AUGUST, 1968'

August, 1968 - 193,125 copies

A19.3.b

Third edition, second printing: New York: New American Library, (1968).

August, 1968 - 20,652 copies (Canada)

A19.3.c

Third edition, third printing: New York: New American Library, (1968).

December, 1972 - 21,470 copies

A20 *The*
Sound of Mountain Water

A20.1.a

First edition, first printing (1969)

Title page: 'WALLACE STEGNER / [wavy rule] / The Sound of
/ Mountain Water / 1969 / DOUBLEDAY & COMPANY, INC.
/ GARDEN CITY, NEW YORK'

Copyright: 'Portions of this book have previously appeared in the
following / publications: *Saturday Review; The Atlantic Monthly;
Holiday;* / *The American West*; THE AMERICAN NOVEL,
published by / Basic Books, Inc.; THE OUTCASTS OF POKER
FLAT AND / OTHER TALES, published by Signet; TEACHING
THE SHORT STORY, published by University of California,
Davis; / *Library Journal*; THE ROMANCE OF NORTH
AMERICA, / Copyright © 1958 by Houghton Mifflin Company,
reprinted by / permission of the publisher, and FOUR
PORTRAITS AND ONE / SUBJECT, Copyright © 1963 by
Houghton Mifflin Company, re-/printed by permission of the
Publisher; *Woman's Day*, reprinted / by permission of Woman's

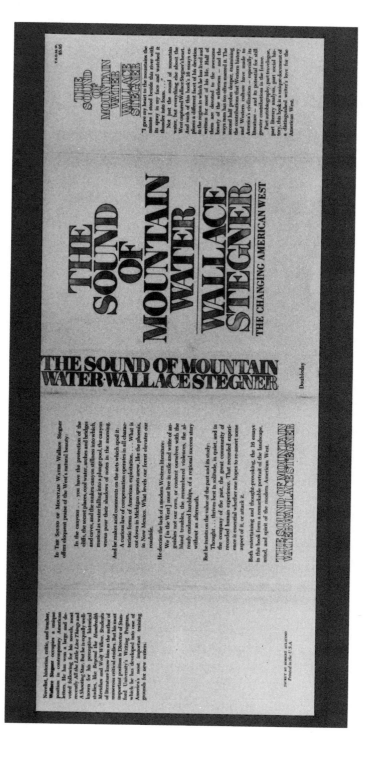

Dust jacket for A20.1.a

Day Magazine, a Fawcett publication. / Library of Congress
Catalog Card Number 69-12196 / Copyright ©1946, 1947, 1950,
1952, 1958, 1959, 1961, 1963, / 1965, 1966, 1967, 1969 by
Wallace Stegner / All Rights Reserved / Printed in the United
States of America / First Edition'

$(1-12)^{12}$

pp. (1-8) 9-38 (39-40) 41-153 (154-156) 157-286 (287-288)

8 3/16" × 5 7/16"

Contents: p. 1: blank; p. 2: 'By Wallace Stegner'; p. 3: half title; p.
4: blank; p. 5: title; p. 6: copyright; p. 7: 'Contents'; p. 8: blank;
pp. 9-38: 'Introduction'; p. 39: Part I title; p. 40: blank; pp.
41-153: text; p. 154: blank; p. 155: Part II title; p. 156: blank; pp.
157-286: text; pp. 287-288: blank.

Text contents: "Overture: The Sound of Mountain Water," "The
Rediscovery of America: 1946," "Packhorse Paradise," "Navajo
Rodeo," "San Juan and Glen Canyon." "Glen Canyon
Submersus," "The Land of Enchantment," "Coda: Wilderness
Letter," "At Home in the Fields of the Lord," "Born a Square,"
"History, Myth, and the Western Writer," "On the Writing of
History," "Three Samples": ("The West Synthetic: Bret Harte,"
"The West Authentic: Willa Cather," "The West Emphatic:
Bernard DeVoto"), "The Book and the Great Community."
Previously published, as described on copyright page.

Paper: Cream wove stock. Top and bottom edges trimmed. Fore
edge rough-cut. Endpapers of heavier medium yellow (c.87) wove
stock.

Binding: Green gray (c.155) cloth with dark green cloth spine.
Front stamped in gold: 'W / S' within gold ruled vertical rectangle.
Back cover blank. Spine stamped in gold: '[double rule] /
WALLACE / STEGNER / [single rule] / The / Sound / of /
Mountain / Water / [double rule] / Doubleday'.

Dust jacket: White with black lined letters, in shades of greens and yellows. Front: '[letters outlined in black with green and yellow within] THE / SOUND / OF / MOUNTAIN / WATER / [black] [narrow rule] / [green and yellow letters] WALLACE / STEGNER / [black] [narrow rule] / THE CHANGING AMERI-CAN WEST'. Spine: '[vertical] [letters outlined in black with green and yellow within] THE SOUND OF MOUNTAIN / WATER [black] [dot] WALLACE STEGNER / [horizontal] Doubleday'. Back: quotations from the book. Front flap: blurb on *The Sound of Mountain Water*. Back flap: biographical information on Stegner. 'JACKET BY ROBERT AULICINO'.

Publication: Copyright Office copy dated May 9, 1969 (A69135). First printing: 5,000 copies. $5.95.

Locations: WS (4), NC (2), LC (1)

Note: All copies of the first printing were recalled because credit lines were left out. A new copyright page was tipped in on the back of the title page.

A20.1.b

Second printing: as A20.1.a, with revised copyright printed on copyright page. 3,000 copies. $5.95.

A20.2.a

Second edition: New York: Ballantine, (1972).

Comstock edition. $1.25. Part I only. Cover title: *The Rockies Filled With The Sound of Mountain Water*. Included: "Introduction," "Overture: The Sound of Mountain Water," "The Rediscovery of America: 1946," "Packhorse Paradise," "Navajo Rodeo," "San Juan and Glen Canyon," "Glen Canyon Submersus," "The Land of Enchantment," "Coda: Wilderness Letter."

A20.3.a

Third edition: New York: E.P. Dutton, (1980).

$6.95. Copyright date for Dutton paperback edition is September 22, 1980. Includes a new introduction.

Remaindered and out-of-print July, 1982.

A20.3.b

Second printing: Lincoln: University of Nebraska, (1985).

Bison book. BB946. Sept., 1985 - 3,066 copies - $7.50 pap.

Reprint of the E.P. Dutton edition (A20.3.a).

A21 *Discovery!*

A21.1.a

First edition, first printing (1971)

Title page: 'DISCOVERY! / [narrow rule] / [gray] The Search for / Arabian Oil / [black] [narrow rule] / By Wallace Stegner / As Abridged for *Aramco World Magazine*'

Copyright: '[publisher's device] / AN / EXPORT / BOOK / Library of Congress Catalog No./ 74-148026 / All Rights Reserved / Printed by / Middle East Export Press, Inc. / Beirut, Lebanon / First Printing, January, 1971'

Perfect bound.

pp. (i-iv) (i) ii-xii, 1-190 (191-192)

7 7/8" × 5 1/4".

Contents: p.i: title; p.ii: copyright; p.iii: 'CONTENTS'; p.iv: blank;

Covers for A21.1.a, A21.1.b, A21.1.c

pp.i-xii: 'INTRODUCTION'; pp. 1-190: text; pp. 191-192: blank.

Paper: Cream wove. Edges trimmed. Inside wraps: maps of the Middle East.

Binding: White paper wrappers with dark red (c.16) and black print. Front: '[illus. of oil rig fire, airplane, figures] / [narrow rule] / [red] DISCOVERY! / [black] [short narrow rule] BY [short narrow rule] / Wallace Stegner / [short narrow rule] / AUTHOR OF / [short narrow rule] / [red] The Big Rock Candy Mountain / All The Little Live Things / [black] [narrow rule]'. Spine: '[vertical] [red] DISCOVERY! [black] Wallace Stegner / [horizontal] AN / EXPORT / BOOK'. Back: blurb on *Discovery!* Photo and biographical sketch of Stegner.

Dust jacket: None.

Publication: Privately printed for ARAMCO. Not for sale. No price (giveaway).

Locations: WS (2), NC (2), FC (1)

Note: Appeared serially in *Aramco World Magazine* January, 1968 through July/August, 1970. See C147-C151, C153-C158, C160-C161, C163.

A21.1.b

Second printing: An Export Book, (no date).

Title page: same as A21.1.a, except for absence of the last line: 'As Abridged for *Aramco World Magazine*'.

Binding: '[5 photographs on front cover] DISCOVERY! / BY / Wallace / Stegner [without mention of Stegner's other books (on cover of A21.1.a)]'.

Twenty pages of photographs between copyright page and 'CONTENTS'. Also, photos interspersed throughout this printing.

Without mapped endpapers.

A21.1.c

Third printing: Beirut, Lebanon: Middle East Export Press, (1971).

This printing obviously dates to 1972, as the front reads: 'BY / Wallace / Stegner / AUTHOR OF THE PULITZER PRIZE NOVEL / Angle of Repose'. The text is the same as A21.1.a, but the wraps are printed in red (on white). No photographs. Maps on inside covers.

Correspondence contains no data regarding the various printings.

A22   *Angle of Repose*

A22.1.a

First edition, first printing (1971)

Title page: 'ANGLE OF REPOSE / [swelling rule] / WALLACE STEGNER / DOUBLEDAY & COMPANY, INC., GARDEN CITY, NEW YORK / 1971'

Copyright: 'LIBRARY OF CONGRESS CATALOG CARD NUMBER 72-144301 / COPYRIGHT © 1971 BY WALLACE STEGNER / ALL RIGHTS RESERVED / PRINTED IN THE UNITED STATES OF AMERICA / FIRST EDITION'

$(1-18)^{16}$

pp. (1-10) 11-12 (13-14) 15-77 (78-80) 81-160 (161-162) 163-204 (205-206) 207-310 (311-312) 313-352 (353-354) 355-371 (372-374) 375-455 (456-458) 459-540 (541-542) 543-569 (570-576)

8 1/8″ × 5 7/16″

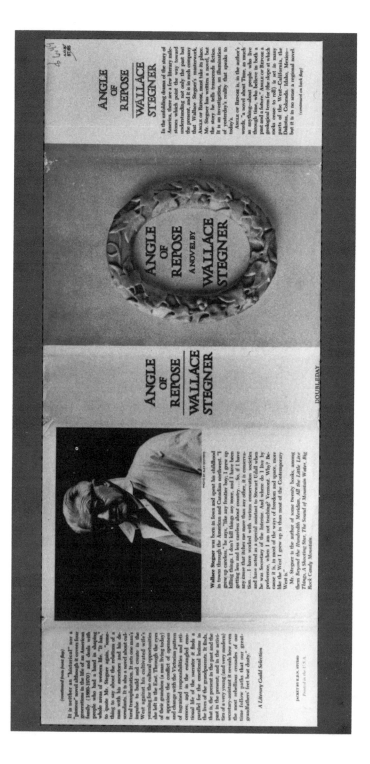

Dust jacket for A22.1.a

Contents: p. 1: half title; p. 2: blank; p. 3: 'BY WALLACE STEGNER [18 titles]'; p. 4: blank; p. 5: title; p. 6: copyright; p. 7: dedication, '*For my son, Page.*'; p. 8: blank; p. 9: 'My thanks to...[8 lines]'; p. 10: blank; pp. 11-12: contents; p. 13: section title, 'GRASS VALLEY'; p. 14: blank; pp. 15-77: text; p. 78: blank; p. 79: section title, 'NEW ALMADEN'; p. 80: blank; pp. 81-160: text; p. 161: section title, 'SANTA CRUZ'; p. 162: blank; pp. 163-204: text; p. 205: section title, 'LEADVILLE'; p. 206: blank; pp. 207-310: text; p. 311: section title, 'MICHOACAN'; p. 312: blank; pp. 313-352: blank; p. 353: section title, 'ON THE BOUGH'; p. 354: blank; pp. 355-371: text; p. 372: blank; p. 373: section title, 'THE CANYON,'; p. 374: blank; pp. 375-455: text; p. 456: blank; p. 457: section title, 'THE MESA'; p. 458: blank; pp. 459-540: text; p. 541: section title, 'THE ZODIAC COTTAGE'; p. 542: blank; pp. 543-569: text; pp. 570-576: blank.

Paper: Cream wove. Top and bottom edges trimmed; fore edge rough-cut. Gray yellow green (c.122) endpapers of heavier wove stock.

Binding: Gray yellow green (c.122) cloth. Front lettered in gilt: 'ANGLE / OF / REPOSE' within an oval blind-stamped wreath design. Back cover blank. Spine stamped in gilt: 'ANGLE / OF / REPOSE / [narrow rule] / WALLACE / STEGNER / DOUBLEDAY'.

Dust jacket: Front printed in dull dark red-shadowed (c.16) letters on light gray green (c.154) background within a photo of an engraved, light gray green oval, marble wreath: 'ANGLE / OF / REPOSE / A NOVEL BY / WALLACE / STEGNER'. Spine: '[dark red shadowed on white] ANGLE / OF / REPOSE / [black rule] / [black and red] WALLACE / STEGNER / [black] DOUBLEDAY'. Back: Photo of Wallace Stegner by Alex Gotfryd and biographical sketch. Front flap has 'A.O.R. / $7.95' and blurb on *Angle of Repose*. Back flap has continuation of blurb.

Publication: $7.95. March 19, 1971 - 35,000 copies. Literary Guild Selection - April, 1971. Recorded by Library of Congress Copyright Office February 9, 1971 (A212376).

Locations: WS (5), NC (4)

Note: Wallace Stegner won the Pulitzer Prize for this novel in 1972.

A22.1.b

Second printing: May 18, 1971 - 3,500 copies.

A22.1.c

Third printing: July 18, 1971 - 2,000 copies.

A22.2

First English edition, first printing (1971) Not from American sheets.

Title page: 'ANGLE OF REPOSE / [orn.rule] / WALLACE STEGNER / [publisher's device] / HEINEMANN: LONDON'

Copyright: 'William Heinemann Ltd / 15 Queen Street, Mayfair, London WIX 8BE / LONDON MELBOURNE TORONTO / JOHANNESBURG AUCKLAND / First published in Great Britain 1971 / Copyright © 1971 by Wallace Stegner / 434 73703 8 / Reproduced and Printed in Great Britain by / Redwood Press Limited / Trowbridge & London'

$(1-18)^{16}$

pp. (1-10) 11-12 (13-14) 15-77 (78-80) 81-160 (161-162) 163-204 (205-206) 207-310 (311-312) 313-352 (353-354) 355-371 (372-374) 375-455 (456-458) 459-540 (541-542) 543-569 (570-576)

8 7/16" × 5 7/16"

Contents: p. 1: half title; p. 2: blank; p. 3: 'OTHER BOOKS BY [9 titles]'; p. 4: blank; p. 5: title; p. 6: copyright; p. 7: dedication, '*For my son, Page*.'; p. 8: blank; p. 9: 'My thanks to...[8 lines]'; p. 10: blank; pp. 11-12: contents; p. 13: section title; p. 14: blank;

pp. 15-569: text [with section titles as in A22.1.a]; pp. 570-576: blank.

Paper: Smooth cream wove stock. Edges trimmed. Cream wove endpapers of heavier stock.

Binding: Gray reddish purple (c.245) paper-covered boards. Front and back covers blank. Spine lettered in gilt: 'ANGLE / OF / REPOSE / [double rule] / Wallace / Stegner / HEINEMANN'.

Dust jacket: Front: '[dark red-shadowed (c.160) letters on red gray (c.22) background within photo of an engraved, red gray oval, marble wreath] ANGLE / OF / REPOSE / A NOVEL BY / WALLACE / STEGNER'. Spine: '[vertical] [red-shadowed on white] ANGLE OF REPOSE / WALLACE STEGNER / [horizontal] [black] [publisher's device] / HEINEMANN'. Front flap: blurb for *Angle of Repose*. Back flap: photograph of Stegner and biographical sketch. Back has quotations from reviews of *Angle of Repose*.

Publication: Heinemann publication date listed as 13 September 1971. Bodleian copy dated 7 October 1971. British Library copy dated 16 September 1971.

Locations: WS (1), NC (1), BL (1), OX (1)

Note: One textual correction made in the English edition: on page 142 "Ten Eyck" was changed to "Van Eyck".

A22.3

Third edition: Greenwich, Conn.: Fawcett, (1972).

December, 1972. A Fawcett Crest Book. Q1768. $1.50.

A22.4

Fourth edition: Franklin Center, Pennsylvania: The Franklin Library, (1978).

Limited edition. Part of the Franklin Library series, "Pulitzer Prize Novels". April, 1978. Illustrated by Kenneth Francis Dewey. Limited to Franklin Library subscribers. Not signed.

Note: A portion of *Angle of Repose* first appeared in *McCall's* magazine in April, 1971. See D55.

There is a Taiwan piracy of *Angle of Repose* (not seen). Binding is dark brown cloth with only spine stamped in gold. On copyright page there are two lines of print in English, followed by eleven lines of Chinese.

A23
Robert Frost & Bernard DeVoto

Only printing (1974)

Title page: Cover title, '[within gray olive (c.110) square panel]
ROBERT / FROST & / BERNARD / DeVOTO / [narrow rule]
/ by Wallace Stegner'

Copyright: 'Copyright 1974 by Wallace Stegner / The text of the
Robert Frost letter repro-/duced herein is contained in *Selected
Letters of / Robert Frost* edited by Lawrance Thompson. / Copyright
©1964 by Lawrance Thompson / and Holt, Rinehart and
Winston, Inc. Repro-/duced by permission of Holt, Rinehart and /
Winston, Inc., and The Estate of Robert Frost / The photograph
of Robert Frost and Wal-/lace Stegner was taken during Frost's
visit to / Stanford in 1958, and is used with the permis-/sion of
the copyright owner, H. Walker Taylor, / Jr., of Oakland, California. / 125 copies printed for the members of the Rox- / burghe
Club of San Francisco.' Copyright printed on verso of front cover.

$(1)^6$

(unpaged) (1-12)

9″ × 7″

Contents: p. 1: 'Published on the occasion of / the Robert Frost Centennial / Exhibit, April 28-August 31, / 1974, by The Associates of the / Stanford University Libraries'; p. 2: photograph of Wallace Stegner and Robert Frost; pp. 3-6: 'ROBERT FROST & BERNARD DeVOTO / by Wallace Stegner'; pp. 7-11: photograph of letter from Robert Frost to Bernard DeVoto; p. 12: blank.

Paper: Cream wove. Edges trimmed. No endpapers.

Binding: Medium yellow green (c.120) wraps. Front: '[within gray olive square panel] ROBERT / FROST & / BERNARD / DeVOTO / [rule] / by Wallace Stegner'. Stapled twice at centerfold.

Dust jacket: None.

Publication: 125 copies were reserved for the members of the Roxburghe Club of San Francisco. Approximately 1,000 copies printed for Friends of the Stanford Libraries.

Locations: WS (5), NC (1)

Note: Copies were printed for the Roxburghe Club. Letter has pages out of order in all copies.

A24 *The Uneasy Chair*

A24.1.a

First edition, first printing (1974)

Title page: 'THE / UNEASY / CHAIR / *A Biography of* / BERNARD DEVOTO / [short narrow rule] / Wallace Stegner / DOUBLEDAY & COMPANY, INC. / GARDEN CITY, NEW YORK / 1974'

Copyright: 'PHOTO CREDITS: / SOOY Ogden, Utah photo 2 / James Woolverton Mason photos 30, 31 / Pix photo by K.W. Hermann photo 35 / Carl E. Vermilya, staff photographer, *The Oregonian*, Portland, Oregon photo 43 / Other photos courtesy Mrs. Bernard DeVoto / ISBN: 0-385-07884-6 / Library of Congress Catalog Card Number 73-81985 / *Copyright* © *1973, 1974 by Wallace Stegner* / ALL RIGHTS RESERVED / PRINTED IN THE UNITED STATES OF AMERICA / FIRST EDITION'

(1-20)[12]

pp. (i-vii) viii (ix) x-xi (xii-xvi) (1) 2-45 (46) 47-77 (78) 79-176 (177) 178-211 (212) 213-245 (246) 247-286 (287) 288-383 (384-385)

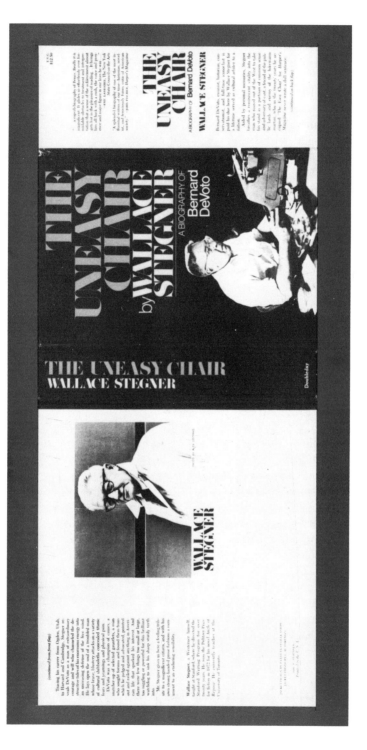

Dust jacket for A24.1.a

386-445 (446-447) 448-464

9 1/4" × 6 1/16"

Contents: p.i: half title; p.ii: 'By *Wallace Stegner*, [19 titles]'; p.iii: title; p.iv: copyright; p.v: dedication, 'to the Tribe of Benny'; p.vi: blank; pp.vii-viii: 'CONTENTS'; pp.ix-xi: 'Author's Note'; p.xii: blank; p.xiii: DeVoto quote; p.xiv: blank; p.xv: half title; p.xvi: poem by Don Marquis; pp. 1-383: text; p. 384: blank; pp. 385-445: 'NOTES'; p. 446: blank; pp. 447-464: 'INDEX'. Photos: 8 pp. between pp. 80 and 81, 8 pp. between pp. 176 and (177), 8 pp. between 272 and 273, and 8 pp. between pp. 368 and 369.

Paper: Cream wove stock. Top and bottom edges trimmed; fore edge rough-cut. Dark reddish orange (c.38) endpapers of a smooth stock.

Binding: Brown orange (c.54) cloth with dark reddish orange (c.38) spine. Front and back covers blank. Spine stamped in gilt: '*Wallace / Stegner* / [three rules] / THE / UNEASY / CHAIR / [three rules] / DOUBLEDAY'.

Dust jacket: Black background with letters in very orange (c.48), brilliant yellow (c.83), and white. Front: '[orange] THE / UNEASY / CHAIR / [yellow] by WALLACE / STEGNER / [narrow rule] / [white] A BIOGRAPHY OF / Bernard / DeVoto / [photo of DeVoto on lower half].' Spine lettered in orange, yellow, and white: '[vertical] [orange] THE UNEASY CHAIR / [yellow] WALLACE STEGNER / [horizontal] [white] Doubleday'. Back: photo of Wallace Stegner by Alex Gotfryd. Front flap has price, 'T.U.C. / $12.50' and blurb on *The Uneasy Chair*. Back flap: continuation of blurb, 'JACKET DESIGN BY PATRICIA SAVILLE VOEHL / JACKET PHOTO BY C.H. DYKEMAN'.

Publication: $12.50. February 11, 1974 - 5,000 copies.

Locations: WS (4), NC (3), LC (2)

A24.1.b

Second printing: February 15, 1974 - 5,000 copies.

A25 *The Spectator Bird*

A25.1

First edition, first printing (1976)

Title page: 'THE FIRST EDITION SOCIETY / [within dark olive green (c.126) decorative border] THE / SPECTATOR / BIRD / [olive green dot] / WALLACE STEGNER / [beneath square] *Illustrated by John Collier* / [olive green dot] / THE FRANKLIN LIBRARY / Franklin Center, Pennsylvania / 1976'

Copyright: 'This limited first edition / has been published / by special arrangement with / Doubleday & Co., Inc. / Copyright © 1976 by Wallace Stegner / All Rights Reserved / Special contents © 1976, Franklin Mint Corporation / *Printed in the United States of America*'

$(1-9)^{16}$

pp. (i-xvi) (1-3) 4-13 (14) 15-20 (21) 22-36 (37) 38-43 (44) 45-58 (59-61) 62-73 (74) 75-83 (84) 85-94 (95) 96-106 (107) 108-111

(112-115) 116-119 (120) 121-124 (125) 126-136 (137) 138-140
(141-143) 144-149 (150) 151-159 (160) 161-189 (190) 191-192
(193-195) 196-214 (215) 216-218 (219) 220-245 (246) 247-248
(249) 250-259 (260) 261-267 (268-272)

8 7/8″ × 5 11/16″

Illustration: The art that illustrates this exclusive first edition is the
work of John Collier. The pastel reproductions are subdued, yet
luminous. The illustrations are integral with the text. The paper
remains the same, although the illustrated pages are without
pagination. 9 pastel reproductions at pages: 14, 44, 74, 95, 125,
160, 190, 215, 249.

Contents: pp.i-ii: blank; p.iii: edition statement; p.iv: blank; p.v:
'Other books by Wallace Stegner [19 titles]'; p.vi: blank; p.vii: half
title; p.viii: blank; p.ix: 'A special message...' signed by Wallace
Stegner; p.x: blank; p.xi: title; p.xii: copyright; p.xiii:
'CONTENTS'; p.xiv: blank; p.xv: half title; p.xvi: blank; p. 1:
'PART ONE'; p. 2: blank; pp. 3-13: text; p. 14: illus.; pp. 15-43:
text; p. 44: illus.; pp. 45-58: text; p. 59: 'PART TWO'; p. 60:
blank; pp. 61-73: text; p. 74: illus.; pp. 75-94: text; p. 95: illus.;
pp. 96-111: text; p. 112: blank; p. 113: 'PART THREE'; p. 114:
blank; pp. 115-124: text; p. 125: illus.; pp. 126-140: text; p. 141:
'PART FOUR'; p. 142: blank; pp. 143-159: text; p. 160: illus.; pp.
161-189: text; p. 190: illus.; p. 191: 'PART FIVE'; p. 192: blank;
pp. 193-214: text; p. 215: illus.; pp. 216-248: text; p. 249: illus.;
pp. 250-267: text; pp. 268-272: blank.

Paper: Cream, fine wove stock. All edges trimmed and gilt in 22
karat gold. Endpapers are very yellow green (c.115) moire, specially
woven fabric.

Binding: Full dark green leather (c.128) with gilt-stamped
decoration on front, back, and spine. Spine stamped in gilt: 'THE /
SPECTATOR / BIRD / [single dot] / WALLACE / STEGNER /
[single dot] / THE / FRANKLIN / LIBRARY / [single dot]'.
Light green ribbon marker. Four raised ribs on spine.

Dust jacket: None.

Publication: Published May 1, 1976, one week before the trade edition. Published for subscribers to the Franklin Library First Edition Society. Printing size not public information. Not a signed limited edition.

Locations: WS (2), NC (1)

A25.2.a

Second edition, first printing (1976)

Title page: '[jagged line with dots] / WALLACE STEGNER / The / Spectator / Bird / 1976 / DOUBLEDAY & COMPANY, INC. / GARDEN CITY, NEW YORK'

Copyright: 'A Limited Edition of this book has been privately printed. / ISBN: 0-385-07870-0 / Library of Congress Catalog Card Number 75-38171 / Copyright © 1976 by Wallace Stegner / All Rights Reserved / Printed in the United States of America'

$(1-12)^9$

pp. (1-5) 6-214 (215-216)

8 3/16" × 5 7/16"

Contents: p. 1: 'BY WALLACE STEGNER [20 titles]'; p. 2: half title; p. 3: title; p. 4: copyright; p. 5: 'ONE'; pp. 6-214: text; pp. 215-216: blank.

Paper: Cream wove. Top and bottom edges trimmed; fore edge rough-cut. Heavier cream wove endpapers.

Binding: White paper-covered boards with black cloth spine. Front and back covers blank. Spine stamped in silver: '[vertical] *The Spectator Bird* WALLACE STEGNER *Doubleday*'.

Dust jacket for A25.2.a

Dust jacket: White and shades of bluish green. Lettering in black, pale yellow (c.89), and light bluish green (c.163). Front: '[narrow rule] / WALLACE / STEGNER / [short rule] / [yellow] THE / [black] [short rule] / [yellow] SPECTATOR / BIRD / [black] [narrow rule] / [light bluish green] A / NOVEL / BY THE PULITZER PRIZE-WINNING / AUTHOR OF "ANGLE OF REPOSE"'. Spine: White. '[vertical] THE SPECTATOR BIRD / [narrow rule] / WALLACE STEGNER / Doubleday'. Back: photo of Stegner by Alex Gotfryd and biographical sketch. Front flap: Price, 'T.S.B. / $6.95' and blurb on *The Spectator Bird*. Back flap: '*continued from front flap*'. Also, 'JACKET TYPOGRAPHY BY JUDITH TURNER'.

Publication: $6.95. May 7, 1976 - 20,000 copies. Library of Congress gives the copyright date as April 9, 1976 (A729759).

Locations: WS (5), NC (3), LC (2)

Note: *The Spectator Bird* was awarded the Commonwealth Club of California Gold Medal for Fiction as the Best Book in Fiction by a California Author in 1976. It was also the National Book Award winner in 1977. Stegner received offers from both the Literary Guild and Book-of-the-Month Club, but took BOMC for a smaller fee.

A25.2.b

Second printing: June 15, 1976 - 2,500 copies.

A25.2.c

Third printing: Lincoln: University of Nebraska, (1979).

Bison book. BB705. April, 1979 - 4,016 copies - $3.50 pap.

A25.2.d

Fourth printing: Lincoln: University of Nebraska, (1979). Bison book. BB705. Jan., 1980 - 7,845 copies - $3.50 pap.

A25.2.e

Fifth printing: Lincoln: University of Nebraska, (1979).

Bison book. BB705. Sept. 2, 1986 - 3.096 copies - $5.95.

A25.3

Large print edition: Boston, Massachusetts: G.K. Hall, (1977).

G.K. Hall Large Print Club Featured Selection. $11.50. June, 1977 - 2,500 copies for the library market. Now out-of-print.

A25.4

Large print edition (English): London: Prior, (1978). Not seen.

A26 *Recapitulation*

A26.1

First edition (1979)

Title page: '[brown decorative edge enclosing all] THE FIRST EDITION SOCIETY / RECAPITULATION / Wallace Stegner / [decorative dot] / ILLUSTRATED BY WALTER RANE / THE FRANKLIN LIBRARY / Franklin Center, Pennsylvania / 1979'

Copyright: 'Portions of the lyric from "Nobody Lied" (When They Said That I / Cried Over You), music by Edwin J. Weber, words by Karyl / Norman and Hyatt Berry. Copyright © 1922 Warner Bros. Inc. / Copyright Renewed. All rights reserved. "Ain't We Got Fun," / words by Gus Kahn and Raymond Egan, music by Richard Whit-/ing. Copyright © 1921 Warner Bros. Inc. Copyright Renewed. All / rights reserved. Used by permission. / Portion of the lyric from "There's A Quaker Down in Quaker / Town," words by David Berg, music by Alfred Solman. Copyright / © 1916 by Edwin H. Morris & Company, Inc. Copyright Re- / newed. International Copyright Secured. All rights reserved. Used /

by permission of Edwin H. Morris & Company, Inc. and
Jerry / Vogel Music Company, Inc. / This limited first edition /
has been published / by special arrangement with / Doubleday &
Co., Inc. / Copyright © 1979 by Wallace Stegner / All Rights
Reserved / Special contents © 1979, Franklin Mint Corporation /
Printed in the United States of America'

(1-11)¹⁶

pp. (i-xvi) (1-4) 5-124 (125-128) 129-174 (175-178) 179-281
(282-286) 287-334 (335-336)

8 13/16″ × 5 7/8″

Illustration: Illustrated with reproductions of watercolor paintings
by artist Walter Rane. 4 double-page illustrations at pages: 2-3,
126-127, 176-177, 284-285. Illustrations are integral with the text.
Same paper as the text, but illustrated pages are without pagination.

Contents: pp.i-ii: blank; p.iii: edition statement; p.iv: blank; p.v:
'Other books by Wallace Stegner [20 titles]'; p.vi: blank; p.vii: half
title; pp.viii-ix: 'A special message...'; p.x: blank; p.xi: title page:
p.xii: copyright; p.xiii: quotations by Ivan Turgenev and Gertrude
Stein; p.xiv: blank; p.xv: second half title; p.xvi: blank; p. 1: 'I'; pp.
2-3: watercolor; p. 4: blank; pp. 5-124: text; p. 125: 'II'; pp.
126-127: watercolor; p. 128: blank; pp. 129-174: text; p. 175: 'III';
pp. 176-177: watercolor; p. 178: blank; pp. 179-281: text; p. 282:
blank; p. 283: 'IV'; pp. 284-285: watercolor; p. 286: blank; pp.
287-335: text; p. 336: blank.

Paper: Text and illustrations on 60-pound Eggshell Wove Cream
paper stock. All edges trimmed and gilt. Medium reddish brown
(c.43) endpapers in moire fabric.

Binding: Medium reddish brown (c.43) leather with gilt design on
front, back, and spine. Spine stamped in gilt: '[square with decorative leaves] / [narrow rule] / FIRST / EDITION / [narrow rule] /
[arch of decorative leaves] / RECAPITULATION / [single dot] /
WALLACE / STEGNER / [reversed arch of decorative leaves] /

[narrow rule] / THE / FRANKLIN / LIBRARY / [narrow rule] / [square with decorative leaves]'. Rust ribbon marker. Four raised ribs on spine.

Dust jacket: None.

Publication: Franklin Library gives January 12, 1979 as the publication date for *Recapitulation*. Regarding the number of copies printed, Franklin Library responded to enquiry thus: "Corporate policy dictates that your question about size of print runs not be answered—and in fact this is not something the editors have records on. However, all of the editions mentioned above...were limited to series subscribers, plus a few author's and office reference copies. We have always adhered strictly to our statements of limitation of edition." Not a signed, limited edition.

Locations: WS (2), NC (3)

Note: Original title was *The Tourist.*

A26.2.a

Second edition, first printing (1979)

Title page: 'Wallace Stegner / RECAPITULATION / 1979 / Doubleday & Company, Inc. / Garden City, New York'

Copyright: 'Portions of the lyric from "Nobody Lied" (When They Said That I / Cried Over You), music by Edwin J. Weber, words by Karyl Norman and / Hyatt Berry. Copyright © 1922 Warner Bros. Inc. Copyright Renewed. / All rights reserved; "Ain't We Got Fun," words by Gus Kahn and Raymond / Egan, music by Richard Whiting. Copyright © 1921 Warner Bros. Inc. / Copyright renewed. All rights reserved. Used by permission. / Portion of the lyric from "There's a Quaker Down in Quaker Town" / words by David Berg, music by Alfred Solman. Copyright © 1916 by / Edwin H. Morris & Company, Inc. Copyright Renewed. International Copy-/right Secured. All rights reserved. Used by permission of Edwin H. Mor-/ris & Company, Inc., and Jerry Vogel

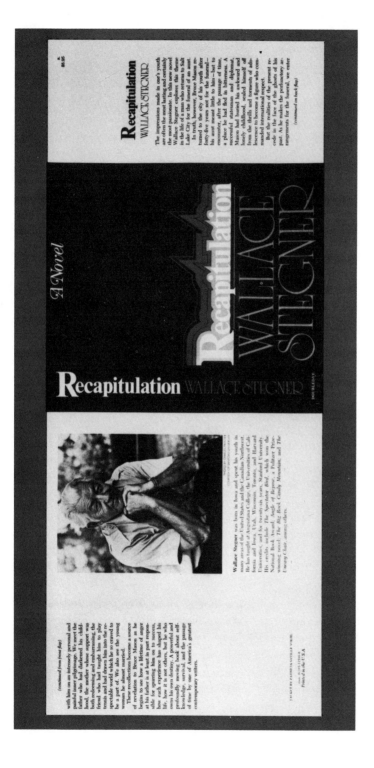

Dust jacket for A26.2.a

Music Company, Inc. / ISBN 0-385-11580-6 / Library of Congress
Catalog Card Number 78-8203 / Copyright © 1979 by Wallace
Stegner / All Rights Reserved / Printed in the United States of
America / First edition after a privately printed limited edition'

$(1-12)^{12}$

pp. (i-viii) (1-3) 4-15 (16-17) 18-24 (25) 26-30 (31) 32-48 (49)
50-60 (61) 62-71 (72-73) 74-87 (88-89) 90-104 (105-107) 108-118
(119) 120-144 (145-147) 148-152 (153) 154-164 (165) 166-175
(176-177) 178-190 (191) 192-206 (207) 208-213 (214-215) 216-233
(234-237) 238-245 (246-247) 248-265 (266-267) 268-278 (279-280)

8 1/16" × 5 7/16"

Contents: p.i: half title; p.ii: blank; p.iii: title; p.iv: copyright; p.v:
quotations by Ivan Turgenev and Gertrude Stein; p.vi: blank; p.vii:
second half title; p.viii: blank; p. 1: chapter number 'I'; p. 2: blank;
pp. 3-104: text; p. 105: chapter number 'II'; p. 106: blank; pp.
107-144: text; p. 145: chapter number 'III'; p. 146: blank; pp.
147-233: text; p. 234: blank; p. 235: 'chapter number IV'; p. 236:
blank; pp. 237-278: text; pp. 279-280: blank.

Paper: Cream wove stock. Top and bottom edges trimmed. Fore
edge rough cut. Cream wove endpapers.

Binding: Medium blue (c.182) paper-covered boards with black
cloth spine. Front and back covers blank. Spine stamped in gilt:
'[vertical] RECAPITULATION / Wallace Stegner / [horizontal]
Doubleday'.

Dust jacket: Black with dark blue (c.183), deep green (c.142), and
very orange yellow (c.66) design around title. Front: '[white] A
Novel / Recapitulation / [split narrow rule] / [gray] WALLACE /
STEGNER'. Spine: '[vertical] [white] Recapitulation [gray]
WALLACE STEGNER / [horizontal] [white] DOUBLEDAY'.
Back: photograph of Wallace Stegner by Charles Painter and
biographical sketch. Front flap: 'R. / $8.95' at upper right corner
and blurb for *Recapitulation*. Back flap: blurb continued from front

flap; below: 'JACKET BY PATRICIA SAVILLE VOEHL / ISBN: 0-385-11580-6 / *Printed in the U.S.A.*'

A variant dust jacket has a different order for colors outlining the letters of the title. The ideal copy has the blue, green, and orange yellow as described above, while the variant has white letters outlined in blue, yellow, and green.

Publication: $8.95. Publication date was February 23, 1979 (first printing), although the 17,000 copies were off the press before January 10, 1979. Library of Congress copy dated January 24, 1979. Copyright Office copy dated January 31, 1979.

Locations: WS (5), NC (4), LC (2)

A26.2.b

Second printing: February 23, 1979 - 2,000 copies.

A26.2.c

Third printing: March 6, 1979 - 2,000 copies.

A26.2.d

Fourth printing: April 5, 1979 - 2,000 copies.

A26.2.e

Fifth printing: Lincoln: University of Nebraska, (1986).

Bison book. February, 1986 - 3,580 copies - $7.95 pap.

A26.3

Third edition: New York: Fawcett Crest, (1980).

First Fawcett Crest printing February, 1980. $2.50.

A27 *American Places*

A27.1.a

First edition, first printing (1981)

Title page: 'ELIOT PORTER / [narrow rule] / American / Places / [narrow rule] / WALLACE STEGNER & PAGE STEGNER / *Edited by John Macrae, III* / E.P. DUTTON NEW YORK'

Copyright: *'Acknowledgments* / CHAPTERS FROM THIS BOOK have appeared in the following periodicals, / in slightly different forms: "Inheritance" in *American Heritage*; "The / Northeast Kingdom," "Crow Country," "The River," and "Remnants" / in *Country Journal*; "There It Is: Take It" in *Harper's*; "Life Along the / Fault Line" in *Esquire*. / We are grateful to the Van Wyck Brooks Estate for permission to / reprint material from *The World of Washington Irving* by Van Wyck / Brooks (E.P. Dutton, 1944). / All rights reserved under International and Pan-American Copyright / Conventions / First published in the United States in 1981 by ELSEVIER-DUTTON / PUBLISHING CO., INC., 2 Park Avenue, New York, N.Y. 10016 / (Library of Congress cataloging

data) / Published simultaneously in Canada by CLARKE IRWIN &
COMPANY / LIMITED, Toronto and Vancouver / 10 9 8 7 6 5
4 3 2 1 / FIRST EDITION / *Production Director*: David Zable /
Managing Editor: Linda Spencer / *Type Composition*:
Mackenzie-Harris Corp., San Francisco, California / *Printed and
bound*: Amilcare Pizzi - S.P.A., Milan, Italy'

(1-14)^8

pp. (1-8) 9-16 (17-32) 33-64 (65-96) 97-128 (129-160) 161-192
(193-208) 209-224

12" × 10 3/8"

Illustrations: 89 color photographs taken especially for the book by
Eliot Porter. Plates on pages: 17-32, 65-96, 129-160, 193-208.
Plates are counted in collation, but are without pagination. Not
printed on text stock, but on coated paper.

Contents: p. 1: half title; p. 2: blank; p. 3: title; p. 4: copyright; p.
5: 'Contents'; p. 6: blank; pp. 7-8: 'List of Plates'; pp. 9-10:
'Foreword'; pp. 11-16: text; pp. 17-32: plates; pp. 33-64: text; pp.
65-96: plates; pp. 97-128: text; pp.129-160: plates; pp. 161-192:
text; pp. 193-208: plates; pp. 209-217: text; pp. 218-222:
'Bibliography'; pp. 223-224: 'Index'.

Text contents: Chapters from this book have appeared in periodicals
in slightly different form. Wallace Stegner and Page Stegner retained
serial rights for *American Places*. *New West, Country Journal,
American Heritage*, and *Sierra Club Bulletin* all include articles from
this book:
   Country Journal - "Northeast Kingdom" (August 1979) -
C195.
      "Remnants" (December 1979) - C197.
      "Crow Country" (July 1980) - C198.

   American Heritage - "By Chaos Out of Dream" (February
/March 1981) - C204.

New West - "The Call of the Wild" (August 1981) - C209.

Sierra - "High Plateaus" (September/October 1981) - C213.

Paper: Cream wove stock. Edges trimmed. Plates on coated paper. Cream wove endpapers similar to text stock.

Binding: Yellow gray (c.93) rough cloth. Front and back covers blank. Spine stamped in gilt: '[vertical] [small type] ELIOT PORTER [large type] American Places [small type] WALLACE STEGNER / & PAGE STEGNER / [horizontal] DUTTON'.

Dust jacket: Dark gray yellowish brown (c.81) with gold print. Front: '[small type] ELIOT PORTER / [narrow rule] / [large type] American / Places / [narrow rule] / [small type] WALLACE STEGNER & PAGE STEGNER'. Spine: '[vertical] [small type] ELIOT PORTER [large type] American Places [small type] WALLACE STEGNER / & PAGE STEGNER / [horizontal] DUTTON'. Back: color photograph of the Colorado Plateau (Plate #72). Front flap: Two prices in upper right corner, '$29.50 until 1/1/82' and '$39.75'. Blurb on *American Places*. Back flap: continuation of front flap.

Publication: Pre-publication price $29.50 until 1-1-82. Thereafter $39.75. First printing: 20,000 copies. Publication date October 12, 1981.

Locations: WS (3), NC (2)

Note: Chapters 1, 3-8, and 13 are by Wallace Stegner; chapters 9-12 are by Page Stegner. Chapter 14 was written jointly by Wallace Stegner and Page Stegner. Chapter 2 was from THE WORLD OF WASHINGTON IRVING BY Van Wyck Brooks, published in 1944. The bibliography is the work of the authors and Jack Macrae.

A27.1.b

Second printing: New York: Greenwich House, (1983)

'Originally published at $39.75. This 1982 edition is published by Greenwich House, a division of Arlington House, Inc., distributed by Crown Publishers, Inc., by arrangement with E.P. Dutton, Inc.' No other printed price. Usually sells at remainder prices ($12.98, for example).

A27.2

Second edition: Moscow, Idaho: University of Idaho Press, (1983). 1,000 copies printed in January, 1986. Copyright page cites the 1983 date.

Text only of chapters by Wallace and Page Stegner. Foreword abridged. Chapter 2 of original volume, by Van Wyck Brooks, not included.

A28
One Way to Spell Man

A28.1

First edition (1982)

Title page: 'ONE WAY / TO SPELL MAN / [short decorative rule] / *Wallace Stegner* / DOUBLEDAY & COMPANY, INC. / GARDEN CITY, NEW YORK / 1982'

Copyright: 'ISBN: 0-385-17720-8 / Library of Congress Catalog Card Number: 81-43428 / *Foreword Copyright* © *1982 by Wallace Stegner* / ALL RIGHTS RESERVED / PRINTED IN THE UNITED STATES OF AMERICA / FIRST EDITION'

$(1-8)^{12}$

pp. (i-vii) viii (ix-xi) xii (1-3) 4 (5) 6-17 (18) 19-25 (26) 27-34 (35) 36-50 (51) 52-68 (69) 70-71 (72-75) 76-83 (84) 85-98 (99) 100-108 (109) 110-117 (118) 119-123 (124) 125-135 (136) 137-143 (144) 145-160 (161) 162-177 (178-180)

8 1/8″ × 5 1/2″

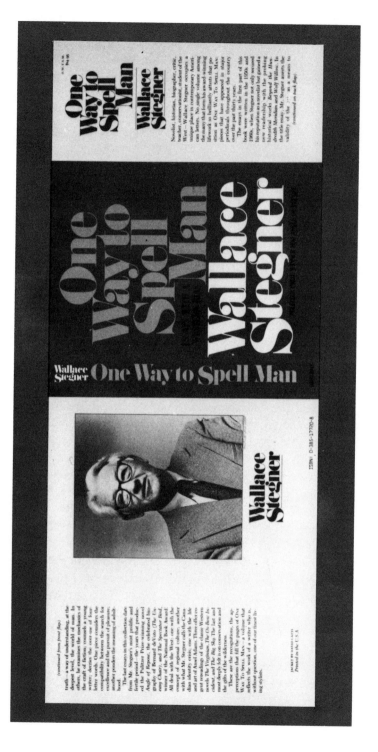

Dust jacket for A28.1

Contents: p.i: half title; p.ii: blank; p.iii: 'by Wallace Stegner'; p.iv: blank; p.v: title; p.vi: copyright; pp.vi-viii: 'Acknowledgments'; p.ix: 'Contents'; p.x: blank; pp.xi-xii: 'Foreword'; p. 1: 'PART I'; p. 2: blank; pp. 3-177: text; pp. 178-180: blank.

Text contents: "This I Believe," (B30) "One Way to Spell Man," (C101) "Fiction: A Lens on Life," (C67) "To a Young Writer," (C110) "The Writer and the Concept of Adulthood," (C185) "Excellence and the Pleasure Principle," (C196) "Good-bye to All T-t!" (C127) "That New Man, the American," (C173) "The Provincial Consciousness," (C177) "The West Coast: Region with a View," (C108) "Making a Myth," (B109) "A.B. Guthrie," (B82) "Walter Clark's Frontier," (C170) "A Desert Shelf," (C187) "Ansel Adams and the Search for Perfection," (B110) and "The Gift of Wilderness" (C209, C210).

Paper: Cream wove. Top and bottom edges trimmed. Fore edge rough-cut. White wove endpapers.

Binding: Light gray (c.264) paper-covered boards with black cloth spine. Front and back covers blank. Spine: '[vertical] [gilt-stamped] Wallace Stegner ONE WAY TO SPELL MAN / [horizontal] DOUBLEDAY'.

Dust jacket: Gray with very orange yellow (c.66), white, and black lettering. Front: '[orange yellow] One / Way to / Spell / Man / [black] [to left of 'Man'] ESSAYS WITH A / WESTERN BIAS / [white] Wallace / Stegner / [black] PULITZER PRIZE WINNER FOR *ANGLE OF REPOSE*'. Spine: '[vertical] [white] Wallace / Stegner / [orange yellow] One Way to Spell Man / [horizontal] [black] DOUBLEDAY'. Back: photo of Wallace Stegner by Layle Silbert. Front flap: Price in upper right corner, 'O.W.T.S.M. / $14.95' and blurb on *One Way to Spell Man*. Back flap: continuation of blurb; below: 'JACKET BY DAVID GATTI'.

Publication: 8,300 copies printed April 16, 1982. Library of Congress copy received March 17, 1982. $14.95.

Locations: WS (5), NC (3), LC (1)

A29   20-20 Vision:
In Celebration of the Peninsula Hills

Only printing (1982)

Title page: '20-20 VISION: / In Celebration of the Peninsula Hills / *Dedicated to Kathryn and Morgan Stedman.* / *Words by Wallace Stegner* / *and members of the* / *Committee for Green Foothills* / *Phyllis Filiberti Butler, Editor*'

Copyright: '[photo of the foothills] / *...to leave for our children and* / *grandchildren a heritage that has* / *not been dug up and paved over* / *and—it is an ironic word—*/ *humanized.* / Copyright 1982 by Committee for Green Foothills / Published May 1982 by Green Foothills Foundation / Peninsula Conservation Center / 2253 Park Blvd. / Palo Alto, CA. 94306 / (415) 327-5906 / Distributed by Western Tanager Press / ISBN 0-934136-20-3'

(1)[18]

pp. (1-4) 5-36

8 1/2" × 9 1/2"

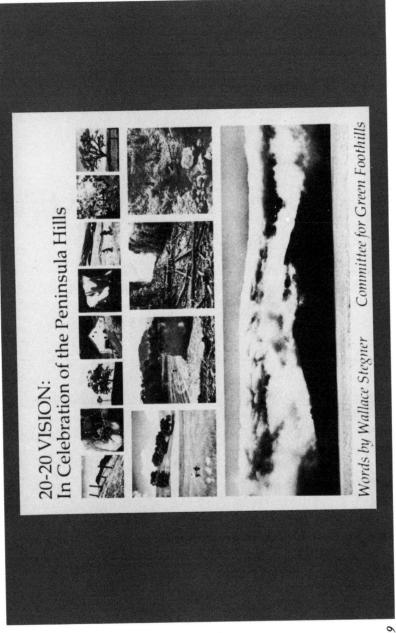

20-20 VISION:
In Celebration of the Peninsula Hills

Words by Wallace Stegner   Committee for Green Foothills

Cover for A29

Contents: p. 1: title; p. 2: copyright; p. 3: credits; p. 4: committee members, presidents, and quotation; p. 4: 'In the Beginning...'; p. 6: photo; pp. 7-35: text and photos; p. 36: 'Key to Cover Photos and Photo Credits'.

Paper: Smooth white wove stock. Edges trimmed. No endpapers.

Binding: White wrapper with photos and black printing. Stapled at centerfold. Front: '20-20 VISION: / In Celebration of the Peninsula Hills / [thirteen photos] / *Words by Wallace Stegner Committee for Green Foothills*'. Back: $4.95 / ISBN 0-934136-20-3 / GREEN FOOTHILLS FOUNDATION'.

Dust jacket: None.

Publication: Printed by Guardian Printing. Typeset by Landford's Typesetting. $4.95. 1500 copies printed.

Locations: NC (10)

A30 *Conversations with Wallace Stegner on Western History and Literature*

A30.1

First edition, first printing (1983)

Title page: 'Conversations with / Wallace Stegner / on Western History / and Literature / Wallace Stegner / and / Richard W. Etulain / UNIVERSITY OF UTAH PRESS SALT LAKE CITY 1983'

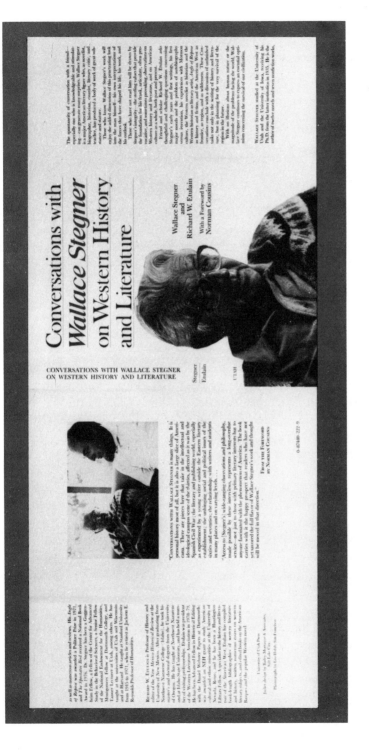

Conversations with
Wallace Stegner
on Western History
and Literature

Wallace Stegner
and
Richard W. Etulain

With a Foreword by
Norman Cousins

CONVERSATIONS WITH WALLACE STEGNER
ON WESTERN HISTORY AND LITERATURE

Stegner
Etulain

UTAH

The spontaneity of conversation with a friend—especially one who is knowledgeable and stimulating—can generate many surprises. Wallace Stegner is a major American literary figure who, as novelist, biographer, historian, essayist, literary critic, and teacher, has produced a body of work of great substance and stature.

Those who know Wallace Stegner's work will enjoy the added dimension of this penetrating book into the man himself—his own interpretations of the forces that have shaped his life, his work, and his outlook.

Those who have not read him will be drawn by Stegner's integrity—the sterling values that provide the foundation for his frank, articulate, often provocative, and sometimes provoking, observations on Western history and literature, and on American culture as a whole, both past and present.

Friend and scholar Richard W. Etulain asks thoughtful and challenging questions concerning Stegner's early years and first writings, his first major novels and the problem of autobiography versus invention, his experiences with Mormon culture, the Western novelist as historian and the Western historian as literary artist, *Angle of Repose* as history and fiction, and the American West as frontier, as region, and as wilderness. These Conversations conclude with a discussion of unfinished tasks not only in the writing of history and literature, but in planning for the very survival of the region for the future.

With so much discussion about human nature or the magnitude of the problems facing the world, Wallace Stegner continues to express an essential optimism concerning the survival of our civilization.

WALLACE STEGNER studied at the University of Utah and the University of Iowa, receiving his Ph.D. from the latter institution in 1935. He is the author of twelve novels and seven nonfiction works,

as well as numerous articles and reviews. His *Angle of Repose* was awarded a Pulitzer Prize in 1971, and *The Spectator Bird* received a National Book Award in 1976. Dr. Stegner has been a Congdon-Bohn Fellow, a Fellow of the Center for Advanced Study in the Behavioral Sciences, a Senior Fellow of the National Endowment for the Humanities, Montgomery Fellow at Dartmouth College, and Lamar Lecturer at Utah, among others. He has taught at the universities of Utah and Wisconsin and at Harvard. He taught at Stanford University from 1945 to 1971, when he retired as Jackson E. Reynolds Professor of Humanities.

RICHARD W. ETULAIN is Professor of History and editor of the *New Mexico Historical Review* at the University of New Mexico. Also graduating from Northwest Nazarene College (Idaho), he took his master's and doctoral degrees from the University of Oregon. He has taught at Northwest Nazarene and at Idaho State University, and was for a number of years visiting professorships. Etulain was president of the Western Literature Association in 1978-79. He has been a Huntington Fellow in History, a Visiting Fellow at Dartmouth, and was awarded an NEH grant to study American cultural and ethnic minorities at the University of Nevada, Reno. A specialist in the history and literature of the American West, Etulain has compiled book-length bibliographies of western literature and history—not just to those with primary literary interests but to anyone fascinated with the American Renaissance, and edited books on the American Renaissance and the popular Western novel.

University of Utah Press
Jacket design by Bailey Montague & Associates, Salt Lake City, Utah

Photograph of Stegner by Leo Holub, San Francisco

"CONVERSATIONS WITH WALLACE STEGNER is many things. It is personal history most of all, but it is also a large slice of Americana. There are pieces here that take in the intellectual and ideological campus scene of the sixties, affected as it was by the Spanish Civil War; the literary and publishing world, especially as experienced by a young writer outside the Eastern literary establishment; the ambitious social and political issues of the sixties and seventies; the relationship with writers and students in many places and on varying levels. . . .

"Access to [Stegner's] wide-ranging observations and philosophy, made possible by these interviews, represents a long-overdue service—not just to those with primary literary interests but to anyone fascinated with the phenomenon of America. The book carries with it the happy prospect that readers who have not yet savored the full flavor of Wallace Stegner's work and thought will be moved in that direction."

FROM THE FOREWORD
BY NORMAN COUSINS

0-87480-222-9

Dust jacket for A30.1

Holub of San Francisco, California'

(1-7)¹⁶

pp. (i-iv) v-viii (ix-x) 1-19 (20) 21-143 (144) 145-183 (184) 185-207 (208-214)

9 1/8" × 6"

Contents: p.i: half title; p.ii: photo of Wallace Stegner; p.iii: title; p.iv: copyright; p.v: 'Contents'; p.vi: 'Books by Wallace Stegner'; pp.vii-viii: 'Foreword'; p.ix: second half title; p.x: photo of Richard Etulain; pp. 1-19: text; p. 20: photo; pp. 21-143: text: p. 144: photo; pp. 145-183: text; p. 184: photo; pp. 185-200: text; pp. 201-207: 'Index'; pp. 208-214: blank.

Paper: Cream wove stock. Edges trimmed. Rough cream wove stock.

Binding: Medium reddish brown (c.43) cloth. Front and back covers blank. Spine gilt-stamped: '[vertical] CONVERSATIONS WITH WALLACE STEGNER / ON WESTERN HISTORY AND LITERATURE / [horizontal] Stegner / [rule] / Etulain / UTAH'.

Dust jacket: White with black and medium reddish brown (c.43) print. Front: 'Conversations with / [brown] [narrow rule] / Wallace Stegner / [narrow rule] / [black] on Western History / [brown] [narrow rule] / [black] and Literature / [brown] [narrow rule] / [photo of Wallace Stegner] / [black] Wallace Stegner / and / Richard W. Etulain / With a Foreword by / Norman Cousins'. Spine: '[vertical] CONVERSATIONS WITH WALLACE STEGNER / ON WESTERN HISTORY AND LITERATURE / [horizontal] [brown] Stegner / [short narrow rule] / Etulain / UTAH'. Back: '[photo of Etulain and Stegner] / [portions of the Foreword by Norman Cousins]'. Front flap: blurb on *Conversations* and biographical sketch of Stegner. Back flap: continuation of front flap. Biographical sketch of Etulain. 'Jacket design by Bailey-Montague & Associates, / Salt Lake City. / Photographs by

Leo Holub, San Francisco.'

Publication: Published September, 1983. First printing: 2,000 copies. $15.00.

Locations: WS (5), NC (10)

A31
Memo to the Mountain Lion

First (and only) printing (1984)

Title: '[medium reddish brown (c.43)] Memo to / the Mountain Lion'

Copyright: '[last line] DESIGNED BY WOLFGANG LEDERER [dot] PRINTED AND COPYRIGHT ©1984 BY HAROLD BERLINER [dot] NEVADA CITY [dot] CALIFORNIA'

1-page broadside

18 1/2" × 12 3/4"

Illustration: Illustration of a mountain lion preceding text. Illus. by Wolfgang Lederer, in medium olive green (c.127) and shades of yellowish brown.

Contents: Five parargraphs, printed in medium reddish brown (c.43), gray yellow green (c.122), and black.

Paper: Cream wove stock.

Publication: 500 copies, numbered and signed by Wallace Stegner.

Locations: WS (1), NC (1)

A32   *The Sense of Place*

First edition, first (and only) printing (1986)

Title page: '[double title page] [both] [illus. in dark brown (c.59), light brown (c.57), and light green gray (c.154) of a man looking toward a "river" of "places" and "things" of the land] / [left] Published by the Wisconsin Humanities Committee / With support from the National Endowment for the Humanities / Printed by the Silver Buckle Press at the University of Wisconsin-Madison / [right] [light green gray] The Sense of Place / Wallace Stegner'

Copyright: '[light green gray] Copyrighted in December, 1986 to the author Wallace Stegner.'

(1)⁸

pp. (i-iv) 1-9 (10-12)

8 1/2″ ↑× 6 7/8″

Contents: p.i: half title; pp.ii-iii: double title page; p.iv: copyright;

pp. 1-9: text; p. 10: illus.; p. 11: biographical information and colophon; p. 12: blank.

Typography and paper: Printed on Mohawk Superfine paper using handset 14 point Baskerville monotype.

Binding: Pamphlet bound in two sheets of blue gray (c.191) Teton Sage cover stock. Sewn with a single strand of white thread, tied on outside edge at centerfold. Front and back covers blank.

Dust jacket: Full paper dust jacket in same heavy blue gray (c.191) stock as in binding. Front: '[light green gray (c.154)] The Sense of Place'. Back cover blank. Flaps blank.

Publication: Published in December, 1986. Printed by the Silver Buckle Press, a working typographical museum located in the Helen C. White Library at the University of Wisconsin-Madison. 200 numbered copies.

Location: WS (2)

Note: From page 11: 'To encourage reading and discussion on the relationship / of myth, story and history, the Wisconsin Humanities Comm-/ittee has selected as a theme: A Sense of Place in History and / Literature. The choice of Wallace Stegner to keynote this / theme was a natural consequence. Throughout his career, Mr. / Stegner has explored the mythical, literary and historical dim-/ensions of the human psyche. The sense of place has been / central to his search.'

A33 *Crossing to Safety*

A33.1

First edition, first printing (1987)

Title page: 'FIRST EDITION / [black and deep blue (c.179) inverted triangular orn.] / [black] CROSSING / TO / SAFETY / [black and deep blue orn.] / [deep blue (c.179)] WALLACE STEGNER / [black] FRANKLIN LIBRARY / FRANKLIN CENTER, PENNSYLVANIA / 1987'

Copyright: 'This signed limited first edition has been published by special arrangement with / Random House, Inc., and Brandt & Brandt Literary Agents, Inc. / Copyright ©1987 by Wallace Stegner. All rights reserved. / Special comments copyright ©1987 The Franklin Library.'

(1)² (2)⁸ (4-20)⁸ (21)⁷

pp. (i-xiv) (1-7) 8-15 (16) 17-20 (21) 22-29 (30) 31-44 (45) 46-56 (57) 58-86 (87) 88-104 (105) 106-109 (110) 111-124 (125) 126-133

(134) 135-142 (143) 144-170 (171-175) 176-185 (186-197) 198-210 (211) 212-234 (235) 236-237 (238-243) 244-253 (254) 255-265 (266) 267-275 (276) 277-289 (290-292)

9 1/16″ × 6 1/8″

Illustration: The illustrations consist of black and white paintings by William Low and were specially commissioned by the Franklin Library for this first edition of *Crossing to Safety*. The paper remains the same, but without pagination: 1, 5, 173, and 241.

Contents: pp.i-ii: blank; p.iii: half title; p.iv: blank; p.v: edition statement; p.vi: blank; p.vii: 'ALSO BY WALLACE STEGNER'; pp.viii-ix: '*A special message for the first edition / from Wallace Stegner*'; p.x: blank; p.xi: title; p.xii: copyright; p.xiii: dedication; p.xiv: blank; p. 1: half title, with black and white illustration and quotation by Robert Frost; p. 2: blank; p. 3: 'PART ONE'; p. 4: blank; p. 5: illustration; p. 6: blank; pp. 7-170: text; p. 171: 'PART TWO'; p. 172: blank; p. 173: illustration; p. 174: blank; pp. 175-237: text; p. 238: blank; p. 239: 'PART THREE'; p. 240: blank; p. 241: illustration; p. 242: blank; pp. 243-289: text; p. 290: 'ABOUT THE AUTHOR'; p. 291: edition statement; p. 292: blank.

Paper: 'The acid-free paper is 70-pound Franklin Library Vellum White Offset, made to archival standards by the P.H. Glatfelter Paper Company of Spring Grove, Pennsylvania, for The Franklin Library.' All edges trimmed and gilt. Marbled, colored endpapers.

Binding: Dark blue (c.183) leather with gilt designs on front, back, and spine. Spine stamped in gilt: '[design with triangles] / CROSS-ING / TO / SAFETY / WALLACE / STEGNER / [panel of design with triangular designs] [with center blue square] / SIGNED / FIRST / EDITION / [design with triangles]'. Blue ribbon marker. Three raised ribs on spine.

Dust jacket: None.

Publication: A signed first edition. The limitation of this edition is

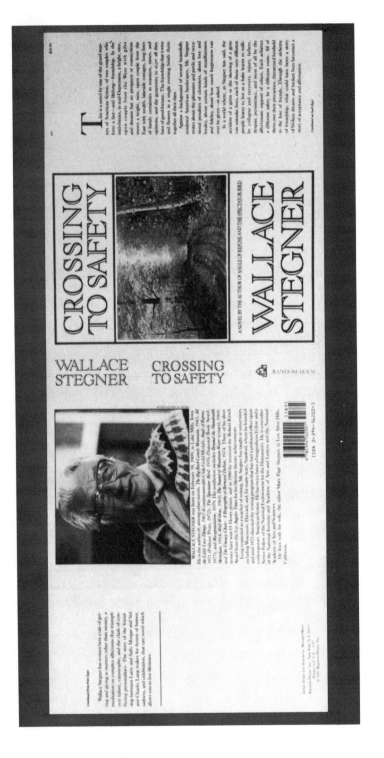

Dust jacket for A33.2.a

not stipulated in the book, nor will The Franklin Library make that information available. The limitation is based on the number of subscribers, which is confidential information.

Locations: WS (1), Franklin Library (1)

A33.2.a

Second edition, first printing (1987)

Title page: '[two double-lined panels, with space left for the title beneath the upper and above the lower] / CROSSING / [narrow rule] TO [narrow rule] / SAFETY / WALLACE STEGNER / [publisher's device] / RANDOM HOUSE NEW YORK'

Copyright: 'Copyright ©1987 by Wallace Stegner / First Random House Edition / A signed first edition of this book has been privately printed by / The Franklin Library.'

$(1-9)^{16}$

pp. (i-x) (1-3) 4-277 (278)

9 1/4" × 6 1/4"

Contents: p.i: blank; p.ii: 'BOOKS BY WALLACE STEGNER'; p.iii: half title; p.iv: blank; p.v: title; p.vi: copyright; p.vii: dedication; p.viii: blank; p.ix: quotation by Robert Frost; p.x: blank; p. 1: half title; p. 2: blank; pp. 3-277: text; p. 278: 'ABOUT THE AUTHOR'.

Paper: Cream wove. Top and bottom edges trimmed; fore edge rough-cut. Smooth, heavier, cream endpapers.

Binding: Medium orange (c.53) paper-covered boards with brown orange (c.54) cloth spine. Front cover with brown orange gilt double panels as on title page, with 'WS' in the center. Spine stamped in gilt: '[horizontal] WALLACE / STEGNER / [vertical] CROSSING / [narrow rule] TO [narrow rule] / SAFETY /

[horizontal] [publisher's device] / RANDOM / HOUSE'.

Dust jacket: Cream-colored with glossy finish. Lettering in black. Double letters for author and title on front and spine. Front: '[within divided brown orange ruled panel] [upper panel] CROSS-ING / TO SAFETY / [middle panel] [painting of autumn leaves and dirt road] / [lower panel] / A NOVEL BY THE AUTHOR OF *ANGLE OF REPOSE* AND *THE SPECTATOR BIRD* / WALLACE / STEGNER'. Spine: '[vertical] [brown orange] WALLACE / STEGNER / [black] CROSSING / TO SAFETY / [horizontal] [publisher's device] / [vertical] RANDOM HOUSE'. Back: photo of Stegner by Leo Holub and biographical information. Front flap: Price at $18.95 and blurb. Back flap: '*continued from front flap*'. Jacket design and illustration by Wendell Minor.

Publication: $18.95. August 13, 1987 - 17,500 copies.

Locations: NC (3)

Note: Book-of-the-Month Club Alternate Selection. Exclusive Quality Paperback Book Club feature for June, 1988.

A33.2.b

Second printing: September 30, 1987 - 2,500 copies.

A33.2.c

Third printing: December 9, 1987 - 2,500 copies.

A33.2.d

Fourth printing: November 10, 1987 - 5,000 copies.

A33.2.e

Fifth printing: December 10, 1987 - 3,500 copies.

A33.2.f

Sixth printing: February 8, 1988 - 2,500 copies.

A33.3

Viking Penguin edition: New York: Viking Penguin, (1988).

Trade paperback edition. $8.95. First printing: September 6, 1988 - 42,162 copies.

A34 *The*
American West as Living Space

A34.1

First edition, first printing (1987)

Title page: '[double title page] [dotted rule across both pages] [right] WALLACE / STEGNER / The / American / West as / Living / Space / The University of / Michigan Press / Ann Arbor'

Copyright: 'Copyright © by The University of Michigan 1987'.

(1-2)¹⁶ (3)⁴ (4)¹⁶

pp. (i-v) vi (vii-x) (1-2) 3-6 (7) 8-27 (28-30) 31-33 (34-35) 36-60 (61-62) 63-65 (66-67) 68-89 (90-94)

8″ × 5 1/16″

Illustration: Three black and white photographs, courtesy of The Wilderness Society. The paper remains the same, but without pagination: 7, 34-35, and 66-67.

Contents: p.i: half title; pp.ii-iii: title page; p.iv: copyright; pp.v-vi: preface; p.vii: 'CONTENTS'; p.viii: blank; p.ix: half title; p.x: blank; p. 1: 'ONE'; p. 2: blank; pp. 3-6: text; p. 7: photo; pp. 8-27: text; p .28: blank; p. 29: 'TWO'; p. 30: blank; pp. 31-33: text; pp. 34-35: photo; pp. 36-60: text; p. 61: 'THREE'; p. 62: blank; pp. 63-65: text; pp. 66-67: photo; pp. 68-89: text; pp. 90-94: blank.

Text Contents: "Living Dry," "Striking the Rock," "Variations on a Theme by Crevecoeur," and "Bibliography."

Paper: Cream wove. All edges trimmed. Heavier cream endpapers.

Binding: Gray yellow (c.90) cloth. Spine: '[vertical] STEGNER The American West as Living Space / [horizontal] [publisher's device]'.

Dust jacket: None.

Publication: $18.00 cloth / $10.00 paper. Publication date (both cloth and paper) is November 13, 1987. Print size was 1,000 paper, 300 cloth.

Locations: Cloth: NC (1), JH (1) Paper: WS (1) NC (1)

Note: Derives with only minor changes from a series of three William W. Cook Lectures delivered at the Law School of the University of Michigan in Ann Arbor on October 28, 29, and 30, 1986.

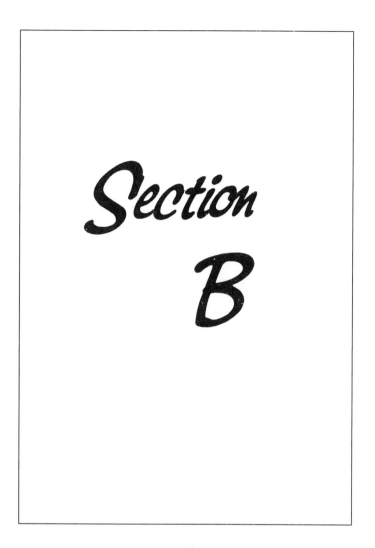

Section

B

B. First-appearance Contributions and Books Edited by Wallace Stegner

1930

B1 HERMITAGE

Hermitage / A Collection of Undergraduate Manuscripts / [pen and ink drawing of person reading a book under a tree] / Salt Lake City MCMXXX

"Introductory Note" and "Bloodstain." Unpaged. D4.

1939

B2 AN EXPOSITION WORKSHOP

AN / Exposition / WORKSHOP / *Readings in Modern Controversy* / CLAUDE M. SIMPSON / STUART G/ BROWN / WALLACE STEGNER / *Department of English, University of Wisconsin* / [publisher's device] / BOSTON / LITTLE, BROWN AND COMPANY / 1939

Editor, with others.

1941

B3   AMERICAN READER

THE / AMERICAN / READER / EDITED BY CLAUDE M.
SIMPSON, / *Harvard University,* AND ALLAN NEVINS, /
Columbia University / WITH A FOREWORD AND EDITORIAL
ADVICE / BY HENRY SEIDEL CANBY / [publisher's device] /
D.C. HEATH AND COMPANY / Boston 1941

"Remembering Laughter," pp. 752-802. A2; D7.

B4   BEST SHORT STORIES

THE / [red] BEST / SHORT STORIES / 1941 / [decorated rule]
/ *and The Yearbook of the American Short Story* / [narrow rule]
Edited by / EDWARD J. O'BRIEN / [1941 and rule broken by
red publisher's device] / HOUGHTON MIFFLIN COMPANY
[dot] BOSTON / [Gothic] The Riverside Press Cambridge

"Goin' to Town," pp. 302-314. D14.

B5   ROCKY MOUNTAIN STORIES

Rocky Mountain / Stories / *Edited by* / RAY B. WEST, JR.
/ SB SAGE BOOKS: :1941 / SWALLOW AND CRITCHLOW,
ALBUQUERQUE

"Dam Builder," pp. 40-48. D5.

1942

B6   BEST AMERICAN SHORT STORIES 1942

THE / [red] Best / [black] AMERICAN / SHORT STORIES /
1942 / [decorative rule] / *and The Yearbook of the American Short
Story* / [rule] / Edited by MARTHA FOLEY / 1942 [date and

rule broken by red publisher's device] / HOUGHTON MIFFLIN COMPANY [dot] BOSTON / [Gothic] / The Riverside Press Cambridge

"In the Twilight," pp. 279-290. A10; D20.

B7   O. HENRY MEMORIAL AWARD PRIZE STORIES OF 1942

O. HENRY MEMORIAL AWARD / PRIZE STORIES / OF / 1942 / [decorated rule] / SELECTED AND EDITED BY / HERSCHEL BRICKELL / ASSISTED BY MURIELL FULLER / [decorated rule] / THE LITERARY GUILD OF AMERICA / NEW YORK

"Two Rivers," pp. 33-48. A10; D21.

Note: The O. Henry competition determines the best short stories published by American authors in American magazines. The selections are chosen by the Society of Arts and Sciences. Wallace Stegner has twice won second prize in the competition, with "Two Rivers" in 1942 and "Beyond the Glass Mountain" in 1948. In 1954 he won first prize with "The Blue-Winged Teal," which appears in several "First-Prize Stories" collections (i.e. 1919-1954 and 1919-1963). He is also represented in the 1955 volume with "The City of the Living." The 1964 volume published his "Carrion Spring."

1943

B8   BEST AMERICAN SHORT STORIES 1943

THE / [red] Best / [black] AMERICAN / SHORT STORIES / 1943 / [decorative rule] / and The Yearbook of the American Short Story / [narrow rule] / Edited by / MARTHA FOLEY / [1943 and rule broken by red publisher's device] / HOUGHTON MIFFLIN COMPANY [dot] BOSTON / [Gothic] The Riverside Press Cambridge

"Chip Off the Old Block," pp. 310-326. A7; A10; D22.

B9   READINGS FOR CITIZENS AT WAR

READINGS / for Citizens at War / [wavy double rule] / Edited by / THEODORE MORRISON / *Director of English A, Harvard University,* / and PHILIP E. BURNHAM / CARVEL E. COLLINS / C.P. LEE / MARK SCHORER / RICHARD P. SCOWCROFT / WALLACE STEGNER / *of the English A* Staff / [wavy double rule] / [Harper device] / HARPER & BROTHERS / New York PUBLISHERS London / [wavy double rule]

"Pecking at a Sandstone Cliff," pp. 250-261. Excerpt from *Mormon Country.* A6.

1944

B10   MODERN WRITING

MODERN / WRITING / Willard Thorp / PRINCETON UNIVERSITY / & / Margaret Farrand Thorp / [publisher's device] / American Book Company / NEW YORK CINCINNATI CHICAGO BOSTON ATLANTA / DALLAS SAN FRANCISCO

"Regionalism in Art," pp. 291-298. C8.

1945

B11   MID COUNTRY

[double title page] [right] [drawing of farmland and telephone wires] / [across double title page] [green] [script] Mid Country / [black] WRITINGS FROM THE HEART OF AMERICA / *Edited by* / Lowry C. Wimberly / *With an Introduction* / *by B.A. BOTKIN* / [left] [green] [publisher's device] NEW YORK - SOLE DISTRIBUTORS IN / THE UNITED STATES AND CANADA / [right] UNIVERSITY OF NEBRASKA PRESS / [University Press device] LINCOLN, NEBRASKA - 1945

"The Colt," pp. 187-198. A7; A10; D24.

1946

B12   ROCKY MOUNTAIN READER

[outlined letters] ROCKY / [solid] MOUNTAIN / READER /
Edited by / Ray B. West, Jr. / 1946 / E.P. DUTTON & CO.,
INC. / NEW YORK

"Arcadian Village," pp. 84-98. An excerpt from *Mormon
Country.* A6.

B13   STANFORD SHORT STORIES

STANFORD SHORT STORIES / [rule] / NINETEEN
FORTY-SIX / [rule] / STANFORD SHORT STORIES / [rule] /
NINETEEN FORTY-SIX / [rule] / DONALD ALLAN-EUGENE
BURDICK / [rule] / STANFORD SHORT STORIES / [rule] /
NINETEEN FORTY-SIX / [rule] / JEAN BYERS-OLIVER
LAWRENCE / [rule] / STANFORD SHORT STORIES / [rule] /
NINETEEN FORTY-SIX / [rule] / BARBARA BELLOW
WATSON / [rule] / STANFORD SHORT STORIES / [rule] /
NINETEEN FORTY-SIX / [rule] / [repeat of last three lines twice
without final rule]

"Preface," pp. vii-viii.

Note: Fifteen volumes of *Stanford Short Stories* were published
between 1946 and 1964. Edited by Wallace Stegner and Richard
Scowcroft, these annual volumes include one hundred and
seventy-five stories written in creative writing classes at Stanford
University. In 1966, Stanford University Press published a selection
of stories published in the preceding fifteen volumes, *Twenty Years
of Stanford Short Stories.* In 1968 the last volume appeared and the
series has been discontinued. Stegner has written prefaces in
volumes 1-4, 7-8, and 12. There is also a lengthy introduction in
the 1966 collection, *Twenty Years of Stanford Short Stories* (B88).

#1 - 1946 - 750 copies	#10 - 1956 - 750 copies
#2 - 1948 - 750 copies	#11 - 1957 - 850 copies
#3 - 1949 - 750 copies	#12 - 1958 - 1000 copies
#4 - 1950 - 750 copies	#13 - 1960 - 900 copies
#5 - 1951 - 1000 copies	#14 - 1962 - 1000 copies
#6 - 1952 - 1000 copies	#15 - 1964 - 1000 copies
#7 - 1953 - 800 copies,	#16 - 1966 - 1000 copies
#8 - 1954 - 1000 copies	pap. - 3000 copies
#9 - 1955 - 1000 copies	#17 - 1968 - 900 copies

B14 WRITER'S HANDBOOK

Title page for 1946 edition not seen.

"'Truth' and 'Faking' in Fiction," pp. 95-101. C14.

1947

B15 BEST AMERICAN SHORT STORIES 1947

THE / [maroon] Best / [black] AMERICAN / SHORT STORIES / 1947 / [decorative rule] / and The Yearbook of the American Short Story / [narrow rule] / Edited by / MARTHA FOLEY / 1947 [date and rule broken by publisher's device] / HOUGHTON MIFFLIN COMPANY [dot] BOSTON / [Gothic] The Riverside Press Cambridge

"The Women on the Wall," pp. 440-460. A10; D33.

B16 LOOK AT AMERICA

[double title page] [left] [photo of canyons] [camera and book] [white] a LOOK / PICTURE / BOOK / [right] [black] LOOK AT AMERICA / [left] The [right] Central / Northwest / BY THE EDITORS OF LOOK / IN COLLABORATION WITH WALLACE STEGNER / A HANDBOOK IN PICTURES, MAPS AND TEXT FOR THE / VACATIONIST, THE TRAVELER AND THE STAY-AT-HOME / ONE OF THE LOOK AT AMERICA REGIONAL VOLUMES / HOUGHTON MIFFLIN

COMPANY [dot] BOSTON / THE RIVERSIDE PRESS
CAMBRIDGE

"Introduction," pp. 9-34.

1948

B17 BEST AMERICAN SHORT STORIES 1948

THE / [red] Best / [black] AMERICAN / SHORT STORIES /
1948 / [decorative rule] / *and The Yearbook of the American Short
Story* / [rule] / *Edited by* / MARTHA FOLEY / [1948 and rule
broken by publisher's device] / HOUGHTON MIFFLIN
COMPANY BOSTON / [Gothic] The Riverside Press Cambridge

"Beyond the Glass Mountain," pp. 294-304. A10; D35.

B18 CONFERENCE ON UNESCO

[blue] UNITED STATES / NATIONAL COMMISSION FOR /
unesco / Report on / Pacific Regional / Conference on /
UNESCO / [beige on blue rectangle] SAN FRANCISCO,
CALIFORNIA / MAY 13, 14, 15, 16, 1948

"A Delegate's View of the Conference," pp. 7-17.

B19 LITERARY HISTORY OF THE UNITED
STATES

LITERARY HISTORY / OF THE / UNITED STATES / *Editors*
/ ROBERT E. SPILLER [dot] WILLARD THORP / THOMAS
H. JOHNSON [dot] HENRY SEIDEL CANBY / *Associates* /
HOWARD MUMFORD JONES [dot] DIXON WECTER /
STANLEY T. WILLIAMS / VOLUME II / 1948 / THE MAC-
MILLAN COMPANY [dot] NEW YORK

"Western Record and Romance," pp. 862-877, Volume 2,
Section 53.

B20   OPINIONS AND ATTITUDES IN THE
TWENTIETH CENTURY

OPINIONS / and / ATTITUDES / in the Twentieth Century /
Compiled and Edited by / STEWART MORGAN / the Agricul-
tural and Mechanical College of Texas / Fourth Edition / THE
RONALD PRESS COMPANY / NEW YORK

"Admirable Crichton," pp. 66-72. D34.

B21   PRIZE STORIES OF 1948: THE O. HENRY
AWARDS

Prize Stories / of 1948 THE O. HENRY AWARDS /
SELECTED AND EDITED BY HERSCHEL BRICKELL /
DOUBLEDAY & COMPANY, INC., GARDEN CITY, NEW
YORK, 1948

"Beyond the Glass Mountain," pp. 15-25. B17.

1949

B22   ASPIRIN AGE

[double title page] [left] WRITTEN BY / SAMUEL HOPKINS
ADAMS / THURMAN ARNOLD / HERBERT ASBURY /
HODDING CARTER / ROBERT COUGHLAN / JONATHAN
DANIELS / ROSCOE DRUMMOND / HOWARD FAST /
HARRY HANSEN / MARGARET CASE HARRIMAN /
CHARLES JACKSON / JOHN LARDNER / MORRIS MAR-
KEY / WILLIAM McFEE / CAREY McWILLIAMS / KEITH
MUNRO / JOEL SAYRE / ARTHUR M. SCHLESINGER, JR. /
WALLACE STEGNER / IRVING STONE / PHIL STRONG /
GENE TUNNEY / NEW YORK [dot] 1949 / [publisher's device
and beginning of rule running length of double title page] / [right]
THE / ASPIRIN / AGE / 1919 ["sun spot"] 1941 / EDITED
BY / ISABEL LEIGHTON / SIMON AND SCHUSTER

"The Radio Priest and His Flock," pp. 232-257.

B23   MODERN AMERICAN SAMPLER

[double rule frame with break at either side at title] A MODERN /
AMERICAN SAMPLER / Edited by / EDD WINFIELD PARKS
/ Professor of American Literature, University of Georgia / Visiting
Professor, University of Brazil, 1949 / In Collaboration with /
OLIVE SHAW AND MICHAEL KELLER / BOOK II /
[publisher's device] / INSTITUTO BRASIL - ESTADOS UNIDOS
/ RIO DE JANEIRO

"Beyond the Glass Mountain," pp. 40-51. B17.

B24   U.S. STORIES

[narrow rule] / [row of stars] / [narrow rule] / U.S. STORIES /
[narrow rule] / [row of stars] / [narrow rule] / REGIONAL
STORIES FROM / THE FORTY-EIGHT STATES / [narrow
rule] / [row of stars] / [narrow rule] / Selected with a Foreword
by MARTHA FOLEY and / ABRAHAM ROTHBERG /
Hendricks House - Farrar Straus [dot] New York / [narrow rule] /
[row of stars] / [narrow rule]

"Chip Off the Old Block," pp. 566-580. B8.

1950

B25   PRIZE STORIES OF 1950

[double title page] [left] DOUBLEDAY & COMPANY, INC.,
GARDEN CITY, NEW YORK, 1950 / [right] prize / stories / of
/ 1950 / [publisher's device] the / O. Henry Awards /
SELECTED AND EDITED BY HERSCHEL BRICKELL

"The Blue-Winged Teal," pp. 1-17. A14; D39.

Note: This prize-winning story was frequently reprinted in
anthologies and textbooks. It was published separately by the
Perfection Form Company in 1979, as "A Tale Blazer Book" in
a simplified version. It also appears in a Japanese short story

collection. These reprintings are not described as they are not first appearances.

B26   WRITER'S ART

Wallace Stegner / Richard Scowcroft / Boris Ilyin / THE / [publisher's device] WRITER'S ART / A Collection of Short Stories / D.C. HEATH AND COMPANY [dot] BOSTON

Reprinted by Greenwood Press, October, 1972.

"The Women on the Wall," pp. 299-317. B15.

"A Problem in Fiction," pp. 317-324. C61.

1951

B27   STORIES FOR HERE AND NOW

[double title page] Stories / [decorative floral rule] for here and now / [left] Other Bantam Anthologies edited by / JOSEPH GREENE and ELIZABETH ABELL / FIRST LOVE / HUSBANDS AND LOVERS / [right] edited by JOSEPH GREENE / and ELI-ZABETH ABELL / [decorative floral rule] / [publisher's device] Bantam Books [dot] NEW YORK

"The Traveler," pp. 267-277. A14; D40.

1952

B28   BEST AMERICAN SHORT STORIES 1952

THE / [red] Best / [black] AMERICAN / SHORT STORIES / 1952 / [decorative rule] / *and The Yearbook of the American Short Story* / [narrow rule] / *Edited by* / MARTHA FOLEY / ASSISTED BY JOYCE F. HARTMAN / 1952 [date and narrow rule broken by publisher's device] / HOUGHTON MIFFLIN COMPANY BOSTON / [Gothic] The Riverside Press Cambridge

"The Traveler," pp. 289-297. B27.

B29   BEST OF THE BEST AMERICAN SHORT STORIES 1915-1950

The Best / OF THE / *Best American* / *Short Stories* / 1915-1950 / EDITED BY / MARTHA FOLEY / [narrow rule broken by publisher's device] / HOUGHTON MIFFLIN COMPANY BOSTON / [Gothic] The Riverside Press Cambridge

"The Women on the Wall," pp. 300-319. B15.

B30   THIS I BELIEVE

This I Believe: / THE LIVING PHILOSOPHIES / OF ONE HUNDRED THOUGHTFUL / MEN AND WOMEN IN ALL WALKS / OF LIFE—AS WRITTEN FOR / AND WITH A FOREWORD BY / EDWARD R. MURROW / *Edited by* EDWARD P. MORGAN / [publisher's device] / SIMON AND SCHUSTER / NEW YORK [dot] 1952

"Everything Potent is Dangerous," pp. 173-174.

1953

B31   EXPANDING HORIZONS

[decorative rule] / EXPANDING / HORIZONS / [decorative rule] / *A Reader for English Composition* / ERNEST W. KINNE / *Purdue University* / and / ARNOLD P. DREW / *Purdue University* / THE ODYSSEY PRESS [publisher's device] / NEW YORK

"Butcher Bird," pp. 37-48. See A7; A10; D17.

1954

B32   AMERICAN ACCENT

AMERICAN ACCENT / Fourteen stories by authors associated /

/ with the Bread Loaf Writer's Conference / with a Foreword by
Theodore Morrison / edited by / ELIZABETH ABELL /
BALLANTINE BOOKS [dot] NEW YORK

"The Blue-Winged Teal," pp. 4-21. B25.

B33   FIRST-PRIZE STORIES 1919-1954

FIRST-PRIZE STORIES / 1919-1954 / *from the O. Henry
Memorial Awards / Introduction by Harry Hansen* / HANOVER
HOUSE, GARDEN CITY, N.Y.

"The Blue-Winged Teal," pp. 452-466. B25.

Also appears in later editions of *First Prize Stories*: 1957, 1960,
1965, and 1966. These are not first appearances, therefore they are
not listed separately.

1955

B34   BEST AMERICAN SHORT STORIES 1955

THE / [red] Best / [black] AMERICAN / SHORT STORIES /
1955 / [decorative rule] / *and the Yearbook of the American Short
Story* / [narrow rule] / Edited by / MARTHA FOLEY /
[publisher's device] / HOUGHTON MIFFLIN COMPANY [dot]
BOSTON / [Gothic] The Riverside Press Cambridge / 1955

"Maiden in a Tower," pp. 282-294. A14; D44.

B35   OUT WEST

[double title page] OUT WEST / [right side] AN ANTHOLOGY
OF STORIES / *edited by* JACK SCHAEFER / BOSTON /
HOUGHTON MIFFLIN COMPANY / [rule] / 19 [Gothic] The
Riverside Press Cambridge 55 / [left side] *Shane / First Blood / The
Big Range / The Canyon / The Pioneers* / [rule with silhouette of
two men sitting over a campfire] / *Books by / Jack Schaefer*

"The Colt," pp. 288-299. B11.

B36   PRIZE STORIES 1955

PRIZE STORIES 1955: *The O. Henry Awards / Selected and Edited by / PAUL ENGLE and HANSFORD MARTIN / Doubleday & Company, Inc., Garden City, N.Y., 1955*

"The City of the Living," pp. 278-290. A14; D43.

B37   SPECTATOR SAMPLER

SPECTATOR / SAMPLER / [publisher's device] / Essays by / BERNARD DEVOTO, C.S. FORESTER, JOSEPH WOOD / KRUTCH, DIXON WECTER, WALLACE STEGNER, HAR- / OLD H. FISHER, JACK JAMES, JOSEPH B. HARRISON, PAUL / S. TAYLOR, RUSSELL A. FITZGIBBON / LOUIS B. WRIGHT, / and S. CHANDRASEKHAR / *Edited by* / Robert C. North *and* Edith R. Mirrielees / *Introduction by* John Dodds / STANFORD UNIVERSITY PRESS, STANFORD, CALIFORNIA

"A Problem in Fiction," pp. 17-24. B26.

B38   THIS IS DINOSAUR

[double title page] [color photo across both pages] [left] [blue] EDITED BY WALLACE STEGNER / [black] [narrow rule] [both] [red] This Is Dinosaur / [right] [black] ECHO PARK COUNTRY AND ITS MAGIC RIVERS / [left] [blue] [publisher's device] [right] ALFRED [dot] A [dot] KNOPF, NEW YORK, 1955

"Foreword," pp. v-vi.

"The Marks of Human Passage," pp. 3-17.

1956

B39   GREAT TALES OF THE FAR WEST

Great Tales / of the / FAR WEST / edited by / Alex Austin / [publisher's device] Lion Library Editions / 655 Madison Avenue / New York City

"Chip Off the Old Block," pp. 76-90. B8.

B40   NEW SHORT NOVELS 2

NEW SHORT / NOVELS 2 / by / NORMAN MAILER / JOHN PHILLIPS / DACHINE RAINER / WALLACE STEGNER / BALLANTINE BOOKS [dot] NEW YORK

"THIS IS AN ORIGINAL COLLECTION—NOT A REPRINT—PUBLISHED BY BALLANTINE BOOKS, INC. ©1956"

"Field Guide to the Western Birds," pp. 97-147. A14.

1957

B41   BEST SHORT STORIES OF WORLD WAR II

[two large asterisks] / THE BEST SHORT STORIES / OF WORLD WAR II / [large asterisk] AN AMERICAN ANTHOL-OGY / [three large asterisks] / *Edited by* / CHARLES A. FENTON / [publisher's device] / *New York* [large asterisk] THE VIKING PRESS [large asterisk] 1957

"The Women on the Wall," pp. 275-296. B15.

B42   BOOK OF THE EARTH

[double title page] [left] Being a collection of writings / about the Earth / in all its aspects; / with 64 pages of illustrations / in gravure, / and many line drawings. / Edited by A.C. Spectorsky / Appleton-Century-Crofts, Inc. / New York / [right] THE BOOK OF THE / EARTH

"Canyon Voyage," pp. 50-59. Excerpts from *Beyond the*

Hundredth Meridian. A13.

B43   EXPLORATION OF THE COLORADO RIVER

THE / [double letters] EXPLORATION / [single] OF THE / [double letters] COLORADO / RIVER / BY JOHN WESLEY POWELL / *Abridged from the First Edition of 1875* / *with an Introduction by Wallace Stegner* / [publisher's device] THE UNIVERSITY OF CHICAGO PRESS

Editor.

"Introduction," pp. xi-xxi.

B44   GREAT AMERICAN SHORT STORIES

Great American / Short Stories / edited by Wallace / and Mary Stegner / [publisher's device] LAUREL / EDITION

On copyright page: 'First printing - August, 1957.' Dell edition LC 103.

New edition 3060: three printings (Nov., 1961, Sept., 1962, Nov., 1962). Copyright renewed 1985. Laurel TM 674623: first printing Nov., 1985.

Also in Spanish as: *Antologia de la Novela Corta Norteamericana* (1964). F21.

"Introduction," pp. 9-28 by Wallace and Mary Stegner.

B45   TRIUMPH OVER ODDS

TRIUMPH OVER ODDS / An Anthology of Man's Unconquerable Spirit / Edited with a Foreword and Introductory Notes / By J. DONALD ADAMS / DUELL, SLOAN and PEARCE / New York

"The Descent of the Colorado: Major Powell," pp. 123-136.

Excerpt from *Beyond the Hundredth Meridian.* A13.

1958

B46   DICTIONARY OF AMERICAN BIOGRAPHY

DICTIONARY / OF / American Biography / VOLUME XI / SUPPLEMENT ONE / *Edited by* HARRIS E. STAFF / [double rule] / SUPPLEMENT TWO / *Edited by* / ROBERT LIVING- STON SCHUYLER / EDWARD T. JAMES, *Associate* / Charles Scribner's Sons *New York*

Supplement Two, ©1958.

"Owen Wister," pp. 728-730.

B47   ROMANCE OF NORTH AMERICA

The Romance of / NORTH AMERICA / Edited by HARDWICK MOSELEY / With an Introduction by / PRESTON E. JAMES / *Illustrated with maps and photographs* / CONTRIBUTING AUTHORS / Donald G. Creighton Steward Holbrook / Marshall B. Davidson William Weber Johnson / Bernard DeVoto Philip A. Knowlton / Waldo Frank Ralph McGill / Ernest Gruening Scott O'Dell / Walter Havighurst Jack Schaefer / Wallace Stegner / HOUGHTON MIFFLIN COMPANY [dot] BOSTON

"The Rocky Mountain West," pp. 363-392.

B48   SELECTED AMERICAN PROSE

[script] Selected American Prose / 1841-1900 [illus. of man in hat leaning back on a chair against a wall] / [Roman] THE REALISTIC MOVEMENT / [short rule] / EDITED WITH AN INTRODUCTION BY / WALLACE STEGNER / NEW YORK [script] Rinehart & Company Inc. [Roman] TORONTO

"INTRODUCTION," pp. v-xxvi.

B49   WESTWARD, WESTWARD, WESTWARD

[double title page] / [right] [covered wagon pulled by oxen] /
[across both] WESTWARD, WESTWARD, WESTWARD / The
Long Trail West and the Men Who Followed It / [right]
SELECTED BY ELIZABETH ABELL / *Pictures by Leonard Everett
Fisher* / [publisher's device] / FRANKLIN WATTS, NEW YORK

"Ordeal by Handcart," pp. 81-98. A17; C94.

1959

B50   GENTLEMEN, SCHOLARS AND
SCOUNDRELS

[left side of title page] [statue on pedestal decorated with books and
flowers] / [right side] GENTLEMEN, / SCHOLARS and /
SCOUNDRELS / A Treasury of the Best of / Harper's *magazine* /
from 1850 to the Present / edited by HORACE KNOWLES /
Harper & Brothers [publisher's device] New York

"The Blue-Winged Teal," pp. 478-494. B25.

1960

B51   ADVENTURES OF HUCKLEBERRY FINN

The Adventures of / HUCKLEBERRY / FINN / MARK TWAIN
/ *with an introduction by* / *Wallace Stegner* / [publisher's device]
LAUREL EDITION

On copyright page: 'Copyright, 1960, by Wallace Stegner / First
Dell printing—June, 1960.'

"Introduction," pp. 9-21.

B52   ESSAYS TODAY 4

ESSAYS / Today / 4 / Editor, RICHARD M. LUDWIG /

PRINCETON UNIVERSITY / [publisher's device] / HAR-
COURT, BRACE AND COMPANY / NEW YORK [dot]
BURLINGAME

"One Way to Spell Man," pp. 140-148. A28; C101.

B53   FIFTY MODERN STORIES

[double title page] [left] FIFTY MODERN / Edited by Thomas
M.H. Blair / *Kent State University* / [right] [alphabetical list of
contributors along left side] / STORIES / Row, Peterson and
Company / *Evanston, Ill., Elmsford, N.Y.*

"Maiden in a Tower," pp. 287-297. B34.

B54   FORM AND THOUGHT IN PROSE

[double title page] / FORM and / THOUGHT in PROSE [wavy
hyphen] *Second / Edition* / Edited by WILFRED H. STONE /
Stanford University / ROBERT HOOPES / *Michigan State
University, Oakland* / THE RONALD PRESS COMPANY / [wavy
hyphen] NEW YORK

"The Making of Paths," pp. 255-259. See A16; C104.

B55   40 BEST STORIES FROM *MADEMOISELLE*

[double title page] 40 *best stories from Mademoiselle* 1935-1960 /
EDITED BY CYRILLY ABELS AND MARGARITA G. SMITH
/ [rule] / *Harper & Brothers, Publishers New York*

"The City of the Living," pp. 467-479. B36.

B56   THE PAPERS OF BERNARD DE VOTO

THE PAPERS OF BERNARD DE VOTO / [typographical design]
/ A Description and a Checklist of his Works / with a Tribute by
Wallace Stegner / on the occasion of an / Exhibition in The Albert
M. Bender Room / The Stanford University Libraries /

[typographical design] / October 1 through November 26, 1960

"Benny DeVoto's America," pp. 7-28.

B57   PRIZE STORIES 1960

PRIZE STORIES / 1960: / THE [script] O. / HENRY / [Roman]
AWARDS / EDITED BY MARY STEGNER / DOUBLEDAY &
COMPANY, INC., GARDEN CITY, / NEW YORK 1960

"Introduction," pp. 5-17.

1961

B58   COMPTON'S ENCYCLOPEDIA

1961 edition not seen.

"Creative Writing." There is an unsigned article on "writing" in
the 1981 COMPTON'S, which may be Stegner's.

B59   MIDLAND

[double title page] [right] MIDLAND / [across both pages]
*Twenty-five Years of Fiction and Poetry Selected from the Writing
Workshops of the State University of Iowa* / [right] EDITED BY *Paul
Engle* / ASSISTED BY *Henri Coulette* AND *Donald Justice* / [left]
[publisher's device] / [right] RANDOM HOUSE [dot] NEW YORK

"The Blue-Winged Teal," pp. 285-304. B25.

B60   OUTCASTS OF POKER FLAT

[within laurel leaf border] the / Outcasts / of / Poker Flat / and
other tales / by BRET HARTE / *With an Introduction by* /
WALLACE STEGNER / [publisher's device] / A SIGNET
CLASSIC / PUBLISHED BY THE NEW AMERICAN LIBRARY

On copyright page: 'First Printing, August, 1961.'

"Introduction," pp. vii-xvi. Reprinted as "The West Synthetic: Bret Harte" in *The Sound of Mountain Water*. A20.

B61 WILDERNESS: AMERICA'S LIVING HERITAGE

CONTRIBUTORS / *Ansel Adams* / *Edmund S. Brown* / *Everett Carter* / *John Walton Caughey* / *Charles Connaughton* / *William O. Douglas* / *Fred Farr* / *David R. Forbes* / *Harold Gilliam* / *Edward Higbee* / *Hans Huth* / *Joseph Wood Krutch* / *Grant McConnell* / *Sigurd Olson* / *Joseph W. Penfold* / *Gerard Piel* / *John P. Saylor* / *Eivind Scoyen* / *Robert C. Stebbins* / *Wallace Stegner* / *Stewart Udall* / *Catherine Bauer Wurster* / *Howard Zahniser* / WILDERNESS / *America's Living Heritage* / Edited by DAVID BROWER / SIERRA CLUB [diamond] SAN FRANCISCO

"THE WILDERNESS IDEA: A Letter by Wallace Stegner read aloud by Secretary Udall," pp. 97-102.

Later appearances:

ORRRC Report
Washington Post - Sunday, June 17, 1962. See C118.
The Sound of Mountain Water. See A20.
American Environment. See B92.
Literature of the American West. See B105.
Voices for the Earth. See B132.
"Caribou on River Icing" (1977 poster). See E10.
Poster from Rhodesia. See E16.
A Land Set Apart. Publication of the Minnesota Historical Society.

1962

B62 COUNTRY IN THE MIND

A COUNTRY IN THE MIND / *An Anthology of Stories and Poems*/ from the / *Western Review* / Edited by RAY B. WEST / *Contact Editions* [dot] Sausalito, California

"Balance His, Swing Yours," pp. 65-73. A10; D31.

B63   THE COURSE OF EMPIRE

The Course / *of* Empire / *by* / BERNARD De VOTO / with maps by Erwin Raisz / [publisher's device] / HOUGHTON MIFFLIN COMPANY BOSTON / '[Gothic] The Riverside Press Cambridge'

'Copyright, 1952, by Bernard DeVoto'. BL has this printing, with the Stegner introduction, dated 1962.

"Introduction," pp. (vii)-xxii.

B64   ESSAYS TODAY 5

ESSAYS / Today / 5 / *Editor* RICHARD M. LUDWIG / PRINCETON UNIVERSITY / HARCOURT, BRACE AND WORLD, INC. / NEW YORK [dot] BURLINGAME

"To a Young Writer," pp. 81-87. C110.

B65   IDEA AND IMAGE

[double title page] / [left] Hans P. Huth / SAN JOSE STATE COLLEGE / [right] [staggered] idEa / & / ImAge / [both pages] READING FOR COLLEGE ENGLISH / Wadsworth Publishing Company, Inc., Belmont, California

Second printing: 1965.

"The Mounties at Fort Walsh," pp. 215-223. A16; C102.

B66   PENINSULA

[double title page] [left] The Peninsula / A STORY OF THE OLYMPIC COUNTRY / IN WORDS AND PHOTOGRAPHS / [right] [photograph of coastline] / BY Don Moser / SIERRA CLUB [diamond] SAN FRANCISCO

"Foreword," pp. 9-11.

B67 REPORT ON THE LANDS OF THE ARID REGION

REPORT ON / THE LANDS OF THE ARID REGION / OF THE UNITED STATES / *with a More Detailed Account of the Lands of Utah* / By / JOHN WESLEY POWELL / [short rule] / Edited by Wallace Stegner / [short rule] / [publisher's device] THE BELKNAP PRESS OF / HARVARD UNIVERSITY PRESS / *Cambridge, Massachusetts* / 1962

"Introduction," pp. vii-xxv.

B68 TWO AND TWENTY

TWO / AND / TWENTY / *A Collection of Short Stories* / *Ralph H. Singleton* / OBERLIN COLLEGE / [publisher's device] / *St. Martin's Press* [dot] *New York*

"Chip Off the Old Block," pp. 285-306. B8.

1963

B69 AMERICAN HERITAGE BOOK OF NATURAL WONDERS

[double title page] [left] *The* AMERICAN HERITAGE *Book of* / [both] NATURAL WONDERS / [photograph of Mount St. Helens, Washington, with Mount Adams in the background, photographed by George Hunter] / [left] *By the Editors of* / AMERICAN HERITAGE / *The* Magazine of History / *Editor in Charge* / ALVIN M. JOSEPHY, JR. / *Chapters by* PETER MATTHIESSEN / WILLIAM O. DOUGLAS / JAN DE HARTOG / BRUCE CATTON / PAUL ENGLE / WALLACE STEGNER / GEORGE R. STEWART / HAROLD GILLIAM / Published by / AMERICAN HERITAGE PUBLISHING CO., INC. / *Book Trade Distribution by* / SIMON AND SCHUSTER, INC.

"The Great Mountains," pp. 209-303.

B70   BEST-IN-BOOKS

[blue] Best-in-Books / [narrow rule] / [black] The Windfall Child / by LOUISE FIELD COOPER [dot] / *Complete Novel* 3 / A Thousand Springs / by ANNA CHENNAULT [dot] *Complete Book* 197 / Wolf Willow / by WALLACE STEGNER [dot] *Excerpt* 365 / Is It Safe to Drink the Water? / by ART BUCHWALD [dot] *Excerpt* 437 / Fire on the Mountain by EDWARD ABBEY [dot] *Complete Novel* 471 / [narrow rule] / [blue] NELSON DOUBLEDAY, INC. / *Garden City New York*

"Genesis," excerpt from *Wolf Willow*. A16.

B71   FOUR PORTRAITS AND ONE SUBJECT

Four Portraits / and One Subject / Bernard DeVoto / *The Historian* / BY CATHERINE DRINKER BOWEN / *The Writer* / BY EDITH R. MIRRIELEES / *The Citizen* / BY ARTHUR M. SCHLESINGER, JR. / *The Personality* / BY WALLACE STEGNER / WITH / A BIBLIOGRAPHY OF HIS WRITINGS / PREPARED BY JULIUS P. BARCLAY / WITH THE COLLABORATION / OF ELAINE HELMER PARNIE / 1963 / HOUGHTON MIFFLIN COMPANY BOSTON / [Gothic] The Riverside Press Cambridge

"Introduction," pp. vii-ix.

"The Personality," pp. 79-108.

B72   PERSONALITY OF THE HORSE

The Personality / of the Horse / Edited by BRANDT AYMAR / and EDWARD SAGARIN / BONANZA BOOKS NEW YORK

"The Colt," pp. 32-43. B11.

B73   THE PLACE NO ONE KNEW

[double title page] / [left] / *Wall and rivers edge* / *Past these towering monuments, past these mounded billows of orange sandstone,* / *past these oak-set glens, past these fern-decked alcoves, past these mural* / *curves, we glide hour after hour, stopping now and then, as our attention is* / *arrested by some new wonder*—JOHN WESLEY POWELL, 1869 / by ELIOT PORTER / THE PLACE / NO ONE KNEW / EDITED BY DAVID BROWER / [right] / [photo of wall and river edge] / Glen Canyon on the Colorado / *Sierra Club [dot] San Francisco*

Excerpts from:

Beyond the Hundredth Meridian: pp. 30, 40, 52, 54, 64. A13.
Mormon Country: p. 28. A6.
Wilderness: America's Living Heritage: pp. 62, 150, 152, 162. B61.

1964

B74   CANADIAN REFLECTIONS

CANADIAN / REFLECTIONS / AN ANTHOLOGY OF CANADIAN PROSE / PHILIP PENNER AND JOHN McGECHAEN / TORONTO / THE MACMILLAN COMPANY OF CANADA LIMITED

"The Wolfer," pp. 83-101. D52.

B75   MODERN COMPOSITION

High school text, published by Holt. Later edition, 1969.

Editor, with others.

B76   OPINIONS AND PERSPECTIVES

OPINIONS / AND PERSPECTIVES / from / The New York Times Book Reivew / EDITED AND WITH AN INTRODUC-TION / BY FRANCIS BROWN / [publisher's device] / HOUGHTON MIFFLIN COMPANY BOSTON / [Gothic] The

Riverside Press Cambridge / 1964

"Yarn-Spinner in the American Vein," pp. 93-96. First printed in a review of *The Complete Short Stories of Mark Twain*, by Charles Neider. C99.

B77   PRIZE STORIES 1964: THE O. HENRY AWARDS

[double title page] [left] PRIZE / STORIES / 1964: / [right] THE / O. HENRY / AWARDS / [both] EDITED AND WITH AN INTRODUCTION BY RICHARD POIRIER / [right] DOUBLEDAY & COMPANY, INC., GARDEN CITY, NEW YORK, 1964

"Carrion Spring, " pp. 270-286. A16; D54.

B78   VANISHING AMERICA

A / Vanishing America / [short rule] / THE LIFE AND TIMES OF / *The Small Town* / [short rule] / TWELVE REGIONAL TOWNS BY / Hodding Carter, Thomas D. Clark, William O. Douglas, / James Gray, A.B. Guthrie, Jr., David Lavender / W. Storrs Lee, Oscar Lewis, Conrad Richter, / Winfield Townley Scott, John Edward Weems, / William E. Wilson / [short rule] / INTRODUCTION BY WALLACE STEGNER / Edited by Thomas C. Wheeler / *Illustrated with photographs and drawings* / [short rule] / HOLT, RINEHART AND WINSTON / NEW YORK [dot] CHICAGO / SAN FRANCISCO

"Introduction," pp. 9-12.

B79   WILDLANDS IN OUR CIVILIZATION

[double title page] / [left] [photograph by Cedric Wright] / *Wildlands* / [right] CONTRIBUTORS / *John Collier / Bruce M. Kilgore / A. Starker Leopold / Wallace Stegner / Lowell Sumner / Lee Merriman Talbot / Howard Zahniser / and participants in the discussions / of the first five Biennial Wilderness Conferences, 1949-1957 /*

edited, with contributions, by David Brower / *in Our Civilization* /
SIERRA CLUB [dot] SAN FRANCISCO

"Introduction," pp. 33-43. This introduction first appeared in the
Sierra Club Bulletin, May 1959, under the title, "The War Between
the Rough Riders and the Bird Watchers." C107.

1965

B80 AMERICAN LITERARY MASTERS

[double title page] / [left] UNDER THE GENERAL EDITORSHIP
OF / *Charles R. Anderson* / JOHNS HOPKINS UNIVERSITY /
ASSOCIATE EDITORS / *Richard P. Adams* / TULANE
UNIVERSITY / *Roger Asselineau* / THE SORBONNE / *James
Baird* / CONNECTICUT COLLEGE / *Roy R. Male* /
UNIVERSITY OF OKLAHOMA / *Wallace Stegner* / STANFORD
UNIVERSITY / *Carl F. Strauch* / LEHIGH UNIVERSITY /
Hyatt H. Waggoner / BROWN UNIVERSITY / [narrow rule] /
[right] AMERICAN / LITERARY / MASTERS / VOLUME
TWO / [three stars] [slash] JAMES [slash] CRANE / ADAMS
[slash] O'NEILL [slash] ROBINSON / FROST [slash] DREISER
[slash] ANDERSON / ELIOT [slash] STEVENS [slash]
FITZGERALD / HEMINGWAY [slash] WOLFE [slash]
FAULKNER / [narrow rule] / HOLT, RINEHART and WIN-
STON, INC. / *New York* [slash] *Chicago* [slash] *San Francisco* [slash]
Toronto

"Introduction to Theodore Dreiser," pp. 631-641.

"Introduction to Thomas Wolfe," pp. 1071-1081.

B81 AMERICAN NOVEL FROM JAMES FENIMORE
COOPER TO WILLIAM FAULKNER

THE / AMERICAN / NOVEL / FROM JAMES FENIMORE
COOPER / TO WILLIAM FAULKNER / *Edited by WALLACE
STEGNER* / BASIC BOOKS, INC., PUBLISHERS / *New York
London*

Editor. Essays originally prepared for presentation over the Voice of America.

"Preface," pp. vii-xiii.

"Willa Cather: *My Antonia*," pp. 144-153. Collected as "The West Authentic: Willa Cather in *The Sound of Mountain Water.*" A20.

B82 THE BIG SKY

[double title page] [map of the U.S. from the Mississippi River west to the Pacific] / [right] *The* / BIG SKY / A.B. GUTHRIE, JR. / [publisher's device] / SENTRY EDITION / HOUGHTON MIFFLIN COMPANY *Boston* / THE RIVERSIDE PRESS *Cambridge*

On copyright page: 'Introduction copyright © 1965 by Wallace Stegner.'

Bantam edition began August, 1972.

"Foreword," pp. vii-xii.

Introduction appears in *One Way to Spell Man* as "A.B. Guthrie." A28.

B83 FIFTY GREAT AMERICAN SHORT STORIES

50 GREAT / AMERICAN SHORT STORIES / EDITED AND / WITH AN INTRODUCTION BY / MILTON CRANE / Professor of English, / George Washington University / [publisher's device] / BANTAM BOOKS / [narrow rule] / NEW YORK [slash] TORONTO [slash] LONDON

"The Blue-Winged Teal," pp. 392-409. B25.

1966

B84 CALIFORNIA: THE DYNAMIC STATE

California / the Dynamic State / Ansel Adams Maurice L. Peterson / Hugo Fisher Herbert L. Phillips / Erle Stanley Gardner Wallace Stegner / C.J. Haggerty Stewart Udall / Louis H. Heilbron William L.C. Wheaton / Introduction by / Governor Edmund G. Brown / 1966 / McNally and Loftin, Publishers / Santa Barbara

"California," pp. 210-224.

B85   CURRENT VOICE

[double title page] / [left] *Indiana University* / Don L. Cook / James H. Justus / Wallace E. Williams / PRENTICE-HALL, INC., ENGLEWOOD CLIFFS, N.J. / [right] THE / CURRENT / VOICE / Readings in Contemporary Prose

Alternate edition: 1971. B103.

"Mormon Trees," pp. 52-54. A6; C37.

B86   FIRST-PRIZE STORIES 1919-1966

FIRST-PRIZE STORIES / 1919-1966 / from the *O. Henry Memorial Awards* / Introduction by Harry Hansen / DOUBLEDAY & COMPANY, INC., GARDEN CITY, NEW YORK

"The Blue-Winged Teal," pp. 452-466. B25.

B87   PATTERNS OF EXPOSITION

RANDALL E. DECKER / *Hartnell College* / *Salinas, California* / PATTERNS OF EXPOSITION / Little, Brown and Company / [publisher's device] / *Boston* [dot] *Toronto*

"That Lieth Four-Square," pp. 211-216. Excerpt from *Mormon Country*. A6.

B88   TWENTY YEARS OF STANFORD SHORT STORIES

Twenty Years of / Stanford Short Stories / Edited by / Wallace Stegner and Richard Scowcroft / with Nancy Packer / *Stanford University Press* / *Stanford, California*

On copyright page: '©1966 / Original edition 1966 / Reprinted 1967.' Paper and cloth.

"Introduction," pp. ix-xx. B13.

B89 TWICE-TOLD TALES

[double title page] / [left] [red] Nathaniel Hawthorne / [right] [illus. of a farm] / [both] TWICE-TOLD TALES / [black] *Selected and Introduced by* / WALLACE STEGNER / and *Illustrated by* VALENTI ANGELO / PRINTED FOR THE MEMBERS OF THE LIMITED EDITIONS CLUB [dot] NEW YORK [dot] 1966

"Introduction," pp. vii-xv.

Heritage Press reprint also issued in 1966.

1967

B90 GREAT WESTERN SHORT STORIES

GREAT / WESTERN / SHORT STORIES / *Edited by J. Golden Taylor* / *With an Introduction by Wallace Stegner* / [wavy rule] / THE AMERICAN WEST PUBLISHING COMPANY / PALO ALTO, CALIFORNIA [dot] 1967

"History, Myth, and the Western Writer," pp. xiii-xxv. (Introduction) A20; C137.

"Carrion Spring," pp. 338-355. B77.

Reissued in two volumes in 1971. B104.

B91 SHORT STORIES FOR INSIGHT

SHORT / STORIES / FOR / INSIGHT / *Edited by* / TERESA
FERSTER GLAZIER / COLLEGE OF SAN MATEO /
[publisher's device] / Harcourt, Brace, & World, Inc. / NEW
YORK [slash] CHICAGO [slash] SAN FRANCISCO [slash]
ATLANTA

"Butcher Bird," pp. 141-152. B31.

1968

B92   AMERICAN ENVIRONMENT

THE AMERICAN ENVIRONMENT: / *Readings in the History of*
Conservation / *edited by Roderick Nash*

"The Meaning of the Wilderness in American Civilization," pp.
192-197. ("The Wilderness Letter") B61.

B93   FROM SOURCE TO STATEMENT

From Source / to Statement / JAMES M. McCRIMMON / *with*
the assistance of / FLORENCE TREFETHEN / *and* BARBARA S.
McCRIMMON / HOUGHTON MIFFLLIN COMPANY [dot]
BOSTON / NEW YORK ATLANTA GENEVA, ILL DALLAS
PALO ALTO

"History is a Pontoon Bridge," pp. 104-111. A16.

1969

B94   GRAND COLORADO

[double title page] / [both] THE GRAND COLORADO / [photo]
Glen Canyon bend above Klondike / [right] *The Story of* / *a River*
/ *and its Canyons* / [photo of hand-crafted wooden horse] / By
T.H. Watkins / and Contributors / William E. Brown, Jr. Roger
Olmsted / Robert C. Euler Wallace Stegner / Helen Hosmer Paul
S. Taylor / Roderick Nash Robert A. Weinstein / *With a Foreword*
by Wallace Stegner / *Color Photography by Philip Hyde* / Published by

American West Publishing Company

"Foreword," pp. 10-13.

"Excerpts from *Beyond the Hundredth Meridian*," pp. 93, 95-108 *passim*, 125-137 *passim*, 148, 263, 265, 282-283. A13.

B95   MICHAEL/FRANK

MICHAEL [slash] FRANK / Studies on Frank O'Connor / [narrow rule] / *edited by Maurice Sheehy* / [publisher's device] / [narrow rule] / Alfred A. Knopf *New York 1969*

"Professor O'Connor at Stanford," pp. 94-102.

B96   VOICES FOR THE WILDERNESS

Voices / for the / Wilderness / EDITED BY / WILLIAM SCHWARZ / BALLANTINE BOOKS / [dot] / NEW YORK / An Intext Publisher

On copyright page: 'All books copyrighted by the Sierra Club. "The War Between the Rough Riders and the Bird Watchers" from WILDLANDS IN OUR CIVILIZATION, ed. by David Brower, Copyright 1964 / copyright 1969 by Ballantine Books'.

"The War Between the Rough Riders and the Bird Watchers," pp. 63-76. B79.

1970

B97   ANYBODY'S GOLD

[small square photo of people before a town hall-type building] / Anybody's Gold / The Story / of California's / Mining Towns / [short rule] / [narrow short rule] / Joseph Henry Jackson / [narrow short rule] / [thicker short rule] / *with an introduction by* / Wallace Stegner / [publisher's device] / Chronicle Books / San Francisco

"Introduction," pp. vii-xiv.

B98   DICTIONARY OF SCIENTIFIC BIOGRAPHY

DICTIONARY / OF / SCIENTIFIC BIOGRAPHY / CHARLES COULSTON GILLISPIE / *Princeton University* / EDITOR IN CHIEF / Volume 4 / RICHARD DEDEKIND—FIRMICUS MATERNUS / CHARLES SCRIBNER'S SONS [dot] NEW YORK

"Clarence Dutton," pp. 265-266.

B99   DICTIONARY OF SCIENTIFIC BIOGRAPHY

DICTIONARY / OF / SCIENTIFIC BIOGRAPHY / CHARLES COULSTON GILLISPIE / *Princeton University* / EDITOR IN CHIEF / Volume 11 / A. PITCAIRN—B. RUSH / CHARLES SCRIBNER'S SONS [dot] NEW YORK

"John Wesley Powell," pp. 118-120.

B100   FIFTY YEARS OF THE AMERICAN SHORT STORY

Fifty Years / OF THE AMERICAN / SHORT STORY / [short rule] / *From the O. Henry Awards* / *1919-1970* / Edited and with an introduction by / WILLIAM ABRAHAMS / DOUBLEDAY & COMPANY, INC. / *Garden City, New York* / 1970

"Beyond the Glass Mountain," Volume II, pp. 337-346. B17.

1971

B101   ATLANTIC BRIEF LIVES

Atlantic / BRIEF LIVES / *A Biographical Companion to the Arts* / *Edited by* LOUIS KRONENBERGER / *Associate Editor* EMILY MORISON BECK / [publisher's device] / *An Atlantic Monthly Press Book* / LITTLE, BROWN AND COMPANY [dot] BOSTON

[dot] TORONTO

"Anton Chekhov," pp. 155-157.

"Guy de Maupassant," pp. 510-511.

B102   ATTACKS OF TASTE

[within black ruled rectangle and then within rust border design] [rust] ATTACKS / OF TASTE / [black] [fancy rule] / Compiled and Edited by / EVELYN B. BYRNE / & / OTTO M. PENZLER / ON TEENAGE READING: / [quote by Archibald Macleish] / [outside ruled rectangle] New York GOTHAM BOOK MART 1971

Untitled contribution by Wallace Stegner (on reading for enjoyment), pp. 42-43.

B103   CURRENT VOICE

[double title page] / [both] THE CURRENT VOICE / [left] don l. cook / james h. justus / wallace e. williams / *indiana university* / Prentice-Hall, Inc., Englewood Cliffs, N.J. / [right] readings / in contemporary prose / *alternate edition*

"Mormonism," pp. 27-29. Excerpt from *The Gathering of Zion.* A17.

B104   GREAT SHORT STORIES OF THE WEST

Great Short Stories / Of The West / Volume II of / GREAT WESTERN SHORT STORIES / *Edited by* / J. Golden Taylor / *With an Introduction by* / Wallace Stegner / BALLANTINE BOOKS [dot] NEW YORK / An Intext Publisher

See B90 for 1967 edition.

"History, Myth, and the Western Writer," pp. xiii-xxv. (Introduction to volumes I and II). B90.

"Carrion Spring," Volume I, pp. 89-106. B77.

B105 LITERATURE OF THE AMERICAN WEST

[double rule] The Literature of the American West / [narrow rule] / *Edited by* / J. GOLDEN TAYLOR / *Colorado State University* / HOUGHTON MIFFLIN COMPANY [dot] BOSTON / New York [dot] Atlanta [dot] Geneva, Illinois [dot] Dallas [dot] Palo Alto / [double rule]

"Wilderness Letter," pp. 446-450. B61.

B106 REDISCOVERIES

REDISCOVERIES / [rule] / Informal Essays in Which Well-Known Novelists / Rediscover Neglected Works of Fiction / by One of Their Favorite Authors / EDITED AND WITH AN INTRODUCTION BY / DAVID MADDEN / CROWN PUBLISHERS, INC. NEW YORK

"Wallace Stegner on Glenway Wescott's *Good-bye Wisconsin*," pp. 47-56. C162.

1972

B107 CROSSROADS

CROSSROADS / Quality of Life Through / Rhetorical Modes / TOM E. KAKONIS / Wisconsin State University / at Whitewater / JAMES C. WILCOX / Boston University / D.C. HEATH AND COMPANY / Lexington, Massachusetts Toronto London

"Conservation Equals Survival," pp. 124-130. C159.

B108 GREAT SHORT STORIES OF THE WORLD

GREAT / SHORT / STORIES / OF / THE / WORLD / [red] Selected / by the Editors / of / the Reader's Digest Association / Pleasantville, New York / Montreal, Canada

"Carrion Spring," pp. 412-428. B77.

B109 MY DEAR WISTER

[script] My dear Wister [slash] / The Frederic Remington- / Owen Wister Letters / By Ben Merchant Vorpahl / With a Foreword by Wallace Stegner / [publisher's device] / AMERICAN WEST PUBLISHING COMPANY / PALO ALTO / CALIFORNIA

"Forward," pp. vii-viii.

1974

B110 ANSEL ADAMS: IMAGES

ANSEL ADAMS / Images 1923-1974 / FORWARD BY WALLACE STEGNER / NEW YORK GRAPHIC SOCIETY BOSTON, MASSACHUSETTS

"Forward," pp. 7-19.

B111 CONTEMPORARY LITERARY SCENE

THE / CONTEMPORARY / LITERARY / SCENE / 1973 / Edited by FRANK N. MAGILL / Associate Editor / DAVID MADDEN / Introduction by R.V. CASSILL / SALEM PRESS / INCORPORATED / Englewood Cliffs, N. J.

On Copyright page: 'Copyright ©1974 by Frank N. Magill / FIRST EDITION / First Printing.'

"The Tension Between the Outlaw and the Law," pp. 1-5. Address delivered in symposium on the teaching of fiction, Library of Congress, January 30, 1973.

B112 CONVERSATIONS WITH FREDERICK MANFRED

Conversations / with Frederick / Manfred / *Moderated by John R.*

Milton / with a Foreword by Wallace Stegner / The University of Utah Press Salt Lake City

"Forword," pp. x-xvi.

B113 WESTERN WRITING

Western Writing / Gerald W. Haslam, editor / *California State College, Sonoma* / UNIVERSITY OF NEW MEXICO PRESS / Albuquerque

"On the Writing of History," pp. 25-39. C129.

1975

B114 ANALYSIS: THE SHORT STORY

ANALYSIS: / The / Short / Story / by Arthur Myers / SOL III Publications / Farmington, Maine

"Impasse," pp. 3-18. A14; D42.

B115 LETTERS OF BERNARD DE VOTO

THE / Letters of Bernard DeVoto / WALLACE STEGNER / 1975 / DOUBLEDAY & COMPANY, INC. / GARDEN CITY, NEW YORK

Editor. "Introduction," pp. xi-xiv. Comprehensive notes and commentary by Stegner throughout this book.

1976

B116 CALIFORNIA EXPERIENCE: A LITERARY ODYSSEY

The California / Experience: / A Literary Odyssey / [illus. of scenes showing California history] / Warren A. Beck / [publisher's device] / Peregrine Smith, Inc. / SANTA BARBARA AND SALT

LAKE CITY / 1976

Excerpt from *Angle of Repose*, pp. 330-335. A22.

B117 WATER OF LIGHT

[light blue] THE / WATER / OF LIGHT / [narrow rule] [black] / A Miscellany in Honor of / Brewster Ghiselin / Edited by Henry Taylor / University of Utah Press, Salt Lake City

"One Way to Spell Man," pp. 213-224. A28; B52.

1977

B118 COMMUNICATION RESEARCH

Communication Research [slash] / a Half-Century Appraisal / [narrow rule] / *Edited by* / DANIEL LERNER / LYLE M. NELSON / [publisher's device] AN EAST-WEST CENTER BOOK / from the East-West Communication Institute / Published for the East-West Center / by The University Press of Hawaii / Honolulu

"The Iowa Years," pp. 305-310.

B119 CONTEMPORARY LITERARY CRITICISM

Not seen.

"N. Scott Momaday," vol. 19, p. 318.

B120 DICTIONARY OF AMERICAN BIOGRAPHY

DICTIONARY / OF / American Biography / Supplement Five / 1951-1955 / John A. Garraty, *Editor* / WITH AN INDEX GUIDE TO THE SUPPLEMENTS / Charles Scribner's Sons / *NEW YORK*

"Bernard DeVoto," pp. 168-169.

B121 FICTION: THE NARRATIVE ART

FICTION: The Narrative Art / [double rule] / JAMES W.
KIRKLAND / East Carolina University / PAUL W. DOWELL
/East Carolina University / PRENTICE-HALL, INC., Englewood
Cliffs, New Jersey 07632

"Butcher Bird," pp. 420-427. B31.

B122 HORIZON

HORIZON / Writings of the Canadian Prairie / Edited by / Ken
Mitchell / Toronto / Oxford University Press / 1977

"The Question Mark in the Circle," pp. 43-46.

B123 TERTIARY HISTORY OF THE GRAND
CAÑON DISTRICT

UNITED STATES GEOLOGICAL SURVEY / J.W. POWELL,
DIRECTOR / [short rule] / TERTIARY HISTORY / OF THE /
GRAND CAÑON DISTRICT / WITH ATLAS / By
CLARENCE E. DUTTON / CAPTAIN OF ORDNANCE U.S.A.
/ [symbol of Survey] [publisher's device] / Peregrine Smith, Inc. /
SANTA BARBARA AND SALT LAKE CITY / 1977

"Introduction," pp. vii-xiii. C189.

1978

B124 ADULTHOOD

Adulthood / Edited by ERIK H. ERIKSON / [publisher's device]
W [dot] W [dot] NORTON & COMPANY [dot] New York

"The Writer and the Concept of Adulthood," pp. 227-236. C185.

B125 BEST MOUNTED POLICE STORIES

BEST / MOUNTED / POLICE / STORIES / Edited by / Dick
Harrison / [publisher's device] / The University of Alberta Press /
1978

"The Wolfer," pp. 217-236. B74.

B126 CONTEMPORARY COLLEGE READER

Third Edition / CONTEMPORARY / *[narrow horizontal rule]* /
COLLEGE READER / *Joyce S. Steward* / *Emerita, University of*
Wisconsin-Madison / Scott, Foresman and Company / Glenview,
Illinois London, England

On copyright page: 'Copyright 1985, 1981, 1978'

"The Town Dump," pp. 106-114. C109.

B127 LIFE ON TWO LEVELS

[double rule] Life on Two Levels / AN AUTOBIOGRAPHY /
[single rule] JOSEPHINE WHITNEY DUVENECK / [double rule]
/ INTRODUCTION BY WALLACE STEGNER / WILLIAM
KAUFMANN, INC. / ONE FIRST STREET, LOS ALTOS,
CALIFORNIA 94022

"Introduction," pp. ix-xiii.

1979

B128 AMERICA IN LITERATURE: THE WEST

AMERICA IN / LITERATURE / *The West* / EDITED BY /
Peter Monahan / Sir Francis Drake High School / San Anselmo,
California / CHARLES SCRIBNER'S SONS [dot] NEW YORK

"This is the Place," pp. 119-124.

B129 THE CHRISTMAS TREASURY

the / Christmas / treasury / and personal / family record [Franklin Library]

"A Frontier Christmas," pp. 57-60. Essay written especially for the Franklin Library's *Christmas Treasury*.

B130 GREAT SALT LAKE PORTFOLIO

GREAT SALT LAKE PORTFOLIO / *John Telford* / *Foreword by Wallace Stegner*

"Foreword," p. (2). Excerpt from *American Places* (A27).

Note: 1 Portfolio [5] leaves, 11 leaves of plates: 11 mounted photographs. 'This Portfolio...is produced in November 1979 in an edition of 75 with 10 artists proofs...'

B131 TRAILS WEST

[double title page] [photo of man with horse, next to wagon] / [left] [black double letters for title] TRAILS / WEST / Prepared by the / Special Publications Division / National Geographic Society / Washington, D.C.

"The Oregon Trail...Road to Destiny," pp. 40-75.

B132 VOICES FOR THE EARTH

VOICES FOR / THE EARTH / A TREASURY OF / THE SIERRA CLUB / BULLETIN / Edited by Ann Gilliam / INTRODUCTION BY HAROLD GILLIAM / [sketch of pine grove] / Sierra Club Books / SAN FRANCISCO

"Wilderness and the Geography of Hope," pp. 546-550. B61.

B133 WEST COAST FICTION

West Coast Fiction / Modern Writing from California, / Oregon and Washington / [flag symbol] / Edited and with an Introduction by / JAMES D. HOUSTON / [publisher's device]

"New Almaden," pp. 290-301.

1980

B134 WILDERNESS READER

[narrow rule running through top line] THE / WILDERNESS / [rule running through third line] READER / EDITED BY / FRANK BERGON / [publisher's device] / A MENTOR BOOK / *NEW AMERICAN LIBRARY* / TIMES MIRROR / New York and Scarborough, Ontario / The New English Library Limited, London

"Packhorse Paradise," pp. 315-327. C50.

"Coda: Wilderness Letter," pp. 327-333. B61.

1981

B135 REMEMBERING

[brown] THE UNIVERSITY OF UTAH / [photo of lion within brown and black ruled frame] / [script] [brown] Remembering / [black] Edited by Elizabeth Haglund / Photograph research and preparation by Allen Thelin

"It is the Love of Books I Owe Them," pp. 111-120.

B136 THE TANNER LECTURES

THE TANNER LECTURES / ON HUMAN VALUES / 1981 / II / Raymond Aron, Brian Berry, Jonathan Bennett, / Robert Coles, George J. Stigler, Wallace Stegner, / and Michel Foucault / Sterling M. McMurrin, *Editor* / UNIVERSITY OF UTAH PRESS—Salt Lake City / CAMBRIDGE UNIVERSITY PRESS [slash] Cambridge, London, Melbourne, Sydney

"The Twilight of Self-Reliance: Frontier Values and Contemporary America," pp. 193-222.

1982

B137 BURIED UNSUNG

[double narrow rule] / BURIED UNSUNG / [double narrow rule] / Louis Tikas and the Ludlow Massacre / [four photos] / Zeese Papanikolas / Foreword by Wallace Stegner / University of Utah Press / Salt Lake City, Utah / 1982

"Foreword," pp. xiii-xix.

B138 LEO HOLUB: PHOTOGRAPHER

[gray] Leo Holub / [black] PHOTOGRAPHER / Foreword by Wallace Stegner / Stanford Alumni Association / Stanford, California

"Foreword," pp. 9-13. Edition limited to 200 copies.

B139 NAMES ON THE LAND

[within frame of laurel leaves and rule] Names / on the land / *A Historical Account / of Placenaming / in the United States* / by George R. Stewart / [laurel leaf rule] / FOURTH EDITION / Lexikos / San Francisco

On copyright page: 'Published in Novemeber 1982 / Introduction copyright © by Wallace Stegner.'

"George R. Stewart and the American Land," pp xv-xxx. (Introduction).

1983

B140 LIBRARY LIT. 13

LIBRARY LIT. 13 / The Best of 1982 / edited by / BILL KATZ / [publisher's device] / The Scarecrow Press, Inc. / Metuchen, N.J., & London / 1983

Copyright 1982 by the University Library, University of California, Santa Barbara.

"The Long Road From Byblos," pp. 143-154. Reprinted from *Soundings*, 13 (1982), pp. 5-19. C217.

B141 STORM

STORM / A NOVEL BY / GEORGE R. STEWART / Foreword by Wallace Stegner / [publisher's device] / University of Nebraska Press / Lincoln and London

On copyright page: 'Copyright, 1941, 1947, 1969, 1975 by George R. Stewart / Foreword Copyright 1983 by the University of Nebraska Press

"Foreword," pp. vii-x.

B142 WALTER VAN TILBURG CLARK: CRITIQUES

WALTER / VAN TILBURG / CLARK: / CRITIQUES / EDITED BY / *Charlton Laird* / [publisher's device] / UNIVERSITY OF NEVADA PRESS / RENO, NEVADA [dot] 1983

"Walter Clark's Frontier," pp. 53-70. C170.

1984

B143 ANSEL ADAMS

[double title page] Ansel Adams / 1902-1984 / [photograph of Half Dome] / *Edited by James Alinder* [diamond] *Untitled 37* [diamond] *The Friends of Photography*

"Miraculous Instants of Life," pp. 51-52.

B144 FLIGHT

[woodcut in rust] *FLIGHT* A STORY BY JOHN STEINBECK / WITH AN AFTERWORD BY WALLACE STEGNER / ILLUSTRATIONS BY KARIN WIKSTROM / CAROLYN AND JAMES ROBERTSON, PUBLISHERS / THE YOLLA BOLLY PRESS

On copyright page: 'Copyright 1938 by John Steinbeck Renewed 1966 by John Steinbeck / *Flight* published by arrangement with The Viking Press / Afterword copyright 1984 by Wallace Stegner / Blocks copyright 1984 by Karin Wikstrom.'

"Afterword," pp. 43-52.

B145 MONTANA AND THE WEST

MONTANA AND THE WEST / Essays in Honor of K. Ross Toole / Edited and with contributions by / Rex C. Myers and Harry W. Fritz / Pruett Publishing Company Boulder Colorado

"Foreword," pp. vii-x.

B146 PASSING FARMS, ENDURING VALUES

[all within narrow, red rule] PASSING FARMS, / ENDURING VALUES / California's Santa Clara Valley [red publisher's device] / Yvonne Jacobson / With a Foreword by Wallace Stegner / WILLIAM KAUFMANN, Los Altos, California / In Cooperation with the California History Center, De Anza College, Cupertino, California

"Foreword," pp. vii-xi.

B147 RIVER REFLECTIONS

RIVER / REFLECTIONS / AN ANTHOLOGY / edited by

Verne Huser / The East Woods Press Inc. / Charlotte, North Carolina / Boston [dot] New York

"The Sound of Mountain Waters," (sic) pp. 113-118. Excerpt from *This is Dinosaur*. B38.

B148 20TH CENTURY ANTHOLOGY

A 20TH / CENTURY / ANTHOLOGY / [decorative rule] / Essays, Stories and / Poems / [decorative rule] / EDITED BY / W.E. MESSENGER W.H. NEW / University of British Columbia

"The Town Dump," pp. 209-213. B126.

B149 THE WILDER SHORE

THE / WILDER SHORE / photographs by Morley Baer / Text by David Rains Wallace / *Foreword by Wallace Stegner* / A YOLLA BOLLY PRESS BOOK PUBLISHED BY / Sierra Club Books / SAN FRANCISCO

Also a signed edition, limited to 500 copies.

"Foreword," pp. xi-xiii.

1985

B150 FINDING THE WORDS

FINDING / THE WORDS / Conversations With / Writers Who Teach / Nancy L. Bunge / [publisher's device] SWALLOW PRESS / Athens Ohio Chicago London / OHIO UNIVERSITY PRESS

"Conversations with Wallace Stegner," pp. 118-127.

B151 A SENSE OF HISTORY

A SENSE / OF HISTORY / [publisher's device] / The Best

Writing from the Pages of / AMERICAN / HERITAGE / Introductory note by Byron Dobell / AMERICAN HERITAGE New York / Distributed by / HOUGHTON MIFFLIN COMPANY BOSTON

"Quiet Earth, Big Sky," pp. 636-644. C89.

B152 THEMES AND VARIATIONS

THEMES AND VARIATIONS / *A College Reader* / W. Ross Winterowd / *University of Southern California* / Charlotte Preston / *University of Southern California* / [publisher's device] / HARCOURT BRACE JOVANOVICH PUBLISHERS / San Diego New York Chicago Atlanta Washington, D. C. / London Sydney Toronto

"From *Beyond the Hundredth Meridian*," pp. 400-401. A13.

B153 THIS IS DINOSAUR

THIS IS [orn.] / DINOSAUR / Echo Park Country and Its Magic Rivers / EDITED BY WALLACE STEGNER / ROBERTS RINEHART, INC., PUBLISHERS

Reprint of 1955 edition with new foreword. B38 $8.95 paper. Cloth edition limited to 250 ($24.95).

'Foreword copyright ©1985 by Wallace Stegner'.

"Foreword," pp. vi-x.

"The Marks of Human Passage," pp. 3-17.

B154 UNKNOWN CALIFORNIA

UNKNOWN / CALIFORNIA / EDITED BY Jonathan Eisen and David Find / with Kim Eisen / COLLIER BOOKS / Macmillan Publishing Company / NEW YORK

"California Rising," pp. 7-11. C214.

1986

B155 BEST OF CALIFORNIA

[within double-ruled frame] The Best of / [open letters] California / [Roman] Some people, places and / institutions of the most / exiting state in the / nation, as featured in / *California* magazine, 1976-86 / [publisher's device] / Capra Press / SANTA BARBARA

"California Rising," pp. 20-24. C214.

B156 BEFORE AND AFTER: THE SHAPE AND SHAPING OF PROSE

[all within double-ruled frame] BEFORE / AND / AFTER / The Shape and / Shaping of Prose / [narrow rule] / Edited by / DONALD L. EMBLEN / ARNOLD SOLKOV / *Santa Rosa Junior College* / *California* / Random House [publisher's device] New York

"The Town Dump," pp. 28-33. B126.

B157 DIMENSIONS: A BOOK OF ESSAYS

Dimensions: / A Book of Essays / *Richard Davies* / *Teacher, J. Percy Page Composite High* / *School, Edmonton* / *Glen Kirkland* / *Teacher, Austin O'Brien Catholic High* / *School, Edmonton* / Consultants: / *Donna Carpenter* / *Halton Board of Education* / *Robert Lebans* / *A. Y. Jackson Secondary School*

"Back to Wolf Willow," pp. 132-139. A16.

B158 LITERATURE OF IDAHO: AN ANTHOLOGY

The Literature of Idaho: / An Anthology / *Selected and edited by* / James H. Maguire / Department of English / Boise State University

/ Hemingway Western Studies / Boise State University / Boise, Idaho / 1986

"The Bridge," pp. 280-292. Excerpt from *Angle of Repose*. A22, pp. 399-419.

1987

B159 COMPANION TO *A SAND COUNTY ALMANAC*

Companion to / *A Sand County Almanac* / Interpretive & Critical Essays / [star] / Edited by J. Baird Callicott / THE UNIVERSITY OF WISCONSIN PRESS

"The Legacy of Aldo Leopold," pp. 233-245.

Originally appeared in *Wilderness* (Spring 1985), under the title, "Living on Our Principal." C228.

B160 THE EXPLORATION OF THE COLORADO RIVER AND ITS CANYONS

THE EXPLORATION OF / THE COLORADO RIVER / AND ITS CANYONS / John Wesley Powell / Introduction by Wallace Stegner / [publisher's device] / PENGUIN BOOKS

'Introduction copyright © Wallace Stegner, 1987'

"Introduction," pp. [vii]-xii.

1988

B161 ALCATRAZ

[double title page] / [left] ALCATRAZ / The Rock / [right] [photo of rain over Alcatraz] / Photographs by Ed Beyeler / Foreword by Wallace Stegner / Essay by Susan Lamb / [publisher's device] NORTHLAND PRESS FLAGSTAFF ARIZONA

Simultaneous hardcover and softcover.

'Foreword copyright 1988 by Wallace Stegner'

"Foreword," pp. [vii-x].

B162 AMERICAN LIBRARY ALMANAC: FROM 1608 TO THE PRESENT

[rule] / [starred rule] / AMERICAN / LITERARY / ALMANAC / FROM 1608 TO THE PRESENT / [rule] / An Original Compendium Of / Facts And Anecdotes About / Literary Life In / The United States of America / EDITED BY KAREN L ROOD / A Bruccoli Clark Layman Book / [publisher's device] / Facts on File / New York [dot] Oxford / [rule]

"Wallace Stegner on the Stanford Writing Program," pp. 98-99.

B163 ANSEL ADAMS: LETTERS AND IMAGES 1916-1984

ANSEL ADAMS / LETTERS AND IMAGES 1916-1984 / Edited by Mary Street Alinder and Andrea Gray Stillman / Foreword by Wallace Stegner / A NEW YORK GRAPHIC SOCIETY BOOK / Little, Brown and Company [small diamond] Boston [small diamond] Toronto [small diamond] London

Copyright © 1988 by the Trustees of the Ansel Adams Publishing Rights Trust.

"Foreword," pp. v-ix.

B164 NORMAN MACLEAN

[gray] [underlined] AMERICAN AUTHORS SERIES / [black] [script] [underlined] Norman McClean / *edited by* / [Roman] Ron Mcfarland and Hugh Nichols / Confluence Press, Inc. Lewiston, Idaho

Copyright © 1988 by Confluence Press, Inc.

"Haunted by Waters," pp. 153-160.

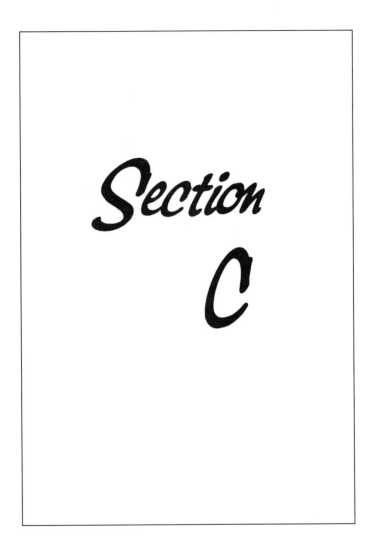

Section

C

C. Articles in
Periodicals and Newspapers

1930

C1. "The Man Who Was Born Too Late," *Daily Iowan*, (16 November 1930), 5.

1931

C2. "A Track in the Snow," *Daily Iowan*, (8 March 1931), 2.

1937

C3. "Can Teachers Be Writers?" *Intermountain Review*, 1 (1 January 1937), 1,3.

C4. "C.E. Dutton, Explorer, Geologist, Nature Writer," *Scientific Monthly*, 45 (July 1937), 82-85.

C5. "What is It?" *Writer*, 50 (November 1937), 342-44.

1938

C6. "The Trail of the Hawkeye," *Saturday Review*, 18 (30 July 1938), 3-4, 16-17.

C7. "Forgive Us Our Neuroses," *Rocky Mountain Review*, 2 (Spring 1938), 1-3.

1939

C8. "Regionalism in Art," *Delphian Quarterly*, 22 (January 1939), 2-7.

C9. "A Decade of Regional Publishing," *Publisher's Weekly*, 135 (11 March 1939), 1060-64.

C10. "Publishing in the Provinces," *Delphian Quarterly*, 22 (July 1939), 2-7, 18.

C11. "Pioneer Record...Earl Douglas and His Work," *Southwest Review*, 24 (July 1939), 369-87.

C12. "A Democracy Built on Quicksand," *Delphian Quarterly*, 22 (October 1939), 12-15, 29.

1940

C13. "Diagnosis and Prognosis," *Delphian Quarterly*, 23 (January 1940), 2-7, 55.

C14. "'Truth' and 'Faking' in Fiction," *Writer*, 53 (February 1940), 40-43.

C15. "Painless Pedestrian," *Tourists' Calendar*, (Spring 1940), 3, 51-52.

1941

C16. "Sword-Words and Words of Wisdom," *Delphian Quarterly*, 24 (July 1941), 2-5.

C17. "Writers Conference in the Rocky Mountains," *Providence Journal*, 6 (24 August 1941), 5.

C18. "The Tourist Revolution," *Delphian Quarterly*, 24 (October 1941), 34-38.

C19. "The Making of Fiction," *Rocky Mountain Review*, 6 (Fall 1941), 1, 3-4.

1942

C20. "Colleges in Wartime," *Delphian Quarterly*, 25 (April 1942), 2-7.

C21. "Shaping of Experience," *Writer*, 55 (April 1942), 99-102.

C22. "The Little Man with the Purchasing Power," *Delphian Quarterly*, 25 (July 1942), 10-15.

C23. "Normalcy Clinic," *Saturday Evening Post*, 215 (15 August 1942), 79.

C24. "Daring the Decibels," *Saturday Evening Post*, 215 (29 August 1942), 59.

C25. "Care and Feeding of Ration Hogs," *Saturday Evening Post*, 215 (5 September 1942), 71.

C26. "The Naturalization of an Idea," *Delphian Quarterly*, 25 (October 1942), 31-36, 43.

C27. "Is the Novel Done For?" *Harper's*, 186 (December 1942), 76-83.

1943

C28. "American Culture: Roadside Variety," *Harper's*, 186 (January 1943), 186.

C29. "The Co-ops in Crisis," *Delphian Quarterly*, 26 (January 1943), 15-18, 50.

C30. "The Cooperatives and the Peace," *Delphian Quarterly*, 26 (April 1943), 15-18.

C31. "Advice to a Young Writing Man," *Pro Tem*, 1 (November 1943), 1.

C32. "Get Out of that Story!" *Writer*, 56 (December 1943), 360-62.

1944

C33. "Crown Thy Good With Brotherhood," *Delphian Quarterly*, 27 (January 1944), 18-22.

C34. "Who Persecutes Boston?" *Atlantic*, 174 (July 1944), 45-52.

C35. "We Reach for the Sky," *Mademoiselle*, 19 (September 1944), 121, 261-63.

1945

C36. "You Meet Such Interesting People," *Publisher's Weekly*, 147 (31 March 1945), 1372.

C37. "Mormon Trees," *Scholastic*, 46 (23 April 1945), 18.

C38. "In America You Say It With Flowers," *Common Ground*, 5 (Summer 1945), 76-80.

C39. "The Nisei Come Home," *New Republic*, 113 (9 July 1945), 45-46.

C40. "They Came to Pick Crops," *Ammunition*, 8 (August 1945), 10-11.

1946

C41. "Jews are the Most Misunderstood Minority," *Glamour*, 12 (July 1946), 75-78.

C42. "One Man's Rediscovery of America," *Saturday Review*, 29 (17 August 1946), 5-6, 26-27.

C43. "Rediscovering America: Part II," *Saturday Review*, 29 (24 August 1946), 12-13.

C44. "Education for Democracy—The Victory of Portola Heights," *Reader's Scope*, 4 (September 1946), 87-89.

C45. "Rediscovering America: Part III," *Saturday Review*, 29 (19 October 1946), 21-23.

C46. "Rediscovering America: Part Four," *Saturday Review*, 29 (23 November 1946), 200-21, 47.

1947

C47. "I Dreamed I Saw Joe Hill Last Night," *Pacific Spectator*, 1 (Spring 1947), 184-87.

C48. "Four Hundred Families Plan a House," *'47 Magazine*, 1 (April 1947), 63-67.

C49. "The Fretful Porcupine," *'47 Magazine*, 1 (May 1947), 87-91.

C50. "Packhorse Paradise," *Atlantic*, 180 (September 1947), 21-26.

1948

C51. "Backroads River," *Atlantic*, 181 (January 1948), 56-64.

C52. "Joe Hill: The Wobblies' Troubadour," *New Republic*, 118 (5 January 1948), 20-24, 38.

C53. "Correspondence: Joe Hill," *New Republic*, 118

(9 February 1948), 38-39.

C54. "New Climates for the *Writer*," *New York Times Book Review*, (7 March 1948), 1, 20.

C55. "Meeting Crisis With Understanding: UNESCO," *Pacific Spectator*, 2 (Summer 1948), 241-252.

C56. "Pattern for Demogogues," *Pacific Spectator*, 2 (Autumn 1948), 399-411.

C57. "Utah," *Holiday*, 4 (September 1948), 34-45, 117-119.

1949

C58. "The Anxious Generation," *College English*, 10 (January 1949), 183-188.

C59. "The Anxious Generation," *English Journal*, 38 (January 1949), 1-6.

C60. "Jack Sumner and John Wesley Powell," *Colorado Magazine*, 26 (January 1949), 61-69.

C61. "A Problem in Fiction," *Pacific Spectator*, 3 (Autumn 1949), 368-375.

C62. "Navajo Rodeo," *Woman's Day*, (November 1949), 48-49, 106-108.

1950

C63. "What Do They Do All Winter," *Woman's Day*, (February 1950), 54-55, 149-153.

C64. "Hometown Revisited: 15. Salt Lake City," *Tomorrow*, 9 (February 1950), 26-29.

C65. "Variations on a Theme by Conrad," *Yale Review*, 39

(March 1950), 512-523.

C66. "The Teaching and Study of Writing," *Western Review*, 14 (Spring 1950), 165-179.

C67. "Fiction: A Lens on Life," *Saturday Review*, 33 (22 April 1950), 9-10, 32-34. *Note*: Published separately by Viking in 1960. 8pp.

C68. "Writing as Graduate Study," *College English*, 11 (May 1950), 429-432.

C69. "Why I Like the West," *Tomorrow*, 9 (July 1950), 5-9.

C70. "Adventures with Trinket," *Woman's Day*, (September 1950), 50-51, 153-156.

C71. "Backroads of the American West," *Tomorrow*, 10 (October 1950), 9-14.

C72. "Wallace Stegner," *New York Herald Tribune Book Review*, (8 October 1950), 14.

1951

C73. "Cairo, 1950," *Pacific Spectator*, 5 (Winter 1951), 42-47.

C74. "Asian Literary Articles," *The Indian P.E.N.*, 17 (1 January 1951), 2-4.

C75. "India: Crowds, Resignation, and the Cominform Line," *Reporter*, 4 (20 February 1951), 6-10.

C76. "Renaissance in Many Tongues," *Saturday Review*, 34 (4 August 1951), 27-28, 52-53.

C77. "Literary Lessons Out of Asia," *Pacific Spectator*, 5 (Autumn 1951), 413-419.

C78. "The Timid Ambassador," *Reporter*, 5 (4 September 1951), 33-35.

1952

C79. "Land of Enchantment," *Woman's Day*, (August 1952), 21, 78-79.

C80. "Workshops for Writers," *Today*, (January 1952), 15.

1953

C81. "Powell and the Names on the Plateau," *Western Humanities Review*, 7 (Spring 1953), 105-110.

C82. "One-Fourth of a Nation: Public Lands and Itching Fingers," *Reporter*, 8 (12 May 1953), 25-29.

1954

C83. "Adding the Stone Age to Human History," *Pacific Spectator*, 8 (Winter 1954), 38-52.

C84. "Battle for the Wilderness," *New Republic*, 130 (15 February 1954), 13-15.

1955

C85. "The Jones Room," *Appreciation*, 2 (Summer 1955), 9-10.

C86. "We Are Destroying Our National Parks," *Sports Illustrated*, 3 (13 June 1955), 28-29, 44-46.

C87. "Boats Hate Me," *Woman's Day*, (August 1955).

C88. "Queen of the Salmon Rivers," *Sports Illustrated*, 3 (8 August 1955), 38-41.

C89. "Quiet Earth, Big Sky," *American Heritage*, 6

(October 1955), 22-27.

1956

C90. "The DeVoto Library and Papers," *Appreciation*, 3 (Winter 1956), 3-5.

C91. "Twenty Years of *Western Review*: a Series of Recollections," *Western Review*, 20 (Winter 1956), 87-89.

C92. "What Besides Talent?" *Author and Journalist*, 41 (March 1956), 11-13, 29.

C93. "America's Mightiest Playground," *Holiday*, 20 (July 1956), 34-43, 122-125.

C94. "Ordeal by Handcart; the Mormon Trek," *Colliers*, 138 (6 July 1956), 78-85.

C95. "Quiet Earth, Big Sky," *Saskatchewan History*, 9 (Autumn 1956), 102-107. Reprint of C89.

1957

C96. "Careful Young Men," *Nation*, 184 (9 March 1957), 201-202.

C97. "The World's Strangest Sea," *Holiday*, 21 (May 1957), 76-77, 176-185.

C98. "History Comes to the Plains," *American Heritage*, 8 (June 1957), 14-19, 108-111.

C99. "Yarn-Spinner in the American Vein," *New York Times Book Review*, (10 February 1957), 1. (Review of Charles Neider's *The Complete Short Stories of Mark Twain*). B76.

1958

C100. "Love Affair with the Heber Valley, U.S.A." *Vogue*, 131 (1 February 1958), 132-133, 192-193.

C101. "One Way to Spell Man," *Saturday Review*, 41 (24 May 1958), 8-11, 43-44.

C102. "The Mounties at Fort Walsh," *Atlantic*, 202 (July 1958), 50-54.

C103. "California's Gold Rush Country," *Holiday*, 24 (August 1958), 64-69, 127.

C104. "The Making of Paths," *New Yorker*, 34 (6 September 1958), 37-38.

C105. "The American Student, a Teacher's View," *Saturday Review*, 41 (13 September 1958), 23.

C106. "Sensibility and Intelligence," *Saturday Review*, 41 (13 September 1958), 24.

1959

C107. "The War Between the Rough Riders and the Bird Watchers," *Sierra Club Bulletin*, 44 (May 1959), 4-11.

C108. "The West Coast, a Region with a View," *Saturday Review*, 42 (2 May 1959), 15-17, 41.

C109. "The Town Dump," *Atlantic*, 204 (October 1959), 78-80.

C110. "To a Young Writer," *Atlantic*, 204 (November 1959), 88-91.

1960

C111. "Celebrated Jumping Freud," *Reporter*, 22 (17 March 1960), 45-46.

1961

C112. "Robert Frost: A Lover's Quarrel with the World," *Stanford Today*, 13 (Spring 1961), unpaged.

C113. "Our Saddest War," *Coronet*, 49 (April 1961), 62-81.

C114. "Corsica Out of Season," *Harper's*, 223 (October 1961), 75-79.

1962

C115. "Megalopolis and the Country All Around," *Living Wilderness*, 82 (Winter 1962), 23-24.

C116. "A Dedication to the Memory of John Wesley Powell," *Arizona and the West*, 4 (Spring 1962), 1-4.

C117. "To an Anonymous Admirer," *Sequoia*, 7 (Spring 1962), 1-7.

C118. "Oh, Wilderness Were Paradise Enow!" *Washington Post*, (17 June 1962), E3.

C119. "Child of the Far Frontier," *Horizon*, 5 (September 1962), 94-95.

1963

C120. "University and the Creative Arts," *Arts in Society*, 2 (Spring-Summer 1963), 33-34.

C121. "Creative Writer as an Image Maker," *Writer*, 76 (October 1963), 24.

1964

C122. "Born a Square: the Westerner's Dilemma," *Atlantic*, 213 (January 1964), 46-50.

C123. "Ordeal at Devil's Gate," *Esquire*, 61 (June 1964), 100-101, 157-159.

C124. "Patterns of Alienation," *Fulbright Review*, 1 (Fall 1964), 3-10.

C125. "Quiet Crisis or Lost Cause?" *Saturday Review*, 47 (19 September 1964), 28, 50.

1965

C126. "Song to the Morning Star," *American West*, 2 (Winter 1965), 23.

C127. "Good-bye to All T—t!" *Atlantic*, 215 (March 1965), 119.

C128. "What Ever Happened to the Great Outdoors?" *Saturday Review*, 48 (22 May 1965), 37-38, 97-98.

C129. "On the Writing of History," *American West*, 2 (Fall 1965), 6-13. *Note*: Speech delivered at University of Utah June, 1965. Reprinted as a keepsake from the *American West* for the Helena meeting of the Western History Association, October, 1965. See E5.

C130. "Correctness and Communication," *Dialog*, (Fall 1965), 15-17.

C131. "Myths of the Western Dam," *Saturday Review*, 48 (23 October 1965), 29-31.

1966

C132. "Lake Powell," *Holiday*, 39 (May 1966), 64-68, 148-151.

C133. "To Save the Grand Canyon," *Saturday Review*, 49 (20 August 1966), 20.

1967

C134. "Legislating to Save the Land," *Saturday Review*, 50 (14 January 1967), 90-92.

C135. "Introduction," *American West*, 4 (February 1967), 4-5.

C136. "Commentary," *American West Review*, 1 (15 March 1967), 12.

C137. "History, Myth, and the Western Writer," *American West*, 4 (May 1967), 61-62, 76-79. *Note*: Reprinted as introduction to *Great Western Short Stories* (J. Golden Taylor - 1967). See B90 and B104.

C138. "Last Chance for the Everglades," *Saturday Review*, 50 (6 May 1967), 22-23, 72-73.

C139. "On Censorship," *Arts in Society*, 4 (Summer 1967), 281-299.

C140. "Commentary," *American West Review*, 1 (15 June 1967), 14.

C141. "Class of '67: The Gentle Desperadoes," *Nation*, 204 (19 June 1967), 775-781.

C142. "Hard Experience Talking," *Saturday Review*, 50 (19 August 1967), 25.

C143. "The People Against the American Continent," *Vermont History*, 35 (Autumn 1967), 177-185.

C144. "For Their Own Sake, and Ours," *American West Review*, 1 (15 September 1967), 14.

C145. "California: The Experimental Society," *Saturday Review*, 50 (23 September 1967), 28.

C146. "Commentary: A Matter of Continuity," *American West Review*, 1 (1 December 1967), 12.

1968

C147. "Beginning!" (DISCOVERY!) *Aramco World Magazine*, 19 (January-February 1968), 11-22. (Chapter 1)

C148. "Chapter 2," (DISCOVERY!) *Aramco World Magazine*, 19 (March-April 1968), 15-21.

C149. "Chapter 3," (DISCOVERY!) *Aramco World Magazine*, 19 (May-June 1968), 8-15.

C150. "Chapter 4," (DISCOVERY!) *Aramco World Magazine*, 19 (July-August 1968), 8-15.

C151. "Chapter 5," (DISCOVERY!) *Aramco World Magazine*, 19 (September-October 1968), 16-23.

C152. "The Book and the Great Community," *Library Journal*, 93 (1 October 1968), 3513-3516. *Note:* From University of Utah Library Dedication Exercises, 1968. Pp. [5-11].

C153. "Chapter 6," (DISCOVERY!) *Aramco World Magazine*, 19 (November-December 1968), 4-11.

1969

C154. "Chapter 7," (DISCOVERY!) *Aramco World Magazine*, 20 (January-February 1969), 12-21.

C155. "Chapter 8," (DISCOVERY!) *Aramco World Magazine*, 20 (March-April 1969), 10-21.

C156. "Chapter 9," (DISCOVERY!) *Aramco World Magazine*, 20 (May-June 1969), 22-31.

C157. "Chapter 10," (DISCOVERY!) *Aramco World Magazine*, 20 (July-August 1969), 20-27.

C158. "Chapter 11," (DISCOVERY!) *Aramco World Magazine*, 20

(September-October 1969), 16-23.

C159. "Conservation Equals Survival," *American Heritage*, 21 (December 1969), 12-15.

1970

C160. "Chapter 12," (DISCOVERY!) *Aramco World Magazine*, 21 (January-February 1970), 17-21.

C161. "Chapter 13," (DISCOVERY!) *Aramco World Magazine*, 21 (March-April 1970), 9-17.

C162. "Re-discovery: Wescott's *Good-bye, Wisconsin*," *Southern Review*, 6 (July 1970), 674-81.

C163. "Chapter 14," (DISCOVERY!) *Aramco World Magazine*, 21 (July-August 1970), 8-21.

C164. "East Palo Alto," *Saturday Review*, 53 (1 August 1970), 12, 15, 54.

C165. "We have met the enemy, and he is us," *Life*, 49 (3 August 1970), 2 pp. between pages 32 and 33.

1971

C166. "Bernard DeVoto and the Mormons: Three Letters," *Dialogue: A Journal of Mormon Thought*, 6 (Autumn-Winter 1971), 39-47.

1972

C167. "Last Exit to America," *Esquire*, 77 (April 1972), 87-89, 168-170, 175.

C168. "Thoughts in a Dry Land," *Westways*, 64 (September 1972), 14-19, 58.

1973

C169. "Selections from the new book Foxfire 2..." (introduction by Stegner), *place*, 3 (June 1973), 73-74.

C170. "Walter Clark's Frontier," *Atlantic*, 232 (August 1973), 94-98.

C171. "Historian by Serendipity," *American Heritage*, 24 (August 1973), 28-32, 92-96.

C172. "The Coast of Oregon," *Travel and Leisure*, 3 (Autumn 1973), 41-43.

C173. "This New Man, the American," *Stanford Magazine*, 1 (Fall/Winter 1973), 14-19. *Note*: Appears as "Variations on a Theme of Discontent," which Stegner delivered as the commencement address at Utah State University June 3, 1972. Also published as a separate pamphlet by Utah State University Press, 1972. See E7.

C174. "DeVoto's Western Adventures," *American West*, 10 (November 1973), 20-27.

1974

C175. "Letter from Canada," *American West*, 11 (January 1974), 28-30.

C176. "The Great Amazonian Plain," *Travel and Leisure*, 4 (February 1974), 31, 47-49.

C177. "The Provincial Consciousness," *University of Toronto Quarterly*, 43 (Summer 1974), 299-310.

C178. "Indians of Otavalo," *Travel and Leisure*, 4 (October 1974), 48, 60, 62.

1975

C179. "I Sing of America," *Holiday*, 56 (March 1975), 36, 49.

C180. "Down Among the Archives," *The Imprint* (of the Stanford Libraries), 1 (April 1975), 16-19.

C181. "Breadloaf in the 40's," *Middlebury College News Letter*, 49 (Summer 1975), 30-31.

C182. "Depression Pop," *Esquire*, 84 (September 1975), 79-83, 154.

C183. "Literary by Accident," *Utah Libraries*, 18 (Fall 1975), 7-21.

C184. "The Writer's Sense of Place," *South Dakota Review*, 13 (Autumn 1975), 49-52.

1976

C185. "The Writer and the Concept of Adulthood," *Daedalus*, 105 (Fall 1976), 39-48.

C186. "Ansel Adams and the Search for Perfection," *Dialogue*, 9 (No. 3, 1976), 33-46. *Note*: Reprint from Ansel Adams' IMAGES.

1977

C187. "A Desert Shelf," *Westways*, 69 (September 1977), 16-19, 80.

C188. "Literary Life Anything But Romantic," *Intellect*, 106 (September 1977), 107.

1978

C189. "Tertiary History of the Grand Cañon District," *Sierra*, 63 (April 1978), 17-19.

C190. "Rocky Mountain Country," *Atlantic*, 241 (April 1978), 44-64, 71-91. (By Wallace and Page Stegner).

C191. "The Scientist as Artist: Clarence E. Dutton," *American West*, 15 (May/June 1978), 18-19, 61.

1979

C192. "Getting to Know the National Domain," *American Heritage*, 30 (February 1979), 60-62.

C193. "Regionalism: No and Yes," *South Dakota Review* (special issue), 3 (Spring 1979), 6-7.

C194. "Regionalism: No and Yes," *New America*, 3 (Spring 1979), 6-7. *Note*: Reprinted from *South Dakota Review*.

C195. "Northeast Kingdom," *Country Journal*, 6 (August 1979), 56-67.

C196. "Excellence and the Pleasure Principle," *Writing*, 1 (3 & 4, 1979), 4-9.

C197. "Remnants," *Country Journal*, 6 (December 1979), 36-42.

1980

C198. "Crow Country," *Country Journal*, 7 (July 1980), 49-55.

C199. "Worst Government in the World—Except for the Others," *U.S. News*, 89 (22 September 1980), 53-54.

C200. "Breaking a New York Monopoly on Books," *Palo Alto Weekly*, 1 (25 September 1980), 1.

C201. "The Geography of Hope," *Living Wilderness*, 44 (December 1980), 12-17.

C202. "The Wild Idea," *Washington Post*, (23 December 1980, A15. *Note*: Reprint of sections of "The Geography of Hope."

1981

C203. "Will Reagan Ride with the Raiders?" *Washington Post*, (20 January 1981), 25, 33, 35, 37. *Note*: Inaugural Edition.

C204. "By Chaos Out of Dream," *American Heritage*, 32 (February/March 1981), 4-13.

C205. "Xanadu by the Salt Flats," *American Heritage*, 32 (June/July 1981), 81-89.

C206. "Land: America's History Teacher," *Living Wilderness*, 45 (Summer 1981), 4-13.

C207. "If the Sagebrush Rebels Win, Everybody Loses," *Living Wilderness*, 45 (Summer 1981), 30-35.

C208. "Lost Horizons," *New West*, 6 (July 1981), 135-136.

C209, "The Call of the Wild," *New West*, 6 (August 1981), 144-146.

C210. "Apples and Oranges," *New West*, 6 (September 1981), 164-165.

C211. "Water Warnings, Water Futures," *Plateau*, 53 (Fall 1981), 2-3.

C212. "Down the Upper Mississippi," *Country Journal*, 8 (September 1981), 74-86.

C213. "High Plateaus," *Sierra*, 66 (September/October 1981), 8-17.

C214. "California Rising," *California*, 6 (October 1981), 187-188.

C215. "Dead Heart of the West: Utah's Great Salt Lake," *Rocky Mountain Magazine*, 3 (November 1981), 56-59.

C216. "Ask the Dust," *California*, 6 (December 1981), 188-189.

1982

C217. "The Long Road from Byblos," *Soundings*, 13 (February 1982), 5-19.

C218. "George R. Stewart, Western Writer," *American West*, 19 (March/April 1982), 64, 67-69.

C219. "Life with My Ancestors," *American Heritage*, 33 (August/September 1982), 21.

1983

C220. "The Best Idea We Ever Had," *Wilderness*, 46 (Spring 1983), 4-13.

C221. "The Geography of Hope: Wilderness Letter," *Orion Nature Quarterly*, 2 (Spring 1983), 42-47.

C222. "Two Artists, Two Friends: A Conversation," *Stanford Magazine*, 11 (Spring 1983), 50-55.

1984

C223. "Ansel Adams and the Search for Perfection," *Arizona Highways*, 60 (January 1984), 11-13.

C224. "Owen Wister: Creator of the Cowboy Myth," *American West*, 21 (January/February 1984), 48-52.

C225. "Ansel Adams 1902-1984," *Wilderness*, 48 (Summer 1984), 2-3.

C226. "Strange Encounter," *California Living*, (7 October 1984), 24-25.

1985

C227. "Claiming Our Cultural Heritage," *Nebraska Humanist*,

8 (Spring 1985), 45-54.

C228. "Living on Our Principal," *Wilderness*, 48 (Spring 1985), 15-21.

C229. "Rivers of My Mind," *San Francisco Chronicle (Great Escapes)*, (24 March 1985), 28-30.

C230. "Bernard DeVoto," *Western American Literature*, 20 (August 1985), 151-164.

C231. "The Power of Homely Detail," *American Heritage*, 36 (August/September 1985), 62-69.

C232. "The Scandinavians Among Us," *Reader's Digest*, 127 (October 1985), 130-134.

C233. "From the Heart of Ansel Adams," *San Francisco Chronicle (Review)*, (6 October 1985), 1, 11.

C234. "Passing Farms, Enduring Values," *The Californian*, 7 (December 1985), 4.

C235. "Water in the West: Growing Beyond Nature's Limits," *Los Angeles Times (Opinion)*, (29 December 1985), V, 3.

1986

C236. "Water in the West," *Los Angeles Times* (letter), (23 January 1986), II, 4.

C237. "A Tribute to Ansel Adams," *Update* (Trust for Public Land), 15 (Winter 1986), 4-5.

1987

C238. "Vision of Light," *Art and Antiques*, (April 1987), 101-105.

C239. "The Spoiling of the American West," *Michigan Quarterly*

Review, 26 (Spring 1987), 293-310.

C240. "Novelist Wallace Stegner Says the West Was Spoiled, Not Won," *Los Angeles Times*, (31 May 1987), v, 5. (Excerpt from C239).

C241. "The Function of Aridity," *Wilderness*, 51 (Fall 1987), 14-18.

C242. "Who Are the Westerners?" *American Heritage*, 38 (December 1987), 34-41.

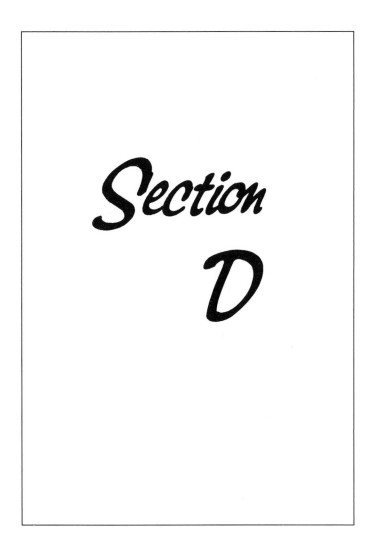

Section

D

D. Short Stories
in Periodicals and Newspapers

D1. "Pete and Emil," *Salt Lake Tribune*, (9 December 1934), 3.

D2. "Saskatchewan Idyll," *Monterey Beacon*, 1 (29 June 1935), 8-9.

D3. "Home to Utah," *Story*, 9 (August 1936), 28-42.

D4. "Bloodstain," *American Prefaces*, 2 (Summer 1937), 150-153.

D5. "The Dam Builder," *Frontier and Midland*, 17 (Summer 1937), 231-236.

D6. "Fish," *Intermountain Review*, 1 (Summer 1937), 1,6,7,10.

D7. "Remembering Laughter," *Redbook*, 71 (September 1937). Complete novel.

D8. "The Two Wives," *Redbook*, 72 (July 1938), 48-52, 65-66.

D9. "Bugle Song," *Virginia Quarterly Review*, 14 (July 1938), 407-415.

D10. "The Potter's House," *American Prefaces*, 3 (Summer 1938), 147-151, 165-176. See A3.

D11. "The Noise Outside," *Redbook*, 73 (January 1939), 20-23, 70, 73.

D12. "One Last Wilderness," *Scribner's*, 105 (January 1939), 16-20, 44, 46-51, 60-65.

D13. "Clash By Night," *Redbook*, 73 (November 1939), 131-162 (unp.) "Novel of the Month," complete in one issue. See *On a Darkling Plain*, A4.

D14. "Goin' to Town," *Atlantic*, 165 (June 1940), 770-776. See A7 and A10.

D15. "The Chink," *Atlantic*, 166 (September 1940), 349-356. See A10.

D16. "One Thing at a Time," *Collier's*, 106 (26 October 1940), 20, 58-61.

D17. "Butcher Bird," *Harper's*, 182 (January 1941), 156-163. See A7 and A10. Many textbook appearances.

D18. "Say It With Flowers," *Mademoiselle*, 12 (June 1941), 60-61, 111-112, 115-116, 119, 122.

D19. "The Four Mules of God," *Decision*, 2 (October 1941), 19-23.

D20. "In the Twilight," *Mademoiselle*, 12 (November 1941), 82-83, 140-142, 144, 150-152. See A10 and B6.

D21. "Two Rivers," *Atlantic*, 169 (June 1942), 745-752. See A7, A10, and B7. Second Prize O. Henry Awards, 1942. Many textbook appearances.

D22. "Chip Off the Old Block," *Virginia Quarterly Review*, 18

(October 1942), 573-590. See A7, A10, and B8.

D23. "The Turtle at Home," *Atlantic*, 171 (April 1943), 123, 127. Abridged version of D25.

D24. "The Colt," *Southwest Review*, 28 (Spring 1943), 267-279. See A7, A10, and B11.

D25. "My Pet Achilles, the Amusing Turtle," *Reader's Digest*, 42 (June 1943), 24-26. See D23.

D26. "Hostage," *Virginia Quarterly Review*, 19 (July 1943), 403-411. See A10.

D27. "The Paradise Hunter," *Redbook*, 82 (August 1943), 24-30, 102-106, 108-110; (September 1943), 24-29, 99-100, 103-108.

D28. "The Berry Patch," *Atlantic*, 172 (September 1943), 51-53. See A10.

D29. "The Volcano," *Harper's*, 189 (September 1944), 315-318.

D30. "The House on Cherry Creek," *Collier's*, 116 (11 August 1945), 16-17.

D31. "Balance His, Swing Yours," *Rocky Mountain Review*, 10 (Autumn 1945), 32-38. See A10.

D32. "Saw Gang," *Atlantic*, 176 (October 1945), 82-84. See A10.

D33. "The Women on the Wall," *Harper's*, 192 (April 1946), 366-376. See A10 and B15.

D34. "Admirable Crichton," *New Yorker*, 22 (15 June 1946), 52. See B20.

D35. "Beyond the Glass Mountain," *Harper's*, 194 (May 1947), 446-452.

D36. "The Double Corner," *Cosmopolitan*, 125 (July 1948), 48-49, 136-141. See A10.

D37. "The Sweetness of the Twisted Apples," *Cosmopolitan*, 124 (March 1948), 190-192. See A10.

D38. "The View from the Balcony," *Mademoiselle*, 19 (July 1948), 68-70, 103-109. See A10.

D39. "The Blue-Winged Teal," *Harper's*, 200 (April 1950), 41-49. First Prize O. Henry Awards, 1950. Included in many anthologies and translations. Appears as a "Tale Blazer" book. See A14 and B25.

D40. "The Traveler," *Harper's*, 202 (February 1951), 79-84. See A14 and B27. Also textbook appearances. Also: *The Diliman Review*, 1 (January 1953), 17-27.

D41. "Pop Goes the Alley Cat," *Harper's*, 204 (February 1952), 42-52. See A14.

D42. "Impasse," *Woman's Day*, 16 (February 1953), 44-45, 112-114, 116-119. See A14 and B114.

D43. "The City of the Living," *Mademoiselle*, 38 (January 1954), 78-79, 135-138. See A14 and B36. O. Henry Award, 1955.

D44. "Maiden in a Tower," *Harper's*, 208 (January 1954), 78-84. See A14 and B34.

D45. "The Volunteer," *Mademoiselle*, 43 (October 1956), 124-125, 146-156. See A14.

D46. "Life Class," *Nugget*, (July 1956), 14-16, 20, 24.

D47. "He Who Spits at the Sky," *Esquire*, 49 (March 1958), 140-154.

D48. "Something Spurious from the Mindanao Deep,"

Harper's, 217 (August 1958), 50-58.

D49. "Genesis," *Contact*, 2 (April 1959), 85-167. Novella published in a periodical. See A16.

D50. "All the Little Live Things," *Mademoiselle*, 49 (May 1959), 90, 132-134, 137-141.

D51. "Indoor-Outdoor Living," *Pacifica*, (September 1959), 16-23. Demonstration issue.

D52. "The Wolfer," *Harper's*, 219 (October 1959), 53-61.

D53. "Chapter 13," *Contact*, 2 (February 1961), 116-122. Chapter from A Shooting Star. See A15.

D54. "Carrion Spring," *Esquire*, 58 (October 1962), 130-133, 160-164. See A16 and B77. O. Henry Award, 1964.

D55. "Angle of Repose," *McCall's*, 98 (April 1971), 103-110. See A22.

D56. "Three Stories by Wallace Stegner," *Scholastic Scope*, 33 (12 October 1984), 1-10. Simplified stories from *The Women on the Wall*: ("Chip Off the Old Block," "The Foreigner," and "In the Twilight.") See A10.

D57. "Amicitia," *Sequoia*, 31 (Centennial Issue 1987), 16-25.

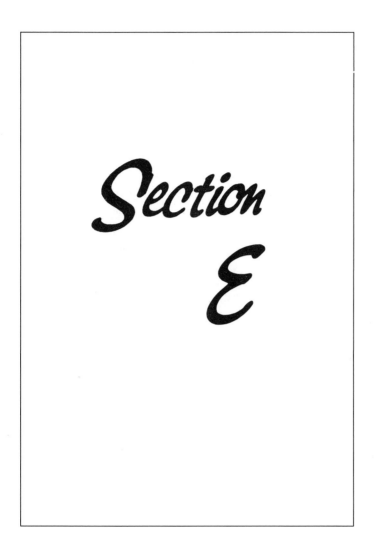

Section

E

E. Miscellaneous

E1. Christmas publication. "Greetings from the Stanford University Libraries," Christmas, 1952. "Work in Progress" includes an excerpt from "City of the Living," (an upcoming short story).

E2. Poster. "The Sound of Mountain Water," Standard Oil of California Western Scenes, 1954. More than 1,000,000 free copies were distributed to motorists and visitors in the West, May through September, 1955.

E3. Voice of America Broadcast, June, 1956. "The Town of Los Altos Hills." Part of a series including contributions from about seventy-five of the country's leading writers. Planned to broadcast the entire series in English and in any of forty languages.

E4. "Assateague." 4″ × 4″ pamphlet with photos and Stegner quotation from "The Wilderness Idea." To support a congressional bill proposing Assateague as a national seashore (to be voted on in 1965). No date.

E5. Keepsake. "On the Writing of History," a keepsake from *The*

American West for the Helena meeting of the Western History Association, October, 1965.

E6. Program. "The Book and the Great Community," program with full text of dedicatory address presented by Stegner at the Library Dedication Exercises, University of Utah, May 17, 1968.

E7. Pamphlet. "Variations on a Theme of Discontent," pamphlet published by Utah State University Press, Logan, Utah, containing the full text of the commencement address presented June 3, 1972.

E8. Opera of *Angle of Repose*. Adaptation composed by Andrew Imbrie with libretto by Oakley Hall. Five performances at the San Francisco Opera House - November 6, 9, 14, 18, and 26, 1976.
    a. Libretto by Oakley Hall. Delaware Water Gap, PA: Shawnee Press, 1976. 36p.
    b. Littlejohn, David, "Novel into Opera," *San Francisco Opera Magazine*, 1976, pp. 18-30, 63, 76-82.

E9. Calendar. "Wilderness Road," Sierra Club Calendar, 1976. Introduction by Stegner for 1976 Wilderness Wall Calendar.

E10. Poster. "Caribou on River Icing," poster, 1977. Excerpt from "Wilderness Letter." Photograph. George Calef, Pub. Northern Environment Foundation, Box 1409, Winnipeg. 24″ × 36″.

E11. "Alcatraz," introductory panel for the traveling exhibit of Beyeler photos, 1978-1979. 16″ × 20″ panel, silk-screened, 300-400 words typeset. Permanently housed at Fort Mason, headquarters for the Golden Gate National Recreation Area.

E12. Christmas Exhibition Catalog, 1983. University of California, Berkeley, The Bancroft Library. "The artist as environmental advocate with an introduction by Ansel Adams." A Regional Oral History office interview funded by the Sierra Club and the National Endowment for the Humanities. On exhibit December 7, 1983 - February 10, 1984.

E13. The 1983 Western Wilderness Calendar. ©1982 by Dream Garden Press. February - Stegner quotations.

E14. The 1984 Western Wilderness Calendar. ©1983 by Dream Garden Press. December - Stegner. Quotation from *The Sound of Mountain Water*: "By such a river it is impossible to believe that one will ever be tired or old."

E15. The 1985 Western Wilderness Calendar. ©1984 by Dream Garden Press. November - Stegner.

E16. Poster from Rhodesia. With excerpt from "Wilderness Letter." No date. Wildlife drawings and calligraphy in black and white. 8" × 10".

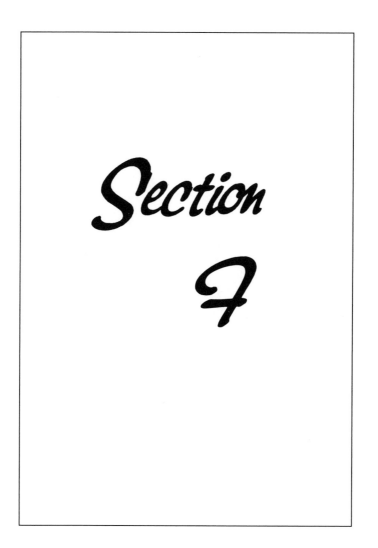

Section

F

F. Translations
of Novels and Stories
into Foreign Languages

French

F1. [From BIG ROCK CANDY MOUNTAIN] ["Chip Off the Old Block"] LA BALLADE DU CAFÉ TRISTE PAR CARSON MAC CULLERS ET AUTRES NOUVELLES AMÉRICAINES. Translated by G.M. Tracy. Paris: Éditions Le Portulan, 1946.

"Bon Chien Chasse De Race," pp. 141-169.

F2. [BIG ROCK CANDY MOUNTAIN] LA MONTAGNE DE MES RÊVES. Translated by Edith Vincent. Paris: Éditions du Bateau Ivre, 1946.

F3. [A SHOOTING STAR] UNE ÉTOILE FILANTE. Translated by Marie Watkins. Paris: Presses de la Cité, 1961.

F4. [THE AMERICAN NOVEL] REGARDS SUR LE ROMAN AMERICAIN, DE JAMES FENIMORE COOPER A WILLIAM FAULKNER. Translated by Jacques Eynesse. Paris: Seghers, 1970.

German

F5. [ON A DARKLING PLAIN] KEINER BLEIBT ALLEIN. Translated by Selma Marie Dege. Gütersloh: C. Bertelsmann Verlag, 1949.

F6. [REMEMBERING LAUGHTER] DAS LACHELN EINES SOMMERS. Translated by Rudolf Wendorff. Gütersloh: C. Bertelsmann Verlag, 1951.

F7. [BIG ROCK CANDY MOUNTAIN] DER BERG MEINER TRÄUME. Translated by Selma Marie Dege. Gütersloh: C. Bertelsmann Verlag, 1952.

F8. [A SHOOTING STAR] JEDER STERN AUF SEINER BAHN. Translated by Margitta de Hervás and Ursula von Wiese. Bern and Stuttgart: Alfred Scherz Verlag, 1962.

F9. [A SHOOTING STAR] JEDER STERN AUF SEINER BAHN. Translated by Margitta de Hervás and Ursula von Wiese. Klagenfurt: Buchgemeinde Alpenland, 1964.

F10. [A SHOOTING STAR] JEDER STERN AUF SEINER BAHN. Translated by Margitta de Hervás and Ursula von Wiese. Zurich: Buchclub Ex Libris, 1964.

F11. [ALL THE LITTLE LIVE THINGS] TAGE WIE HONIG. Translated by Margitta de Hervás. Bern: Alfred Scherz Verlag, 1970.

F12. [ALL THE LITTLE LIVE THINGS] TAGE WIE HONIG. Translated by Margitta de Hervás. Munich: W. Goldmann, 1971.

F13. [ALL THE LITTLE LIVE THINGS] TAGE WIE HONIG. Translated by Margitta de Hervás. Stuttgart: Dt. Bucherbund, 1972. (Also a 1962 printing).

Greek

F14. [WOLF WILLOW] ΜΥΡΟΥΔΙΑ ΤΗΣ ΑΥΓΑΡΙΑΣ.
Translated by ΒΑΣ Λ. ΚΑΖΑΝΤΖΗ. Athens: Biblia, 1964.

F15. [5 Lectures on American Writers] ΑΜΕΡΙΚΑΝΙΚΗ
ΛΟΓΟΤΕΧΝΙΛ ΕΖΗ ΟΜΙΛΕΣ ΤΟΥ ΑΜΕΡΙΚΑΝΟΥ
ΣΥΓΓΡΑφΕϑΕΩΣ ΟΓΛΛΣ ΣΤΕΓΚΝΕΡ ΑΘΗΝΑ, 1964.

Lecture on William Faulkner, pp. 16-22. Translator unknown.

Italian

F16. [ANGLE OF REPOSE] ANGOLO DI RIPOSO. Translated
by Edward Tosques and Ernestina Pellegrini. Firenze: Vallecchi
Editore, 1987.

Japanese

F17. [THE BLUE-WINGED TEAL] Selected Short Stories translated by Mikio Hiramatsu. Tokyo: Hokuseido Press, 1952.

F18. [DISCOVERY] DAIHAKKEN. Translated by Yoroshi Kudo.
Tokyo: Kodansha, 1976.

Polish

F19. [THE BLUE-WINGED TEAL] 26 WSPÓtCZESNYCH
OPOWIADAŃ AMERYKAŃSKICH Wybral Maxim Lieber.
Translated by Jan Dehnel. Warsaw: Iskry, 1966.

"Cyranka," pp. 237-257.

Spanish

F20. [A SHOOTING STAR] UNA ESTRELLA FUGAZ.

Translated by Alfredo Crespo. Buenos Aires and Barcelona: Plaza & Janés, 1962.

F21. [GREAT AMERICAN SHORT STORIES] ANTOLOGIA DE LA NOVELA CORTA NORTEAMERICANA. RECOPILA-CIBON DE WALLACE Y MARY STEGNER. Translated by Andres M. Mateo. Mexico: Editorial Limusa-Wiley, 1964.

F22. [THE AMERICAN NOVEL] LA NOVELA NORTEAMERICANA. Translated by Alfonso Esparza. Mexico, D.F.: Ed. Diana, 1970.

Swedish

F23. [A SHOOTING STAR] SABRINA. Translated by Lisbeth Renner. Stockholm: Gebers Verlag, 1962.

F24. [ALL THE LITTLE LIVE THINGS] TILL LIVETS LOV. Translated by Berit Skogsberg. Stockholm: Gebers Verlag, 1968.

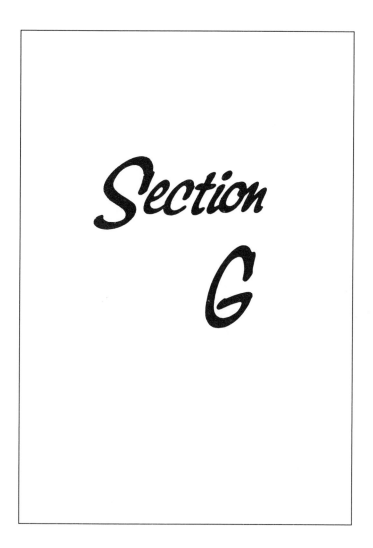

G. Manuscripts and Special Collections

The manuscripts and special collections consist primarily of typescripts. Stegner always uses a manual typewriter and does not have holograph materials.

UNIVERSITY OF IOWA

Iowa Authors Manuscripts - Special Collections Department, University of Iowa Libraries, Iowa City, Iowa.

"Beyond the Glass Mountain."

First draft (under title "Kilroy Was Here").
Printer's copy (with revisions and carbon).

Beyond the Hundredth Meridian.

Early draft of manuscript (with some editorializings and changes indicated).
Early draft of manuscript (including acknowledgments).
Early draft of manuscript (including section titled notes).

Publisher's copy (with corrections).

Big Rock Candy Mountain.

Original draft, transcript.
Printer's setting copy (typescript).

Mormon Country.

Printer's setting copy (typescript).

The Preacher and the Slave.

Preliminary working draft (with notes).
Working draft (with corrections).
"Interview - The Editor."
Notebook (with titles of books and articles on subject).
Another draft (fewer corrections).
Publisher's copy.

Remembering Laughter.

Two incomplete versions of the first draft.
Complete first draft.
Printer's proof.
Printer's setting copy (working title: "Landscape with Figures")

The Women on the Wall.

Printer's setting copy (typescript with revisions).

Letters: To Ronald Rayman (2)
         To Paul Engle (2)
         To John Leggett (3)

STANFORD UNIVERSITY

Department of Special Collections, Stanford University Libraries, Stanford, California.

Angle of Repose.

Materials (1,000 items) related to Mary Hallock Foote (subject fictionalized in *Angle of Repose*).

Beyond the Hundredth Meridian.

Carbon I and notes. Typed.
Table of Contents. Typed.
Second carbon typescript and notes for each chapter.

Women on the Wall.

MS. Typescript.

The Gathering of Zion.

Notes.
Early, fragmentary drafts, typescript and carbon (with autograph corrections).
First draft, typescript (partially carbon).
Late draft, typescript.
Reviews (14).
Correspondence regarding publication, 1961-1965 (65).
Photocopies of diaries or portions of diaries used in research for "The Mormon Trail."
Large segment of material on Mormonism used as background (bibliographies, unidentified journals, etc.)

Wolf Willow.

Typescript and carbon with Viking's directions and corrections. "Genesis" and "Carrion Spring" short stories laid in.

Sabrina (A Shooting Star).

Typescript.
Typescript with corrections.
Fragmentary drafts, carbon typescript.

First draft, incomplete, typescript incomplete.
Early draft and notes.
Semifinal draft (lacks ending).
Final draft (semifinal plus ending, typescript and carbon).
Revisions of final draft, carbon typescript.
Printer's proof.
Reviews (44).
Correspondence regarding publication, 1960-1961 (34).
Photographs (2).

Discovery.

Letter to Stegner from editor Paul Hoye (from *ARAMCO World Magazine*), dated May 5, 1971.

The Preacher and the Slave.

Joe Hill materials housed at the Hoover Library, Stanford.

Miscellaneous

Source material on Robert Frost.

UNIVERSITY OF UTAH

Manuscript Division, Special Collections, Marriott Library, Salt Lake City, Utah.

Papers.

Manuscript of *The Gathering of Zion.*
13 hardcover books, 5 paperback books, 1 pamphlet.
Teaching the Short Story.
2 printed copies of speeches; Library Dedication Exercises and the Commencement Address U.S.U., June 3, 1972.
Dale L. Morgan correspondence.

From *The Papers of Fawn McKay Brodie.*

16 letters, 1969-1979. "Contains information about contemporary figures in the field of history. His letters are full of wit and humor. There are many revealing passages about his own and others' work."

From *The Utah Humanities Research Foundation* (Manuscript Collection)

"This file includes correspondence between Stegner, Houghton Mifflin Company, Harold Bentley, and Don D. Walker regarding a request by Houghton Mifflin to reprint in *Beyond the Hundredth Meridian* a chapter on plateau country place names published in the *Western Humanities Review*, 1953."

From *The Papers of the Walter Daniel Bonner Family.*

Letters from David, 1944. He wrote about Wallace Stegner at Stanford.
Letters from David, 1946. He described a trip down the Colorado River with the Wallace Stegner family.

From *The Papers of A. Russell Mortensen.*

"Utah" in *Holiday*, 1948.
Mormon Country, 1942.
Letters; 1958, 1963-1966. Correspondence about "the possibility of extracting an article from one of his forthcoming books, having Stegner contribute an article, and evaluate other manuscripts as a member of the Editorial Board" (of *American West*) 1965. "On the Writing of History," Fall 1965. Correspondence and drafts of the manuscript.

From *The Papers of Dean R. Brimhall.*

"Stegner, Wallace, 1940-43"
"University of Utah Speeches" (see "Papers" above).

Western Americana (also part of Special Collections).

Clipping file and a vertical file on Stegner, as well as copies of all of his books.

UNIVERSITY OF NEVADA, RENO

Special Collections Department, The University Library, Reno, Nevada.

Mr. Stegner has given the University of Nevada, Reno a number of A, B, C, and D items from his personal collection.

The Special Collections Department is in the process of building a comprehensive Stegner collection.

Appendix

1

Appendix 1
Selected Materials
on Wallace Stegner

1. Ahearn, Kerry. *"The Big Rock Candy Mountain* and *Angle of Repose*: Trial and Culmination," *Western American Literature*, 10 (Spring 1975), 11-27.

2. Ahearn, Kerry. "Heroes vs. Women: Conflict and Duplicity in Stegner," *Western Humanities Review*, 31 (Spring 1977), 125-141.

3. Ahearn, Kerry. "Wallace Stegner and John Wesley Powell: The Real—And Maimed—Western Spokesmen," *South Dakota Review*, 15 (Winter 1977-78), 33-48.

4. Arthur, Anthony. *Critical Essays on Wallace Stegner*. Boston: G.K. Hall, 1982. Three essays written especially for this volume:

    a. Baurecht, William C. "Within a Continuous Frame: Stegner's Family Album in *The Big Rock Candy Mountain*," 98-108.

    b. Lewis, Merrill. "Wallace Stegner's *Recapitulation*: Memory as Art Form," 210-221.

c. Walsh, Mary Ellen Williams. "*Angle of Repose* and the Writings of Mary Hallock Foote: A Source Study," 184-209.

5. Brown, Dixie. "Wallace Stegner: A Writer's Writer," *Peninsula*, 5 (January/February 1980), 46-48.

6. Canzoneri, Robert. "Wallace Stegner: Trial by Existence," *Southern Review*, 9 (October 1973), 796-827.

7. Clayton, James L. "From Pioneers to Provincials: Mormonism as Seen by Wallace Stegner," *Dialogue*, 1 (Winter 1966), 105-114.

8. Devine, Paul. "On Reading a Novel," *Vanderbilt University Graduate English Newsletter*, 7 (May 1979), 3-4.

9. Dillon, David. "Time's Prisoners: An Interview with Wallace Stegner," *Southwest Review*, 61 (Summer 1976), 252-267.

10. Dillon, David. *Wallace Stegner*. [Dallas?]: New London Press, 1978. The greater portion of this interview originally appeared in the *Southwest Review*. The first printing...consists of three hundred copies bound in paper wrappers. Two hundred and fifty copies are numbered and signed by Wallace Stegner.

11. Dillon, Millicent. "Learning From a Feeling of Reality—Stegner," *Stanford Observer*, (April 1974), 7.

12. Dillon, Millicent. "Stegner: When the Bucket's Overflowing, You Write," *Campus Report* (Stanford publication), 6 (20 March 1974), 1-2.

13. Dunbar, Maurice. "The West of Wallace Stegner," *Handicapped Travel Newsletter*, (April 1986), 3.

14. Eisinger, Chester E. *Fiction of the Forties*. Chicago: University of Chicago Press, 1963, 324-328.

15. Eisinger, Chester E. "Twenty Years of Wallace Stegner," *College English*, 20 (December 1958), 110-116.

16. Etulain, Richard W. "Western Fiction and History: A Reconsideration," *The American West: New Perspectives, New Dimensions*. Ed. Jerome O. Steffen. Norman: University of Oklahoma Press, 1979, 152-174.

17. Ferguson, J.M., Jr. "Cellars of Consciousness: Stegner's 'The Blue-Winged Teal.'" *Studies in Short Fiction*, 14 (Spring 1977), 180-182.

18. Fletcher, Peggy and L. John Lewis. "An Interview with Wallace Stegner," *Sunstone*, 5 (January-February 1980), 7-11.

19. Flora, Joseph M. "Stegner, Wallace (Earle)," in *Twentieth Century Western Writers*. Ed. James Vinson. London: Macmillan Publishers, 1982, 728-732.

20. Flora, Joseph M. "Vardis Fisher and Wallace Stegner: Teacher and Student," *Western American Literature*, 5 (Summer 1970), 121-128.

21. Fowler, Carol. "Wallace Stegner and the Literary Life," *Contra Costa Times*, (15 July 1979), 31.

22. Hairston, Joe B. *Wallace Stegner*. Unpublished Master's thesis. Austin: University of Texas, 1966.

23. Hairston, Joe B. "Wallace Stegner and the Great Community," *South Dakota Review*, 12 (Winter 1974-75), 31-42.

24. Hairston, Joe B. *The Westerner's Dilemma*. Unpublished Doctoral dissertation, University of Minnesota, 1971.

25. Hanscom, Leslie. "Wallace Stegner: Brilliant, 'Old-Fashioned' Writer," *Salt Lake City Tribune*, (1 April 1979), 2E.

26. Harlow, Robert. "Whitemud Revisited," *Canadian Literature*, 16 (1963), 63-66.

27. Harrigan, Stephen. "Angle of Reflection," *Texas Monthly*,

(May 1980), 206, 209.

28. Henkin, Bill. "Time is Not Just Chronology: Interview with Wallace Stegner," *Massachusetts Review*, 20 (Spring 1979), 127-139.

29. Hofheins, Roger and Dan Tooker, "Interview with Wallace Stegner," *Southern Review*, 11 (October 1975), 794-801.

30. Houston, James D. "Wallace Stegner—Universal Truths Rooted in a Region," *Los Angeles Times (Book Review)*, (23 November 1980), 3.

31. Hudson, Lois Phillips. "*The Big Rock Candy Mountain*: No Roots and No Frontier," *South Dakota Review*, 9 (Spring 1971), 3-13.

32. Hunter, Mark. "In the Company of Wallace Stegner," *San Francisco Magazine*, 23 (July 1981), 38-43.

33. "Interview [with] Wallace Stegner." *Great Lakes Review*, 2 (Summer 1975), 1-25.

34. Jenson, Sidney L. "The Compassionate Seer: Wallace Stegner's Literary Artist," *Brigham Young University Studies*, 14 (Winter 1974), 248-262.

35. Jenson, Sidney L. *The Middle Ground: A Study of Wallace Stegner's Use of History in Fiction*. Unpublished Doctoral dissertation, Salt Lake City: University of Utah, 1972.

36. Johnson, Mark and Linda Goldston. "Wallace Stegner Talks About His Favorite Subject—the Novel," *San Jose Mercury News*, (12 November 1978), 6B-8B.

37. Larson, Paul. "Wallace Stegner: Surviving Perils of a 'Ruinous Field," *Turlock Daily Journal* (Turlock, California), (10 November 1982), D1.

38. Lewis, Merrill and Lorene Lewis. *Wallace Stegner*. Boise, Idaho:

Boise State College, 1972. (Western Writers Series, No. 4).

39. Lewis, Merrill. "Wallace Stegner (1909—)," in *Fifty Western Writers: A Bio-Bibliographical Sourcebook*. Eds. Fred Erisman and Richard W. Etulain. Westport, Conn.: Greenwood Press, 1982, 465-476.

40. Mach, Tom. "Pulitzer Prize Winning Novelist Wallace Stegner," *Sun Living*, (18 July 1979), 31. (Interview).

41. Martin, Russell. "Writers of the Purple Sage," *New York Times Magazine*, 131 (27 December 1981), 18-22, 40-43. Writes about "William (sic) Stegner."

42. McAllister, Mick. "A Smooth Stone Held Absently in the Hand," *Utah Holiday*, 11 (March 1982), 26-28.

43. Mills, Kay. "A Look at the Real West: Wallace Stegner Wants a More Realistic Line to the Past," *San Francisco Examiner*, (20 August 1977), 11.

44. Mills, Kay. "Looking West: A Conversation With Wallace Stegner," *Los Angeles Times*, (29 July 1979), Part V, 3.

45. Milton, John. "Conversation With Wallace Stegner," *South Dakota Review*, 9 (Spring 1971), 45-57.

46. Mitchell, Henry. "Wallace Stegner and the Wilderness," *Washington Post*, (21 March 1986), B2.

47. Moseley, Richard. "First-Person Narration in Wallace Stegner's *All the Little Live Things*," *Notes on Contemporary Literature*, 3 (March 1973), 12-13.

48. Otis, John Whiteacre. *The Purified Vision: The Fiction of Wallace Stegner*. Unpublished Doctoral dissertation. Drake University, 1977.

49. Paluka, Frank. *Iowa Authors: a Bio-Bibliography of Sixty Native Writers*. Iowa City: Friends of the University of Iowa Libraries,

1967, 217-220.

50. Peterson, Audrey C. "Narrative Voice in Wallace Stegner's *Angle of Repose*," *Western American Literature*, 10 (Summer 1975), 125-33.

51. Putnam, Jackson K. "Wallace Stegner and Western History: Some Historiographical Problems in *Angle of Repose*," *vis-a-vis*, 3 (September 1975), 51-60.

52. Robertson, Jamie. "Henry Adams, Wallace Stegner, and the Search for a Sense of Place in the West," *The Westering Experience in American Literature*. Ed. Merrill Lewis and L.L. Lee. Western Washington State University, 1977, 135-143.

53. Robinson, Forrest G. and Margaret G. Robinson. *Wallace Stegner*. Boston: Twayne (G.K. Hall & Co.), 1977.

54. Robinson, Forrest G. and Margaret G. Robinson. "Wallace Stegner: An Interview," *Quarry* (University of California, Santa Cruz), 4 (1975), 72-84.

55. Robinson, Forrest G. "Wallace Stegner's Family Saga: From *The Big Rock Candy Mountain* to *Recapitulation*," *Western American Literature*, 17 (August 1982), 101-116.

56. Saporta, Marc. "Wallace Stegner," *Informations & Documents*, 187 (15 September-1 October 1963), 23-36. (French)

57. Schindler, Harold. "Stegner Looks at America," *Salt Lake Tribune*, (6 December 1981), E1, E3.

58. Shepherd, Tuck. "Novel Ideas Are Always at Work in the Mind of Wallace Stegner," *Los Altos Town Crier* (Los Altos, California), 29 (18 August 1976), 5.

59. Singer, Barnett. "The Historical Ideal in Wallace Stegner's Fiction," *South Dakota Review*, 1 (Spring 1977), 28-44.

60. *South Dakota Review*, "Wallace Stegner Number," 23 (Winter 1985). Nine essays on Stegner by James D. Houston, Wendell Berry, Edward Loomis, Gary Topping, T.H. Watkins, Forrest G. Robinson, Kerry Ahearn, Melody Graulick, and John Milton.

a. Ahearn, Kerry. "Stegner's Short Fiction," 70-86.

b. Berry, Wendell. "Wallace Stegner and the Great Community," 10-18.

c. Graulich, Melody. "The Guides to Conduct that a Tradition Offers: Wallace Stegner's *Angle of Repose*," 87-106.

d. Houston, James D. "Wallace Stegner: Universal Truths Rooted in a Region," 6-9. See -30.

e. Loomis, Edward. "Wallace Stegner and Yvor Winters as Teachers," 19-24.

f. Milton, John. "Conversation with Wallace Stegner," 107-118. See -45.

g. Robinson, Forrest G. "A Usuable Heroism: Wallace Stegner's *Beyond the Hundredth Meridian*," 58-69.

h. Topping, Gary. "Wallace Stegner and the Mormons," 25-41.

i. Watkins, T.H. "Bearing Witness for the Land: The Conservation Career of Wallace Stegner," 42-57.

61. Thomas, Phil. "Author Wallace Stegner Says the West is Best," *Wisconsin State Journal*, (10 June 1979), Section 8, 2.

62. Tyburski, Susan J. "Wallace Stegner's Vision of Wilderness," *Western American Literature*, 18 (August 1983), 133-142.

63. Tyler, Robert L. "The I.W.W. and the West," *American*

Quarterly, 12 (Summer 1960), 175-187.

64. *University of Utah Review* (Alumni News), "Profile: Wallace Stegner, Author," (December 1969), 4A-4B.

65. West, Don. "3 Books to Write, So Stegner Retires," *San Francisco Examiner and Chronicle*, (5 December 1971), B5.

66. White, Robin and Ed McClanahan. "An Interview with Wallace Stegner," *Per Se*, 3 (Fall 1968), 28-35.

67. Willey, Jill Lucas. *Wallace Stegner: An Annotated Bibliography*. Unpublished Master's thesis, San Jose: San Jose State University, 1975.

68. Williams, Nancy. "Stegner: 'A Gift of Wilderness," *The Herald Journal* (Logan, Utah), (11 June 1981), 17.

Index